The Gardener's Guide
to Growing
PEONIES

The Gardener's Guide
to Growing
PEONIES

Martin Page

David & Charles
Newton Abbot

TIMBER PRESS
Portland, Oregon

To Mair, my wife

PICTURE ACKNOWLEDGEMENTS
All photographs by Martin Page, except pages 58, 72–3, 76, 82–3, 93, 96–7, 102, 104–5, 110, 111, 116–17, 131, 132 by Karl Adamson; pages 2, 29, 126, 135 property of Kelways Ltd.; page 142 by Don Hollingsworth; page 147, property of Penshurst Place. Woodcuts on page 15 from Mattioli's *Commentarii*. Illustrations on pages 16, 17 and 19 by Coral Mula.

NOTE The flowering season for peonies depends to a great extent on the weather. In this book flowering times are mainly referred to as early, mid- or late season, to allow you to adjust expectations to your prevailing conditions. Relative seasons and months for herbaceous peonies are given below. Tree peonies have a slightly different system of seasons and midseason for a tree peony is a month earlier than for an herbaceous one.

VERY EARLY SEASON	EARLY SEASON	MIDSEASON	LATE SEASON
Mid spring	*Late spring*	*Early summer*	*Early to midsummer*
April	May	June	Late June to early July

Copyright © Martin Page 1997
First published 1997

Martin Page has asserted his right to be identified as author of this work in accordance with the Copyright, Designs and Patents Acts 1988.

First published in the UK in 1997 by David & Charles Publishers, Brunel House, Newton Abbot, Devon
ISBN 0 7153 0531 X

First published in North America in 1997 by Timber Press Inc., 133 SW Second Avenue, Suite 450, Portland, Oregon 97204, USA
ISBN 0-88192-408-3
Cataloguing-in-Publication Data is on file with the Library of Congress

Typeset by ACE
and printed in Italy by Lego SpA

Photographs page 1 'Ellen Cowley'; page 2 'Glory of Huish'; page 3 'Niigata Otomenomai'

CONTENTS

Introduction   6

1. History & Botany   10

2. Cultivation   22

3. Peonies in the Garden   30
   Peonies in America
   Peonies in New Zealand

4. Pests & Diseases   38

5. The Peony Species   43

6. Cultivars of Paeonia lactiflora & hybrids   71

7. Tree Peonies   126

8. Itoh or Intersectional Hybrids   142

9. Where to See Peonies   146

Appendices   152
   Glossary
   Bibliography
   Synonyms of Peony Species
   Where to Buy Peonies

Index   158

INTRODUCTION

It will always be a mystery to me why a group of plants as beautiful as the peonies should have been so neglected by modern gardeners. At the end of the nineteenth century peonies were at the zenith of their popularity and widely grown throughout Europe. It may be that modern horticulture is to blame; peonies do not lend themselves to mass propagation and this will have reduced their commercial viability. Another factor may be the paucity of information available to gardeners about them. When I started to write this book I was surprised to find that there was so little written. There were dozens of books about roses and several about rather obscure genera, which were mainly of academic interest. Peonies by comparison seem to have been almost completely ignored by modern authors.

When compared to roses, peonies are very easy to care for: aphids seem completely disinterested in them and slugs, on the whole, cause limited damage. In a world where water is an increasingly valuable commodity peonies have much to offer the modern gardener. Peonies make most of their growth during the spring months and have usually flowered by the time droughts occur. Few herbaceous perennials have the longevity that peonies enjoy; vitality is greatly improved by regular division, but they can easily survive a hundred years if left to their own devices.

The only disease that seriously threatens peonies is a fungal pathogen called *Botrytis paeoniae*, which can be quite lethal. Anyone with a small collection of peonies is unlikely to ever experience this disease, but if you have a large collection the potential risk is much greater. Nevertheless, it can be easily controlled by regular spraying with a systemic fungicide and the destruction

The most readily available peonies, usually varieties of *P. officinalis* and *P. lactiflora*, are relatively resistant to drought.

of dead foliage in the autumn. If you purchase good quality plants you will have few problems growing peonies.

TAXONOMY & DESCRIPTION

The taxonomy of the genus is very confused. A number of species, such as *P. officinalis* and *P. mascula*, are tetraploids and exhibit considerable variation. Both of these species consist of several subspecies, many of which were formerly considered to be species in their own right. Scientists in the former Soviet Union (now the Confederation of Independent States, CIS) also have a different concept of the principle of the 'species'. This has resulted in them describing several species that are not generally accepted by botanists throughout the rest of the world.

In Europe the most readily available peonies are varieties of *P. lactiflora*, the Chinese peony. The majority of these were raised by French breeders during the nineteenth century and are perfectly suited to a European climate. After the First World War, the emphasis changed to breeding hybrids between the different species, which extended the potential flowering period for peonies from mid-spring to midsummer. The majority of this work was undertaken in the USA and has dramatically increased the range of flower colours which are now available. Until very recently many of these varieties were unknown to European gardeners and it was only the publication of *The Peony* by Roy Klehm in 1993 (a revision of two earlier books by Alice Harding) that made European gardeners aware of these plants.

With in excess of five thousand named herbaceous peony varieties it has been impossible, within the scope of this book, to list more than a tiny proportion of them. I have tried to give a balanced selection of those available and while some may be extremely rare I did not feel that this was sufficient justification in excluding a number of very beautiful plants. The great majority of the peonies listed should be available from at least one of the suppliers in Appendix IV. For ease of use I have included the hybrids with the cultivated varieties of *P. lactiflora* in Chapter 6. The selected forms of individual species are listed under the description of that species in Chapter 5.

Wherever possible I have checked the description of the species by referring to both live and herbarium material. The species have been described from specimens of known wild origin, whether derived from living plants or wild-collected seed, the only exceptions being species that are only known from cultivation. In several cases preserved or living specimens have not be available for study and I have had to obtain information from the original published Latin descriptions. These are acknowledged in the bibliography.

Although a number of peony species have been well understood for many years, there remains a lot of confusion about those originating from the Caucasus region and China. Both of these areas remain difficult to visit at the time of writing.

AVAILABILITY

The availability of peonies varies considerably from country to country. They are very popular in the United States of America where there are several specialist nurseries that can supply them. Only a few of these are able to export to Europe due to the large amount of paperwork required.

The situation in Europe is somewhat different. Peonies reached the zenith of their popularity during the latter part of the nineteenth century since when they have declined in public esteem and, as a consequence, a number of the lesser known varieties have disappeared. Fortunately this situation is changing and these beautiful plants appear to be enjoying a renaissance. Gradually the range of available varieties is increasing as plants are propagated and new material is imported from the USA.

Species peonies remain difficult to obtain. They are more readily available in Europe than in America, due to the hard work of SPIN (The 'Species Peony International Network') and Will McLewin of Phedar Nursery in England.

AWARDS

A number of horticultural organizations give awards for highly regarded species and cultivars. While this should, in theory, indicate which are the best varieties, their judgements have been made from a different perspective. In the USA, where peonies are more widely grown than in Europe, comparison will have been made

with several thousand other varieties. Thus a plant with an American Peony Society Gold Medal should be something truly special. The Royal Horticultural Society on the other hand, with less experience of the range of plants available, is more likely to make an award based upon its value as a garden plant.

I have used the following abbreviations for awards:

GM The American Peony Society (APS) Gold Medal

NGC The American Peony Society National Grand Champion

AGM The Royal Horticultural Society (RHS) Award of Garden Merit

EXTINCT VARIETIES

Thousands of varieties of herbaceous and tree peonies have been raised during the last 200 years, many of which are no longer cultivated. To a great extent these have fallen by the wayside because they did not bear comparison with the better modern varieties. In particular, most of the selected varieties of *P. officinalis*, which were grown in Europe during the eighteenth century fell out of favour

when the Chinese peony, *P. lactiflora*, was introduced. It is quite possible that some of these survive, unrecognized, in corners of old gardens. Others, such as the tree peony 'Sybil Stern', were never propagated on a commercial scale and may prove to be impossible to purchase.

PLACE NAMES

The world has changed dramatically during the past hundred years and many of the geographical locations cited in old books and scientific papers now have quite different names. In most cases, I have used the local name for a location, such as Krym for the Crimea and Heilongjiang rather than Manchuria. The majority of the Caucasian peonies in cultivation originated from the Tiflis Botanical Garden, now the Institute of Botany in Tbilisi.

I have used the Pinyin zimu system for Chinese place names. This is the system approved by the Chinese government and replaces the Wade-Giles romanized Chinese used since 1942 in American and British maps. For example, in Pinyin, the Chinese province of Szechwan becomes Sichuan, and Kansu becomes Gansu. The Pinyin system is

'Illini Warrior' is an extremely attractive hybrid peony with single cardinal-red flowers (see p.100).

widely used by scientists and is described in more detail in *The Times Atlas of The World*, which I have consulted on a regular basis during the writing of this book.

COLOURS

It is quite difficult to describe a colour in words. We all use the word scarlet, but how many of us could actually point it out in a garden? Everyone interprets colour in a different way and one person's blood-red is another's cardinal-red. To avoid this ambiguity I have used a set of horticultural colour charts which remove the subjective description of flower colour and can be used to communicate flower colours accurately to people who do not have a visual reference.

One of the most useful colour charts was that produced by the British Colour Council in 1938 and 1941. While extremely useful, the charts were not without fault and some colours, such as crimson, were clearly incorrect. In 1966, the Royal Horticultural Society published a completely new colour chart, comprised of a set of colour swatches illustrating a wider range of colours and using numbers for the colours (eg magenta is 66A). Where necessary these numbers are referred to in the text.

I have tried my best to describe the colour of peony flowers as accurately and objectively as possible. However, colour changes according to the quality of sunlight: a pink flower may have a glowing appearance on a warm sunny evening but look washed out when the sky is overcast. Many varieties of the Chinese peony (*P. lactiflora*) are described as having red flowers in nursery catalogues. I am, therefore, going to upset a lot of people by saying that, in my experience, they are invariably shades of magenta or purple. True red only occurs in hybrids with *P. officinalis* and a few other species, such as *P. anomala*.

Nursery catalogues regularly use the term rose-pink or blush to describe the colour of peony flowers. Rose-pink is the colour of the flowers of the common dog-rose (*Rosa canina*) and has a slightly bluish tint. (Rose-red is the colour of *Rosa officinalis*.) Flesh-pink is a pale pink with a hint of yellow, salmon-pink is yellower still. Scarlet is a yellowish red, crimson is a bluish red. Pure white has no colour at all, milk-white has a yellow hint and creamy white is yellower still. The term blush is frequently used to describe peony flowers; it is a warm pink. Coral-pink has a hint of orange and cherry-red is the colour of black cherries.

1
HISTORY & BOTANY

Peonies have been used as medicinal plants for at least two thousand years. The correct name for the plant is peony, rather than paeony, which is a recent corruption of the Latin name. Man has always held the peony in high esteem; an ancient Greek poem referred to it as 'the Queen of all herbs' and the ancient Chinese considered the tree peony to be the 'King of flowers'. Few wild plants in the ancient world had such striking flowers as the peony.

It is thought to have been named after the Greek mythological figure, Paeon, a pupil of Asclepius, the Greek God of medicine and healing. He reputedly discovered peonies growing on the slopes of Mount Olympus – after Leto (Apollo's mother) told him where to find them – and used them to cure a wound that Pluto had received in a fight with Hercules. Asclepius was so jealous of Paeon's success that he had him killed. However, the grateful Pluto then had him changed into the flower that had cured him (which seems little compensation for his fate!).

MEDICINAL USES

With the notable exception of their use as ornamental garden plants, peonies currently have little economic value in the Western world. However, in medieval times the situation was very different. Peonies were highly valued as medicinal plants; their roots and seeds were extensively used by physicians for the treatment of a wide range of ailments. Much of the knowledge that is found in the medieval herbals actually seems to originate from much earlier in our history.

P. mascula ssp. *mascula* was widely grown in medieval 'Physic Gardens'. It is often found near the sites of old monasteries.

Gaius Plinius Secundus (also known as Pliny, The Elder) was a leading authority on science in Rome during the first century AD. Born in AD23, he rose to become a procurator and commanded the Western Roman Fleet. His scientific curiosity got the better of him when he became asphyxiated by fumes during the eruption of Mount Vesuvius, which destroyed Pompeii in AD79. He was the author of *Historia Naturalis*, a famous book which distilled the knowledge of art and natural history of a hundred authors. This was copied over the centuries, and has survived in the form of seventh-, twelfth- and thirteenth-century manuscripts. His reference to peonies has been much quoted but is well worth repeating, as it shows the level of knowledge about peonies in the first century.

'Glycyside, called by some paeonia or pentorobon, has a stem two spans high; two or three others go with it. This stem is reddish, with bark like that of bay; the leaves resemble those of isatis, only more fleshy, rounder and smaller. The seed is in pods, with some grains red, some black. There are however two kinds of the plant. The one to the roots of which are attached about six or eight rather long bulbs like acorns is regarded as female. The male has no more bulbs, since it is supported only by a single root, a span deep, white, and astringent to the taste. The leaves of the female smell of myrrh, and are closer together. The plants grow in woods. It is said that they should be dug up by night, because to do so in the daytime is dangerous, for the woodpecker called 'bird of Mars' assaults the eyes. That there is a danger, however of prolapsus of the anus when a root is being dug up, I hold to be a very fraudulent lie, calculated to exaggerate the real facts.

'These plants are of manifold use. The red grains check red menstrual discharge about fifteen being taken in dark red wine. The black grains are healing to the uterus, the same number being taken in raisin or ordinary wine. The root in wine relieves all pains of the belly, opens the bowels, cures opisthotonic tetanus, jaundice, and complaints of the kidneys and bladder; for the trachea and the stomach however a decoction in wine is used, which also acts astringently on the bowels. It is eaten too as food but as a medicine four drachmae are enough. The black grains, taken in wine to the number mentioned, also prevent nightmares, while stomach ache and for gnawing colic it is beneficial both to eat them and to apply them locally. Suppurations too are dispersed, recent by the black seed and old by the red. Both kinds are good for snake bites, and to cure stone in children.'

The story about the woodpecker was almost certainly a ruse circulated by the herbalists to ensure that amateurs did not poach their business! It is not surprising that the plant was treated with the same respect as the Mandrake (*Mandragora officinarum*).

In medieval Europe only two peonies were widely used in medicine: *P. officinalis* (the 'female peony') and *P. mascula* (the 'male peony'). Of these *P. mascula* was considered to be the most effective, but was less readily available. Both species are thought to have been introduced into England by the Romans. The famous English herbalist, Nicholas Culpeper (1653), described *P. officinalis* thus:

'The ordinary Female Peony hath as many stalks, and more leaves on them than the Male; the leaves not so large, nicked on the edges, some with great and deep, others with small cuts and divisions, of a dead green colour.'

Of their medical uses:

'Paeoniae, maris, foemellae. Of the Peony male and female. They are meanly hot, but more drying. The root helps women not sufficiently purged after travail, it provokes the menses, and helps in the belly, as also on the reins and bladder, falling sickness, and convulsions in

The roots of *P. delavayi* are sometimes used in traditional Chinese medicine as 'Mu Dan Pi'.

children, being either taken inwardly, or hung about their necks. You may take half a dram at a time, and less for Children.'

In the British Isles peony seeds were made into necklaces or planted outside the house to ward off evil spirits. This practice lingered into the nineteenth century. In his book on English folklore Thiselton-Dyer (1889) wrote: 'to this day Sussex mothers put necklaces of beads turned from the peony root around their children's necks, to prevent convulsions and to assist in their teething'. Herbals of the seventeenth century also recommended peonies as a cure for gall stones, kidney pains, yellow jaundice and insanity. The dry root was powdered and an infusion made in boiling water; this was used to treat convulsive illnesses, such as cholera and epilepsy, or as a sedative. Peonies were indeed a panacea for all ills.

Peonies are still extensively used in traditional Chinese medicine (TCM). Chinese communities around the world have created an important export market for peony products. TCM uses three types of peony preparation: Moutan Radicis Cortex (Mu Dan Pi) is root bark derived from Moutan tree peonies – *P. delavayi*, *P. lutea* and *P. potanini*. Paeoniae Radix Rubra (Chi Shao Yao) is intact peony root harvested from *P. lactiflora* or more rarely *P. obovata*, *P. veitchii* or *P. anomala*. Paeoniae Radix Alba (Bai Shao yao) is obtained exclusively from the roots of *P. lactiflora*. The only significant difference between the latter and Radix Rubra is that the bark is removed during its preparation.

Scientists have investigated members of the genus to establish whether there is any scientific foundation to the claims of the herbalists. Mu Dan Pi has been shown to have an anti-microbial effect on *Escherichia coli*, typhoid, cholera, *Staphylococcus aureus*, *Streptococcus hemolyticus* and pneumococci. It is an anti-inflammatory agent which can reduce arthritic joint swelling. An analgesic, a sedative and an anticonvulsant, it also has a high success rate in curing dysentery and can be used to treat allergic rhinitis.

The most important active ingredient in Chi Shao Yao is paeoniflorin. Experiments have shown that it has a strong antispasmodic effect on mammalian intestines, reduces blood pressure, reduces body temperature caused by fever in mice and protects against stress ulcers in rats.

Bai Shao Yao is usually, but not exclusively, obtained from wild plants. It is prepared by boiling in water and then removing the bark with a knife. Traditionally, the root is dried by laying it out in the sun, which may account for the varying efficacy of this product. The product is said to regulate menstrual bleeding, reduce excessive perspiration, control pain and reduce liver hyperactivity. It is quite possible that Western medicine has seriously underestimated the value of these plants to mankind.

The negative side to this use of peonies in TCM is the excessive demand that it places on the wild populations of these plants. While many species of peony are now cultivated specifically for medical use, large numbers of wild tree peony are still dug up every year to satisfy the demand. This may have serious implications for the survival of wild tree peonies in China.

Finally, there is even a recipe for peony flower tea! This is used in Europe as a cough remedy, for treating haemorrhoids and varicose veins. Boiling water is poured over one teaspoon of the crushed, dried petals and left for 5–10 minutes. The resulting liquor is passed through a tea strainer, it contains paeonidin 3,5-diglucoside, flavonoids and tannins. While there are no known side effects an overdose can produce gastro-enteritis, vomiting and diarrhoea.

FOOD AND SCENT
In medieval England spices were extremely expensive and local substitutes were used wherever possible.

Peonies were one of the few suitable plants that were readily available and their seeds were used to flavour stews. The practice continued into the late eighteenth century, so that *Mrs. Glasse's Cookery Book* (1796), gives the following instruction: 'Stick the cream with Paeony kernels'. The roots of peonies were also cooked and used as a vegetable.

Few people realise that peony flowers have also been used for making perfume. Kelways, the English nurserymen, who were one of the world's leading peony breeders during the latter part of the nineteenth century, had imposing premises in Langport, Somerset, and were known as the 'The Royal Nursery'. Thousands of people travelled by train to see their famous 'paeony valley', and they could boast of royal patronage. Their perfume, introduced in the 1930's, was named, rather predictably, 'Paeony Valley' and was sold in Art Deco bottles. There is no record of how successful this particular enterprise was!

In the former Soviet Union the bright red flowers of *P. caucasica* have been used to dye wool, paper, silk and linen. Oil has been extracted from the seeds and children also use them to make necklaces. In Kazakhstan *P. hybrida* was made into a gruel by boiling the roots in water or milk, while in Siberia the roots of *P. anomala* were dried and cooked with meat. (Although thought by most botanists to be a hybrid between *P. tenuifolia* and *P. anomala*, several Russian scientists have claimed that *P. hybrida* is growing as a wild plant (see p.43).)

TAXONOMY
In the first century AD, the Greek botanist and physician, Pedanios Dioscorides referred to the 'male' and 'female' peonies in his treatise *De materia medica*. Carl Linnaeus (inventor of the Latin binomial for species names) included both of them within his new species *P. officinalis* (1753) but referred to them as *feminea* and *mascula*. In 1768 Philip Miller split the species, retaining *feminea* as *P. officinalis* and coining a new name for the male peony: *P. mascula*.

For many years the genus *Paeonia* was included in the family *Ranunculaceae*, together with plants such as Monk's hood (*Aconitum* spp.), Hellebores (*Helleborus* spp.) and Buttercups (*Ranunculus* spp.). However, in 1830 Rudolphi and Bartling suggested that peonies were sufficiently distinct to justify placing them in their own family, the *Paeoniaceae*, and this has been accepted

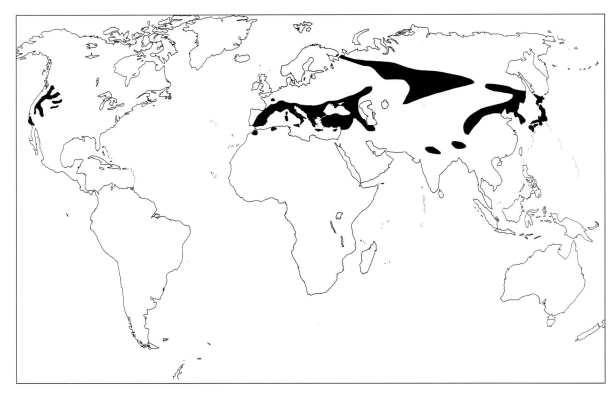

Worldwide distribution of the genus Paeonia

by most modern botanists. Worsdell suggested that, on morphology alone, they were closer to the *Magnoliaceae* than the *Ranunculaceae*. Members of the *Paeoniaceae* differ from those of the *Ranunculaceae* in possessing persistent sepals, petals which were derived from sepals rather than stamens, a perigynous disc, and seeds with arils. In peonies the stamens ripen from the inside out; in the *Ranunculaceae* the reverse is the case.

The family *Paeoniaceae* is restricted to the northern hemisphere. Species have been recorded in areas ranging from northwest America, to North Africa, west and central Europe, the Middle East, Russia, China, Pakistan, and northern India (see map above). Depending upon which classification is selected, there are between 30 and 42 species in the genus, including both woody and herbaceous plants.

ANATOMY

Herbaceous peonies have tuberous roots which store reserves from the previous year. These roots can act as rhizomes and in some species, such as *P. officinalis* and *P. peregrina*, they are also capable of producing adventitious buds. Certain species such as *P. tenuifolia* and *P. potanini* spread by stolons to form large clumps.

The roots of most species contain high concentrations of polyphenols, which prevent micro-biological decay. If the roots of peonies are damaged they can survive in the soil for a considerable period of time without rotting and frequently produce new shoots which are able to grow into independent plants. The roots of some herbaceous species (such as *P. mascula* and *P. mlokosewitschi*), taper from the crown of the plant, while in others (such as *P. officinalis* and *P. parnassica*), they are swollen and attached to the crown by a narrower section of root. This difference is clearly shown in the woodcut illustrations of sixteenth century books (see illustration opposite). Surprisingly, the shape of the roots has been little used to differentiate between the species, although this would obviously entail digging up the plant, which is not always desirable. New shoots arise from large buds on the rootstock, which gardeners often refer to as 'eyes'.

Leaves

The young shoots of herbaceous species are protected above the ground in spring by a number of pointed sheaths. The emerging stems and leaves in many species are coloured red or purple when young, although most of this colour fades as the shoot matures. The lower leaves of peonies are typically divided twice (biternate) and are composed of varying numbers of leaflets, which may be entire or lobed; stipules are absent. The leaf is supported by a long petiole which is divided at its apex into three petiolules. These petiolules then bear three primary leaflets, each with one central and two lateral segments. This layout thus provides a compound leaf with nine leaflets, such as is found in *Paeonia mascula* ssp. *triternata*. In other species the primary leaflets may then be further divided, with each leaflet possessing a secondary petiolule. The central segment is then ternately divided and the lateral segments pinnately divided, to give a leaf with as many as thirty or more segments (as in *P. officinalis* ssp. *humilis*). The final stage of division is where they are tripinnately lobed to form the very narrow linear

Paeonia mascula (left) and *Paeonia officinalis* (right) as shown in sixteenth century woodcuts.
(Mattioli, *Commentarii* 914 and 915.)

segments found in *P. tenuifolia*. The upper leaves are usually less divided than the lower.

The number of leaf segments and lobes is very variable in a number of species and it is often difficult to decide what is a segment and what is a lobe. Peony leaves are consequently very difficult to describe and are best shown by illustration. Nevertheless there is a consistent underlying pattern that has been widely used to distinguish between the various species. The degree of leaflet division has been used to separate the Section PAEON into two sub-sections, the FOLIOLATAE (represented by the *P. mascula* complex) and the DISSECTIFOLIAE (represented by the *P. officinalis* complex). The leaves of plants from different geographical locations can also vary considerably in the degree of hairiness, as well as the presence or absence of a glaucous coating. Anderson (1818) who produced one of the earliest monographs of the genus, used the presence

LEAVES

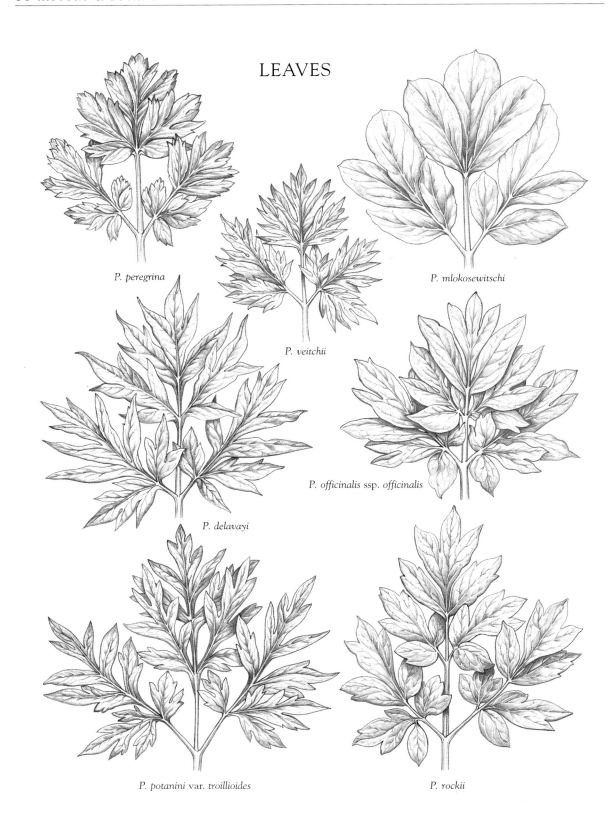

P. peregrina

P. veitchii

P. mlokosewitschi

P. delavayi

P. officinalis ssp. officinalis

P. potanini var. troillioides

P. rockii

LEAVES

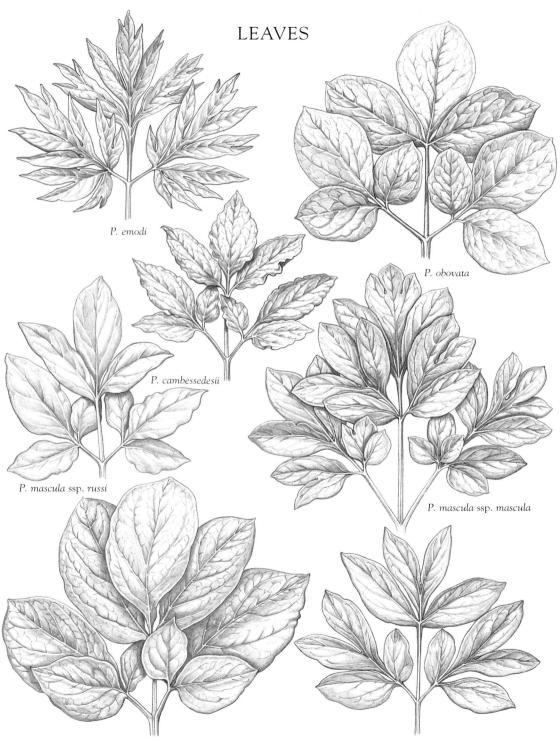

P. emodi

P. obovata

P. cambessedesii

P. mascula ssp. russi

P. mascula ssp. mascula

P. wittmanniana

P. mascula ssp. arietina

or absence of hairs on the leaves to separate some of the species. This character has since been found to be unreliable as the hairs often disappear when a plant is cultivated. One feature found to have taxonomic value is the presence or absence of minute bristles along the main vein of the upper surface of the leaf.

Although commonly called 'tree peonies', the woody species of the Section MOUTAN rarely grow to a height in excess of 2m (6ft) high. Their stems are relatively weak and occasionally branched. Tree peonies have a similar leaf pattern to their herbaceous cousins, but the petioles and petiolules have an abscission layer which allows the leaves to fall from the stem in the autumn, leaving leaf-base scars on the stem. New buds develop in the leaf axils, while the scales of the large terminal bud shrivel to leave a conspicuous ring around the base of the new shoot. If the buds are damaged, new shoots may appear from below soil level. The lower part of the stem is usually bare, glabrous; the leaves confined to the upper part. Flowers may arise from buds in the leaf axils as well as the terminal growing point. The youngest part of the stem is smooth with a few lenticels, while the older lower section is rougher with small amounts of thin peeling bark.

Flowers

Most species of herbaceous peony have a single flower to a stem, although three – *P. emodi*, *P. veitchii* and *P. lactiflora* – have several. The majority produce large and conspicuous flowers up to 15cm (6in) across, but the North American species have dull brown flowers that are rarely more than 3cm (1¼in) wide. Wild peonies typically have 5–10 petals and five green and persistent sepals; in some species leafy bracts may also be present. In the wild peonies are usually pollinated by beetles, but the flowers are also very attractive to bees. Some species, such as *P. delavayi* produce abundant nectar and ants may often be found crawling over the flowers. The flower colour in a population of wild plants is usually very uniform; in cultivation some herbaceous species freely interbreed to give flower colours ranging from reddish magenta to white and every shade between. Peony flowers close at night and when the sky is very overcast. This may have the advantage of protecting the delicate stamens from damage by hail and heavy rainfall.

P. veitchii has very attractive pale purple flowers. It is one of the few species to have more than one flower to a stem.

FLOWERS

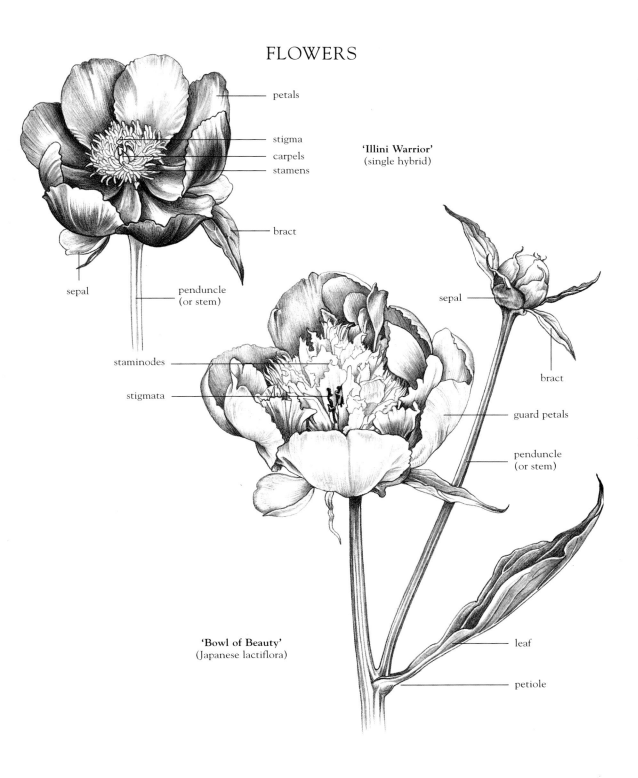

petals

stigma

carpels

stamens

'Illini Warrior'
(single hybrid)

bract

sepal

penduncle
(or stem)

staminodes

stigmata

sepal

bract

guard petals

penduncle
(or stem)

'Bowl of Beauty'
(Japanese lactiflora)

leaf

petiole

The reproductive parts of the flower, the pistils, are divided into the carpels (which hold the ovules), the style, and the stigma (which receives the pollen). In most peonies the stigma and style are the same colour. The style is often very short and I have, therefore, referred to only the stigma in the majority of the descriptions that follow. The number of carpels varies considerably from as few as one in *P. emodi*, to a maximum of eight in *P. cambessedesii*; the carpels are free to the base and carried on a fleshy disc. The seed pods (follicles) are fleshy, becoming leathery or woody as they mature, and bear their fruit in two rows. Peonies may have as many as 140 stamens, arranged centrifugally. The anthers produce large quantities of yellow pollen.

The carpels of some species are covered with hairs, which ranges from a soft tomentum in *P. mascula* ssp. *russi* to coarse yellow hairs in *P. mairei*. The presence or absence of this tomentum has been used by some botanists to distinguish between several species. Its significance is much disputed and its relevance depends upon whether wild peony populations with tomentose carpels are separated from those with glabrous (hairless) carpels. If the two interbreed in the wild, they are the same species, but if this characteristic is inherited (as it appears to be) then they must be separate species. So, depending upon your point of view, *P. wittmanniana* is either one species or two: *P. tomentosa* (with tomentose carpels) and *P. steveniana* (with glabrous carpels).

Moutan tree peony flowers are similar to those of their herbaceous cousins, the main difference being the presence of a membranous sheath covering the carpels. This sheath, which may be strongly coloured, tears as the carpels mature. It is possibly a primitive device for reducing self pollination, achieved in more advanced plants by the delayed development of the stigmatal surface.

Mature fertile seed is usually very dark blue-black or brown-black and broadly ellipsoid to almost globular in shape; sterile ovules are bright red and often occur with fertile seed in the same follicle.

FLOWER TYPES

The process of artificial selection has resulted in a great increase in the number of petals in many peony flowers. Unfortunately, the terms used to describe the different types of flowers are not uniformly used by all growers and breeders. There is a grey area where some authorities consider a variety to be double-flowered, whereas others consider it to be semi-double. While peony species usually have between five and ten petals, cultivated varieties may be single, double, or with the stamens modified to form further petals (staminodes). This doubling-up process can have developed so far that the carpels have also developed into petals (carpelodes). The variety 'Whitleyi Major', considered by many people to be the cultivar closest to the true species of *P. lactiflora*, has ten petals; it can be used as the base line for the doubling-up process in the cultivated varieties.

'Buckeye Belle' is a semi-double hybrid. The flower's centre has numerous narrow petals and pale yellow staminodes.

All species and many hybrid peonies have single flowers. Many gardeners consider them to be more beautiful than the double peonies.

Japanese flowers, sometimes called Imperial in the British Isles, have enlarged outer, or 'guard', petals. The anthers are usually also greatly enlarged and may be edged with yellow, the only remaining vestige of the pollen-carrying organs. In the majority of cases the filaments are also widened; however, in a few varieties at least some of the filaments remain thread-like. Anthers, whether complete or vestigial, must be present for the flower to be considered a Japanese type (eg 'Bowl of Beauty' p.84).

Anemone flowers are a further progression from the Japanese-form, but the term is not universally used. It is, nevertheless, a valid flower type and can be recognized by the complete absence of any functional stamens. The tissues that would have been stamens are much widened to form numerous narrow petals, or petaloids, distributed throughout the centre of the flower (eg 'Gay Paree' p.95).

Semi-double flowers tend to have a mass of loose petals with stamens scattered throughout the bloom. In most cases the petals originate from a duplication of the floral structure so that a flower-within-a-flower is formed. This is often demonstrated by concentric rings of stamens alternating with the petals. Carpels are usually fully developed in semi-double flowers (eg 'Buckeye Belle' p.85).

Crown-type flowers In a narrow sense these have petaloids that differ depending upon whether they have developed from stamens or carpels. In practice the term is often loosely applied and frequently used to describe flowers with a raised dome of petals in the centre (eg 'Monsieur Jules Elie' p.112).

Bomb-type flowers have a central raised mass of petaloids which have developed from both stamens and carpels. The greatly increased number of petals makes these flowers very heavy and, consequently, they need strong stems if they are to survive without being staked. The outer guard petals are well differentiated. It has been suggested that the name 'bomb' refers to a supposed similarity with a 'bombe' ice-cream dessert (eg 'Raspberry Sundae' p.119).

Peony flowers can change considerably after they have first opened. The flowers of most of the Japanese-form peonies, for instance, take several days to develop their typical shape. Flowers on freshly planted peonies are rarely fully developed until the plant is at least three years old. Flower colour is affected by the soil the peony is planted in and may be more intense when the substrate is rich in minerals.

Single flowers normally have between five and ten petals with a centre of functional stamens and carpels.

2
CULTIVATION

The advent of containerization has transformed horticulture, allowing the majority of plants to be planted at any time of the year. While many species are quite happy being handled in this way, peonies definitely benefit from being planted during the spring or autumn, immediately after division. Peonies are long-lived and will only give their best if they have a good start in life. This is one of the reasons why specialist peony growers sell their plants bare rooted. Garden centres on the other hand sell peonies in deep plastic pots full of compost; while this is very convenient it makes it impossible to check the quality of the plant.

If you do buy peonies in plastic pots, avoid plants with only a couple of weak stems, as these will take a long time to get established. If possible, purchase bare-root peonies in the autumn or choose well established containerized plants. The recognised standard for a herbaceous peony in the nursery trade is a division with three to five obvious buds or 'eyes'. It is advisable to avoid any plants that have less than this; they may be cheaper but such a purchase will invariably turn out to be a false economy. Species peonies are the one exception to this rule, many grow at a much slower rate than the more vigorous hybrids and cultivars of *P. lactiflora*.

If you buy a containerized plant, check whether it is growing in compost that is covered with weeds and moss. If this is the case, the compost will probably be exhausted and the plant weakened. Finally, have a close look at the crown of the plant. If the old woody part has split during division the plant can easily become infected and may ultimately die. Also try to avoid plants that are just labelled 'Peony'. These are usually the 'rogues' from the field which the wholesaler wishes

to dispose of. They are likely to be inferior plants and, consequently, a waste of money.

The best peonies are those purchased from a specialist nursery, which will have a much wider range of varieties to choose from. While these nurseries tend to concentrate on supplying bare-rooted peonies in the autumn and spring, they often have a small quantity of containerized plants for sale during the rest of the year. The range of varieties can be daunting. If in doubt ask one of the staff to recommend something: the best known varieties are not always the best! Decide whether you want a single, Japanese or a double flower and which colour you prefer. Some peonies have a very strong fragrance, while others have none at all. Another point to bear in mind is that the flowers of some varieties bleach very quickly in strong sun, while others have a longer lasting colour. It is always best to select plants after having seen them flower, as this will save disappointment. Display gardens at these nurseries are worth visiting during spring to help you decide which plants to order later in the year.

A common problem that may be encountered when purchasing peonies is the incorrect labelling of plants. There is nothing worse than waiting for a couple of years for a plant to flower, only to find that it is not what you expected it to be. Most varieties of *P. lactiflora* look identical when they are not in flower. The plants are raised in fields and it is very easy for them to be mixed up unless the nursery is extremely methodical with its labelling. The demand for species peonies is such that

The flowers of *P. wittmanniana* range from creamy white to very pale yellow. It is a very underrated plant.

some plants sold as species are actually hybrids. Some characteristics of one parent are so dominant that the infertility of the plant may be the only indication that it is a hybrid. Thus *P. wittmanniana*, which should be creamy white, is often sold with pink flowers, indicating the specimen is of hybrid origin and likely to be infertile. While this may not be critical for the average gardener, it is particularly important for anyone who intends to breed peonies.

American breeders have recently succeeded in introducing herbaceous peonies with coral-pink flowers, achieved by crossing *P. peregrina* with other species. These are very striking but tend to be less hardy in Europe than in America, and may produce fewer flowers than expected. North American winters tend to be very cold but have less rainfall than in the Atlantic climate of Western Europe. This does occasionally work to the advantage of gardeners in Western Europe: one of the most beautiful of the species, *P. mlokosewitschi* is considered to be very unreliable in North America, whereas it grows happily in the British Isles.

Tree Peonies

In the British Isles at least, tree peonies are more difficult to obtain. It is common to see these plants sold in garden centres in vividly illustrated cardboard cartons: avoid them like the plague. The varieties are rarely, if ever, marked and the plant cannot be guaranteed to be identical to the illustration on the front of the box. Part of the problem with this type of presentation is that the plant cannot be watered once it is in the box. It is obvious that any plant, starved of water and kept in a dark carton for several weeks (during what should be its main growing season) will be at a disadvantage when compared to a potted specimen. The plants sold in these boxes are usually year-old grafts, much better established plants can be obtained from a specialist nursery for a similar price.

Tree peonies usually become available in the early spring and, in all likelihood, the plants will have small flowers. While it is very tempting to allow the plants to flower, this can considerably weaken a young tree peony. The buds are, therefore, best removed with a pair of secateurs and the shoot pruned to leave three or four leaves. Tree peonies are normally sold in small plastic pots, filled with a peat-based compost. This is a suitable medium for transport, but the plants can deteriorate if

they are not planted out fairly quickly into normal soil. Peat-based compost can easily become waterlogged, resulting in the death of the rootstock, and consequently the grafted scion. If the peony has been bought during the summer months, it should be carefully removed from the pot with its root ball intact and planted out in a spare piece of ground. In the autumn it can be dug up, taking care not to damage the roots, and planted correctly in its permanent home.

Peony Species

The majority of peony species are fairly easy to grow, the main difficulty is obtaining them in the first place. In Great Britain no single nursery has all of the peony species; the *RHS Plant Finder* is a great help, but living material is in short supply and therefore expensive. Another problem is that some peonies hybridize fairly easily, and produce fertile seed. Plants are also mislabelled, either due to an inability to recognize a very young plant or because the label has fallen out at some stage, or the nurserymen may have ignored changes in nomenclature and continued to use names that ceased to be legitimate many years ago. For example, *P. peregrina* is still frequently sold as *P. lobata*.

Certain species, such as *P. mlokosewitschi* are always in short supply and thus fairly expensive to purchase. The demand is such that some nurseries will divide their material to give just one 'eye' or bud. Although this is better than nothing, such plants will take a long time to recover from the shock and it may be several years before they flower. The very rare species often have a waiting list; the plants are divided in the autumn or spring and posted to the customer in bare-root form.

Part of the problem associated with the shortage of desirable species is the pressure that is placed upon the plants in their natural habitat. Several originate from the Caucasus Mountains, an area which is still in a state of political turmoil. As countries where species peonies grow become more accessible to visitors and tourists, there is strong pressure to exploit these natural resources. Avoid adding to the problem by ensuring that any species peony you purchase was either raised from seed or propagated in a nursery.

Many species are available as seed, and this is the most cost effective way of building up a collection. It is a rather long process, however, as seedlings cannot be expected to be flowering until they are least four or five years old. Peony flowers are self-fertile and, in the absence of other peony species, set seed that will usually produce pure offspring. However, most species are also inter-fertile, which can cause problems when trying to obtain pure seed. The majority of peony seed originates from botanic gardens and nurseries, which typically have a number of species growing together. It is impossible to completely isolate these different species, so bees and other insects often cross-pollinate them. Therefore, wild-collected seed is more likely to produce authentic plants than nursery-collected material. An exception is *P. cambessedesii*, which flowers much earlier than most of the other species so nursery-grown seed is more likely to be pure. Check on the origin of the seed before you purchase it: certain threatened species, such as *P. rhodia*, could be irrevocably damaged by excessive seed collection in the wild.

GROWING PEONIES FROM SEED

Peonies are not difficult to grow from seed, in fact this is how most of the species were collected in the first place. They produce quite large seed: that obtained from *P. mascula* is ovoid and measures approximately 5mm x 7mm (³⁄₁₆ x ³⁄₁₆in) while that of *P. mlokosewitschi* is a rather more spherical 7mm x 7mm (³⁄₁₆ x ³⁄₁₆in). The largest seed is that of *P. lutea* var. *ludlowii*; it measures approximately 11 x 14mm (⁶⁄₁₆ x ⁹⁄₁₆in), is somewhat flattened and looks rather like a small black bean. The seeds of most peonies are dark blue when mature, but darken to almost black as they dry. *P. lactiflora* seed is light chocolate-brown when mature.

Peony seed should be collected when it is ripe; unripe seed will almost certainly rot in the soil. The seed should be sown as soon as possible after harvesting, if it is allowed to dry out too much the embryo will enter dormancy and will not germinate for at least a further year. Fresh peony seed normally produces its first root in the autumn after sowing, the aerial shoot appearing during the following spring. Older seed will lie dormant for the whole of the first winter and will not germinate until late in the autumn of the following year. The aerial shoot should then emerge during the second spring. It is possible to break dormancy by placing the seed in a fridge, but the process is not well documented. Germination of the species is somewhat erratic and depends to a great extent on how old the seed is. It is quite common for a few seedlings to appear in the second year and a

further batch during the third.

Older seed can be cleaned of any fungal pathogens by rinsing in a mild solution of *Potassium permanganate* or domestic bleach (10% by volume) then thoroughly rinsed with fresh water before sowing.

Sow the seed of peony species in deep seed trays or 12cm (5in) pots at a depth of approximately 2–3cm (1in). Use sterilized soil-based seed compost and cover the surface with a layer of horticultural grit to reduce the growth of moss and weeds. It is not necessary to protect the seed of the hardy species but the more tender ones should be placed in a unheated coldframe. There are several advantages in using pots, the main being the opportunity to give expensive seed more care and attention. Plants in pots are more securely labelled and less prone to attack by rabbits and other pests. Peony breeders usually sow seed outside in carefully prepared nursery beds.

Peonies germinate in one of two ways: epigeal or hypogeal. Only a few, such as *P. brownii* and *P. tenuifolia*, are epigeal, producing aerial cotyledons before the juvenile leaves. The majority have hypogeal germination where the cotyledons remain in the seed case and the juvenile leaves emerge immediately. The young seedlings have three juvenile leaves and are best left until the end of the second year after germination before transplanting. Plants are more capable of surviving the trauma of being moved when they have a well established root system. Pot-grown seedlings can be pricked out into individual 10cm (4in) pots or planted out in a nursery bed 30cm (12in) apart and in rows 1m (3ft) apart. Tree peony seedlings are larger than those of their herbaceous cousins, if they have been sown in pots they can often be transplanted during the first autumn after germination.

The big advantage of growing peonies from seed is the opportunity to try them in different parts of the garden. Peony species are expensive to buy ready grown and they are not always the easiest of plants to establish. This is particularly the case with species such as *P. rhodia* which is easily damaged by late frosts.

DIVIDING HERBACEOUS PEONIES

Herbaceous peonies are best propagated by division in early autumn. Lift the plant with a fork and clean it thoroughly with fresh water. Leave the excavated crown to stand in the shade for at least a few hours;

they are allowed to dry out slightly they become more flexible and, therefore, easier to divide. Split the crown into pieces with at least four or five buds, using a clean, sharp knife. Dust the cut ends with fungicide before replanting. It is unlikely that the new plants will flower during the following season, the buds are there but they often fail to open. Flowering can be expected to resume during the second year. Smaller pieces with fewer buds, which break off during division, can be planted out in a nursery bed but it will be some time before the resulting plants are large enough to flower.

CULTIVATING HERBACEOUS PEONIES

Herbaceous peonies are best planted in the autumn. This allows the small feeding roots to become well established during the winter. They can be planted in the spring but it is important to water them well in dry weather until they are established.

Plant in good, well-drained garden soil. Peonies grown on sandy soil have a tendency to produce more leaves and less flowers, while those planted on clay soil take longer to become established but produce better blooms. Peonies grow best in neutral or alkaline soil but are unhappy in soil with a pH lower than 6. If the pH is too high, they are likely to suffer from chlorosis; ground limestone should be added if the pH is lower than 6. The majority of peonies prefer an open sunny position, but some species, whose natural habitat is in woodland or among scrub, are happier when planted among shrubs in a mixed border.

While peonies are tolerant of a wide range of soil conditions, they will not survive in situations where the soil becomes waterlogged. Another situation to avoid is beneath large conifers, the soil is far too dry and insufficient light will reach the plants.

Paeonia cambessedesii, *P. clusii*, *P. parnassica* and *P. rhodia* are all considered to be more difficult to grow and maintain than other species. They originate from Mediterranean islands where there are short wet winters and long dry summers. To stand any chance of success in wetter climates, they must be grown in very well-drained soil. They also start to grow very early in the season and, as a consequence, are likely to be damaged by frosts. *P. rhodia* starts to grow in early winter and is very vulnerable to damage by low temperatures in the spring. *P. cambessedesii* survives quite happily outside in mild areas as long as it receives shelter from cold winds and frost. In wetter places it is best protected by a cloche or planted at the foot of a warm sunny wall. While some people consider *P. clusii* to be quite hardy, I recommend it is given some protection. *P. emodi* is best planted in the shade of shrubs or trees where it will be protected from cold winds and the sun: in its natural habitat it grows in dappled shade.

Species peonies have a much shorter flowering period than the more familiar *P. lactiflora* varieties. Individual plants may also vary in their flowering time, depending upon their origin. In a large collection, such as that at the Royal Botanic Gardens at Kew, some plants may be in full flower, while others of the same species are still in bud. Most species will flower for at least two weeks, but this may be shortened if the weather is very hot. The flowering season can be prolonged by planting peonies in semi-shade.

Site

It has always been accepted that a peony should not be planted where another has grown previously. The reasons for this are uncertain, but may be due to the depletion of trace elements in the soil. Another possible cause could be a build up of soil pathogens from a previous resident. If there is no alternative site the soil should be excavated to a depth of 1m (3ft) and replaced with fresh. Peonies should be planted at least 1m (3ft) apart, if space permits 1.2m (4ft).

Dig the soil to a depth of 30–90cm, (12–36in); deeper digging will give better results in the long term. Mix bonemeal, compound fertilizer or well-rotted manure with the soil at the bottom of the hole and, if necessary, add ground limestone. Place the peony in the hole and fill the area around it carefully with topsoil, ensuring that no air cavities are left under the plant or among the roots. It is important to ensure that the buds are planted at a final depth of approximately 5cm (2in). If they are planted too deeply the peony may not flower. In very hot countries peonies should be planted at a maximum depth of 2.5cm (1in) to allow the plant to benefit from any cold weather during the winter months.

The peony will appreciate a liberal amount of well-rotted compost mixed with the top soil at the time of planting. Fresh manure should not be used as it may cause the crown to rot. The recently dug soil will settle in time and this should be borne in mind when planting: soil is likely to be raked into any depression and the

peony may still end up being covered too deeply. Mark the plant with a cane to ensure you do not damage the emerging shoots when they start to grow in the spring. Peonies should be well watered after planting and this should be repeated frequently if the work was carried out during the spring. Regular irrigation is only necessary in very hot countries.

To get the best out of your peonies, give them an application of fertilizer in the autumn. Try to avoid compound fertilizers that are high in nitrogen as this will only produce a large amount of foliage and few flowers. A suitable ratio is 20:20:20 or 10:20:20 (NPK) applied at a rate of 60g (2oz) in the first year after planting; double this in subsequent years. Good organic fertilizers are bonemeal or well-rotted cow manure, if the latter is used, care must taken to avoid applying it near the crown of the plant.

If you accidentally damage the emerging shoots of a peony in the spring, this is not the disaster it may initially appear. Peonies have two sets of buds, primary and secondary. If the primary buds are destroyed, the

Peonies should be planted at least 90cm (3ft) apart, as shown here with the semi-double hybrid 'Postilion'

secondary will develop to take their place, although these stems will not be as strong as those developing from the primary buds. However, if the plant has double flowers it is not unusual for the secondary buds to produce stems with single flowers that have fully functional stamens and pistils. This characteristic is of great importance to the plant breeder. In many double varieties of peony the stamens and carpels have developed into non-functioning petaloids. By removing the primary buds the breeder is able to cross-pollinate plants which would otherwise be infertile.

PROPAGATING TREE PEONIES

While it is possible to propagate tree peonies by layering, the success rate is said to be fairly low. Named varieties are usually increased by grafting on to a herbaceous rootstock in late summer. This is a rather skilled task and is usually carried out by specialist nurseries in Japan or the USA. The best rootstock material is considered to be that produced from five year old plants of *P. lactiflora* or *P. officinalis*, which have been raised from seed specifically for this purpose. These tend to be more resistant to *Botrytis* and other diseases than the roots of cultivated varieties. The roots are dug up and the soil washed off; they are then stored in a cool place while the scions are produced. The rootstocks are stored in damp wood chips or some similar material to prevent them drying out. Each *P. lactiflora* root can then be divided to produce twenty or more rootstocks, each measuring approximately 10–15cm (4–6in) long. The roots are divided from the crown of the plant using a clean, sharp knife.

The best material for grafting is obtained from shoots that have grown up as suckers during the previous season. The first scion, measuring approximately 6–8cm (2.5–3in) long, is taken from the terminal bud, the removal of which stimulates one or two of the lateral buds to grow and mature. These can then also be removed and used in the grafting process. There is a higher success rate with the terminal buds than with the laterals and the terminal bud has the bonus that it may well have a flower bud already developed. If this is grafted on to a rootstock the resulting plant will probably flower in its first year, which helps to sell the plant and confirms that it is true to type. The prepared scions are stored in a polythene bag to prevent dehydration and are best used on the day that they were cut.

Breeders use a number of different types of graft, but one of the most popular is the wedge graft. The best tool for preparing the scion is a single-sided razor blade or a suitable scalpel, both of which can be obtained from suppliers of laboratory equipment. A cut is made along one side of the scion down to its severed end, this is then repeated on the other side to create a triangular-shaped point. Another cut of exactly the same size is made in the side of the rootstock; the scion will fit into this. It is very important that the two cuts match; if they do not the scion may die and the graft fail. The top of the rootstock (opposite the graft) is cut away in a downward direction. This stops rainwater collecting in the graft and reduces the chance of infection. The graft is assembled and bound tightly with grafting tape (available from most good garden centres). If the completed grafts cannot be planted immediately they should be labelled, placed in a polythene bag and stored in a cool place.

The soil for the nursery bed is best prepared several weeks before planting by incorporating well-rotted manure into the soil, together with a slow-release fertilizer such as blood, fish and bone. The grafts are planted upright, approximately 20cm (8in) apart, and covered by 5cm (2in) of soil. The whole area is then covered with a 5cm (2in) layer of wood bark chips, which is in turn covered by a sheet of thick black polythene. This has the dual role of keeping down weeds and reducing the chances of the graft union being damaged by frost in the winter. The plastic sheet is removed in spring. With practice, and a certain degree of luck, it is said to be possible to achieve a 50% success rate with grafting.

The process can also be undertaken on a smaller scale by placing the grafted plants in pots or deep seed trays filled with equal parts of sand and peat. These are placed in a shaded coldframe until the autumn, by which time the graft should have callused over. The grafts are then potted up into 10cm (4in) flower pots filled with a soil-based compost, sprayed with a fungicide, and returned to the coldframe for the winter. In the spring the tree peonies can be planted out into a nursery bed. It is important that the union between rootstock and scion is below ground level as this stimulates the scion to produce its own roots. Some growers recommend cutting off the rootstock when the scion itself is well rooted – the herbaceous rootstock is an obstacle for the roots of the tree peony and can become infected with fungi, which can in turn attack the scion.

The majority of Chinese growers propagate their tree peonies by division. Outside China this has always been the least favoured method of propagation, as there is always a high risk that the plant will die afterwards. Mature plants frequently produce new shoots around the original graft. These usually have their own roots and can be separated to produce new tree peonies. The chances of this occurring are increased if the plant has been regularly mulched with humus-rich material. Great care must be taken when the tree peony is lifted and all of the soil must be hosed off to enable these buds to be seen. Any cuts that are made should be dusted with flowers of sulphur to reduce the risk of infection. Divisions with four or five buds are more likely to survive than those with less.

A method that has shown some promise is the use of rooted cuttings, although this is not widely used. The cuttings are taken from the parent plant in late spring, being cut just below the current season's wood. The top of the shoot is removed above a leaf node to give a cutting approximately 15cm (6in) long. The lower leaves are removed completely and the upper leaves reduced in length by 50%. The prepared cutting is dipped in water and then hormone rooting powder, before being placed in pots filled with a well-drained compost composed of loam, peat or coir and sharp sand at a ratio of 1:2:3. The finished cuttings are placed in a coldframe and should root during the summer. They should be sprayed with a fungicide to prevent infection by *Botrytis* and can be planted out during the following spring.

Micro-propagation has been attempted with tree peonies. While it is possible to divide the meristem and produce young plantlets, these invariably succumb to infection when they are transplanted.

CULTIVATING TREE PEONIES

It is a common misconception that tree peonies are delicate and difficult to grow. Their natural habitat is on mountainous and rocky hillsides where they are subjected to high winds, extreme cold in the winter and dry soil in the summer. In China, tree peonies used to be grown in the mountainous areas of the country and then shipped, bare-rooted, to the cities in the hotter lowlands. They were then potted up and sold to customers for flowering. These were the original disposable plants, it was too hot for them to survive the winter in the south of the country and after flowering the plants were simply thrown away.

Tree peonies are best planted in rich, well-drained soil and tend to prefer slightly alkaline conditions. They should be planted in the open and away from the roots of large trees, but with some protection from early morning frost. Tree peonies benefit from the application of a heavy layer of compost – particularly important if they are grown in sandy soil. It is essential to plant young specimens with the graft union covered by at least 10cm (4in) of soil. If this is not done the scions will be unable to grow their own roots, and the resulting plant will not be well shaped. Grafted plants are more susceptible to fungal attacks and the sooner the scion produces its own roots the healthier it will be. If a plant refuses to produce more than one stem when it is happily rooted, it can be pruned to within 10cm (4in) of the ground in autumn. This should stimulate it to produce more shoots (the author cannot be held responsible for the consequences of this action!). The cut wood

The Kelways tree peony 'Duchess of Kent' (p.135).

should be dusted with a fungicide to avoid any infection. Tree peonies do not require any regular pruning, other than to remove dead or weak stems.

Tree peonies are very rarely damaged by low temperatures in the winter, when they are dormant. They grow happily in many parts of Scandinavia and America, where temperatures can fall as low as -20°C (-4°F), as long as they are protected with straw, bracken or conifer branches. The young shoots often start to grow in the very early spring and the sudden thawing of frozen leaves by bright sunshine causes tissue damage. The branches of tree peonies are very brittle and easily damaged by high winds. In exposed areas it is best to plant them in a sheltered site. This also has the advantage of protecting the flowers in the spring: there is nothing more frustrating than having to wait patiently for the flower buds to open only to have them destroyed the next day by high winds and rain. In Japan, flowering tree peonies are often protected from sun, wind and rain with a canopy of cloth.

Contrary to popular belief, tree peonies can be grown successfully as pot plants when they are young; the ancient Chinese often grew them in this way. They can grow very quickly in the right conditions and require large pots filled with a well-drained soil-based compost. Terracotta is preferable to plastic as this reduces the risk of the roots becoming waterlogged. Potted plants should remain healthy for at least three to four years, after this they should be planted out in open ground.

3

PEONIES IN THE GARDEN

While the majority of herbaceous peonies are large plants with vivacious flowers, there are also a number of species and hybrids that make good rock-garden plants. Many species of peony grow on rocky slopes in their natural habitat and are therefore well adapted to living in well-drained and stony sites. Among the most suitable species are *P. anomala*, *P. officinalis* ssp. *humilis* and ssp. *villosa*, *P. veitchii* and *P. tenuifolia*. The Greek species such as *P. clusii* and *P. rhodia* would also be ideal if they were not such delicate plants. The American breeder, Roy Klehm has introduced several new dwarf hybrid peonies in his 'Rock Gardens Series', many of which were originally bred by William Krekler. *P. officinalis* 'Anemoniflora rosea' is another dwarf plant which makes an ideal subject but its flowers are such a striking colour that it can rather steal the show.

I have already emphasized that tree peonies are not the delicate plants that many people perceive them to be. On the other hand, they do benefit from being grown in a location where they are protected from the worst that the elements can throw at them. They are perfectly suited to open woodland or among shrubs. Here, they can develop their wonderful flowers without being battered by cold winds; the surrounding vegetation also creates a micro-climate which reduces the risk of damage by late frosts. Avoid densely shaded areas as this will reduce the vigour of the tree peony.

P. delavayi and *P. lutea* ssp. *ludlowii* are best treated as specimen plants isolated from other shrubs. Both species have a particularly elegant shape when they are fully grown and this is spoilt if the branches of other shrubs are allowed to mingle with them. The same applies to a certain extent with Moutan tree peonies, but these do benefit from the protection that is afforded by surrounding trees and shrubs.

While tree peonies do eventually become very large shrubs, they can be kept to a manageable size by planting them in large terracotta pots. They make very good specimen plants for the patio and there are very few other shrubs that can compete with a tree peony in full bloom.

BORDERS AND FAMOUS GARDENS

Herbaceous peonies are probably best suited to herbaceous borders, where they can be fitted into many colour schemes. The French Impressionist painter Claude Monet applied the same principles in his garden at Giverny that he used in his paintings. He planted pale pink, single-flowered and Japanese varieties of peony to make the perfect counterfoil for blue and mauve irises. Both flowers thrive in dry well-drained soil and bloom at the same time of the year.

The doyen of British gardening Gertrude Jekyll was sparing in her use of peonies. Seeming to have had a dislike for magenta, she preferred to use peonies with white or pink flowers. Her favourite combination was peonies with roses, as is demonstrated by her plans for the garden at Upton Grey in Hampshire. She also liked planting peonies with irises. It was an eye for colour that was the secret of her success and we can only speculate on how she would have handled the fiery colours of the modern hybrids. It is unfortunate that so many of the gardens she designed no longer exist in their original

These attractive displays of a wide variety of peonies are growing in island beds at Gilbert H. Wild Nurseries in Missouri, USA.

form: many of them were very labour intensive and nowadays few house owners can afford the luxury of a huge team of gardeners. While the original gardens are no longer in existence, the majority of her plans and designs have survived and they remain an inspiration for modern gardeners.

A traditional way of growing peonies in the British Isles is in mixed borders. This is well exemplified by the borders surrounding the walled garden at Spetchley Park in Worcestershire. The majority of the plants here are varieties of *P. lactiflora* planted in groups of three or four and mixed with other herbaceous perennials. In Victorian and Edwardian Britain, most large country houses had a collection of peonies, many of which have survived to this day (unfortunately all too frequently the labels for the plants were lost many years ago). To a great extent this aspect of British gardening is trapped in a time warp: the majority of the varieties that are still grown in these gardens were bred in the latter part of the nineteenth century. The owners of Spetchley Park, who are trying to rectify this, have recently planted a number of modern American hybrids.

Hidcote Manor Garden in Gloucestershire has enthralled many people since it was first laid out by Lawrence Johnston in the early part of the twentieth century. Hidcote's charm is in the way that the garden has been divided into numerous compartments, linked by steps and footpaths. Above all, it is on a manageable scale which visitors can relate to; each compartment has a different character, in a space comparable to their own garden. As holder of a National Collection of peonies, Hidcote has a good collection of species and their cultivated varieties. The majority of them are grown away from the main garden but it is well worth asking permission to see them.

The area of Hidcote where peonies come into their own is the Pillar Garden. Here, the vigorous hybrid 'Avant Garde' (*P. wittmanniana* × *P. lactiflora*) makes a wonderful specimen plant with its large rounded leaves and single pink flowers suffused with magenta. There are a number of other *P. wittmanniana* hybrids in the Pillar Garden, all sharing the same dramatic foliage and massive creamy white flowers. These are no shrinking violets, they shout for attention and crowd out the smaller plants beneath them. *Fuchsia magellanica* var. *aurea* is planted around the peonies and fills the space when they lose their vigour towards the end of the

summer. *P. mascula* ssp. *arietina* 'Mother of Pearl', in contrast, is a much smaller plant, perfect for softening the hard edges of steps and walls, its soft pink flowers contrasting beautifully with its grey-green foliage.

P. officinalis 'Mutabilis Plena' is an old variety, similar to the better known 'Rosea Plena', but with brighter deep pink flowers. Johnston used it to line one of the paths in the Pillar Garden, backed by the purple globes of *Allium giganteum* and the blue *Geranium wallichianum* 'Buxton's Variety'. Companion plants with blue or purple flowers such as these are useful for bringing out the pink colour of peony flowers and suppressing the magenta. Another path runs parallel to the first and is lined along one side with *P. peregrina* 'Fire King' and 'Otto Froebel'. A selection of other peonies is planted

In perfect conditions, *P. rockii* will grow to form a substantial shrub up to 2m (6ft) high. This specimen at 'Highdown' in Sussex is over sixty years old.

beneath a Scot's pine (*Pinus sylvestris*) and a nice specimen of *Magnolia denudata*.

Sadly the gardens at Highdown in West Sussex have lost some of their original inhabitants. The house used to belong to Sir Frederick Stern who wrote an influential monograph about peonies in 1946. A retired merchant banker and soldier, Stern collected a wonderful range of lime-loving plants in his garden, formerly a disused chalk quarry. With dozens of cartloads of manure Stern transformed the barren soil into a suitable home for hundreds of exotic specimens, including all of the

peonies he collected for his monograph. One of the survivors is a massive specimen of *P. rockii*. When this is flowering nothing can compete with it for sheer impact. It was grown from the original seed collected by Dr. Rock (see p.49) when he was in China.

Peonies are at home at Highdown, tumbling over the slopes which mimic their natural habitat so closely. In some places *Paeonia officinalis* ssp. *humilis* and ssp. *villosa* have self-seeded and in late spring cover themselves with bright magenta flowers. Also found in the garden are *P. wittmanniana* and *P. veitchii*, which grow happily beneath the wooded areas. Another plant that is particularly at home here is *P. delavayi*. Over the years it has hybridized with *P. lutea* and produced plants with a diverse range of flower colours. Named hybrids at Highdown include 'Black Pirate' and 'Argosy'. Stern was interested in breeding tree peonies and, although none of these appear to have been offered commercially, they are scattered like jewels around the garden. One of them, 'Sybil Stern', has strawberry-coloured flowers with mauve flares.

The garden at Hodnet Hall in Shropshire was originally laid out by the late Brigadier A. G. W. Heber-Percy. One of the highlights of this attractive English garden is the 'Circular Garden', which uses concentric rings of roses, peonies and hydrangeas to provide a succession of colour throughout the year. The outer circle consists of four varieties of rose. Two hybrid musks, 'Felicia' and 'Penelope' complement the Portland rose, 'Comte de Chambord', and the single rugosa 'Fru Dagmar Hastrup'. All have pink flowers.

Inside this ring of roses and separated by a grass path is a wonderful circle of Chinese peonies. These are varieties of *P. lactiflora*, including 'Sarah Bernhardt', 'Lady Alexandra Duff', 'Kelway's Glorious', 'Bowl of Beauty' and 'Pink Dawn'. The peonies produce a dense mass of pink and white flowers whose scent wafts around the whole area. The single varieties form a soft counterfoil to the more imposing double forms. At the extreme centre of the flower clock is a solid bed with a small statue at its centre. It is planted with *Hydrangea paniculata* 'Grandiflora', lavender and *Caryopteris × clandonensis*.

The gardens at Penshurst Place are redolent of history, having been the home of the Sidney family since 1552. Peonies have a particularly high status in this garden where they have been used to particularly dramatic effect in the Peony Walk. This consists of a pure mass of

The impressive circular bed at Hodnet Hall in Shropshire is an imaginative way to grow peonies in the garden.

pink and magenta peonies and includes 'Monsieur Jules Elie', 'Lady Alexandra Duff', 'Albert Crousse' and 'Sarah Bernhardt' with lavender in the foreground and *Berberis thunbergii* behind.

Herbaceous peonies can be used as massed plants for dramatic effect or blended into herbaceous borders. And it should be remembered that while peonies can look rather sad during the latter months of the summer, many come into their own again in the autumn. Peony species such as *P. mlokosewitschi*, *P. mollis* and *P. veitchii* have wonderful autumn colouring and various cultivars of *P. lactiflora*, 'Whitleyi Major', for example, turn bright reddish brown, while the leaves of the tree peony 'King of White Lion' turn vivid red.

PEONIES IN AMERICA
Don Hollingsworth, Maryville, Missouri

"Peonies have been widely grown in North America, not only because of their extraordinary flowers, but because they are as favourably adapted to the harsher inland climates as they are to the easier gardening areas of east and west. Historically, once they had become known to the settlers of mid-America, peonies became a part of the cherished traditions of home and family, joining such early stalwarts as lilacs (*Syringa* sp.), mock orange (*Philadelphus* sp.), Scotch pines (*Pinus sylvestris*) and perennial food plants around homes in rural and urban areas, alike. Peonies that were planted long ago may still be seen growing around abandoned rural home sites and old cemeteries, often flowering quite well without any current care.

During the early half of the twentieth century, peony flowers came into extensive demand for the florist trade, being equal to rosebuds in their suitability for shipping and storage. There was also a thriving market in local sales, especially around Decoration Day (now the Memorial Day holiday), the late May date set aside for honouring the dead. The pre-World War II demand for long-stemmed cut peonies had a profound influence on the type of peony sought by breeders. Preference was given to long-stemmed cultivars having double flower forms. The sorts most favoured by the trade were, consequently, built up to very large numbers. However, for several decades after the Second World War, the once flourishing demand for cut-flower peonies declined, while exotic tropicals and greenhouse-produced flowers replaced them in the market. So, many cut-flower peony fields were simply abandoned. Others were sold off into the general nursery trade, following the established practice of selling the plants on offer only upon flower descriptions. Many buyers were thus lured into acquiring peonies that were poorly suited for standing against rain in the garden while carrying their heavy flowers. The long-time practice of offering peonies principally upon flower descriptions continues to prevail to this day.

The American Peony Society (1903 to the present) grew strongly for its first half century under the major influence of the cut-flower interests. Therefore, much recognition was given to show table qualities and attributes leading to the reliable production of flowers, with lesser regard for classifying the cultivars on characteristics that were favourable to their presentation while flowering in the landscape.

The traditional peonies of America are the cultivars of the Lactiflora Group (also known as Chinese peonies) and it is these sorts upon which the prevailing image of peonies is based. The very large scale of the typical lactiflora peonies (relative to many garden perennials) imposes certain constraints on how they are used in landscape designs. Even in large estates and public gardens, they have been most often displayed as single genus collections in blocks of plants, although such displays are fitted into the larger landscape plan. This is also seen in large garden's treatment of the Moutan tree peony cultivars. In small gardens, uses typically include planting in blocks or rows along boundaries, driveways or as cutting beds. Other gardens, designed to feature a variety of flowering perennials, have peonies integrated into mixed borders. As traditional images of peony growing have faded, the interest in using them as part of all-season mixed genera landscape decoration has increased.

Not all peonies are created equal. The current North American collection of peonies contains numerous hybrids, as well as less heavily-flowered forms of the lactifloras. The ancestry of the hybrids reflects fifteen or more of the species and has led to appealing innovations of flower, flowering season and bush habit. American peony breeders and specialist propagators are increasingly meeting the requirements of the landscapers and gardeners in their published descriptions of new cultivars and in their lists of offerings. This partly reflects the personal interests of those who are composing the descriptions, but also reflects the increasing market place influence of specialists in landscape design and maintenance – a discriminating lot, at best.

Recent decades have seen a great rise in consciousness of beautiful landscape in America, as evidenced in the proliferation of popular gardening periodicals, gardening products and larger increases in membership of local plant societies and gardening groups. Affluent two-income families with increasing disposable cash, while having less personal time for caring for their exterior surroundings have, simultaneously, become increasingly sensitized to both the larger environment and the possibilities for their own landscape. Consequently, the full range of peony varieties can be expected to come into wider use in coming decades."

PEONIES IN NEW ZEALAND

The first peonies to reach New Zealand were probably introduced by English settlers in the late nineteenth century. Many of these were Kelways varieties such as 'Lady Alexandra Duff', 'Kelway's Majestic', 'King of England' and 'Kelway's Glorious'. A number of old French varieties, such as 'Monsieur Jules Elie', 'Festiva Maxima' and 'Albert Crousse' were also very popular and probably arrived from the same English source.

During the twentieth century further plants were introduced by private individuals from England and Holland. In recent years, growers like Dorothy and Bruce Hamilton have imported a wider range of plants from America and Holland. These have included many new hybrid peonies, a number of which are still unavailable in Britain.

The cut-flower trade is well developed in New Zealand, with blooms finding a ready market in Japan and the United States. The majority of nurseries are members of the New Zealand Peony Grower's Group, which tests new varieties and develops the market for cut blooms. At the present time there is no peony breeding being undertaken in New Zealand. New varieties are being introduced but these have been raised from seed that originated in the United States.

'Monsieur Jules Elie' (above) is an old variety with fragrant, double flowers. It is widely grown and inexpensive. 'Scarlet O'Hara' (right) has single, bright red flowers. The numerous side buds give it a very long flowering season.

In many ways the climate of South Island is very similar to that of the British Isles. Most peonies are grown in the Central Otago district and in the vicinity of Canterbury. The central plateau of South Island has cold dry winters and hot dry summers; perfect for peonies. The North Island is much hotter than the South, with high humidity and warm winter temperatures. This restricts the areas where peonies can be satisfactorily grown. The climate around Auckland and most of the north coast is far too hot but they can be cultivated elsewhere in the south of the island. Botrytis can be a serious problem in New Zealand, particularly in the coastal regions where the humidity is high.

RECOMMENDED PEONIES

The table opposite recommends a number of peony varieties. These are based on my own experience and taste. Flowering time is only an approximate guide.

RECOMMENDED VARIETIES FOR GARDENS

	VERY EARLY SEASON	EARLY SEASON	MIDSEASON	LATE SEASON
Tree Peonies	*Paeonia rockii*	Yachiyo Tsubaki Kaow Kishu Caprice	Golden Era	
Single White		Archangel Requiem	Krinkled White	White Wings
Single Pink	*Paeonia arietina* 'Mother of Pearl'	Paula Fay Salmon Dream	Dawn Pink Honor	Mischief Nymphe
Single Light Red	*Paeonia officinalis* 'Rubra'	Scarlet O'Hara America Postilion	Bethcar	
Single Dark Red		Illini Warrior	Red Velvet	
'Yellow' Peonies	*P. mlokosewitschi*	Claire de Lune Moonrise	Garden Treasure (Itoh)	
Japanese White			Isani Gidui	Jan van Leeuwen Bu-Te
Japanese Pink	*Paeonia officinalis* 'Anemoniflora rosea'	Bowl of Beauty	Gay Paree Comanche	Doreen
Japanese Red			White Cap Chocolate Soldier	Charm
Semi-double White		Miss America	Kelway's Supreme	
Semi-double Pink		Ellen Cowley Lovely Rose	Lady Alexandra Duff Philomèle	Nice Gal Daystar
Semi-double Red		Buckeye Belle	Cherry Ruffles	
Double White	*Paeonia officinalis* 'Lize van Veen'		Baroness Schroeder Kelway's Glorious Charlie's White Festiva Maxima	Marie Lemoine
Double Pink			Mrs. F. D. Roosevelt Dinner Plate Monsieur Jules Elie	Claire Dubois Emma Klehm
Double Red		Auten's 1816 Big Ben Delaware Chief Diana Parks	Kansas Paul M. Wild	

4
PESTS & DISEASES

Peonies are, on the whole, very robust plants which suffer from relatively few diseases. It is quite possible to operate without chemicals, such as fungicides, but vigilance is essential. Diseased material must be destroyed before pathogens can spread.

FUNGAL PATHOGENS

Honey Fungus (*Armillaria mellea*) This is a very serious fungal pathogen which can infect most woody plants and kills many ornamental trees and shrubs: tree peonies are susceptible. An attack by *Armillaria* is not always easy to diagnose as the fruiting bodies are only present in the autumn. These appear as clumps of toadstools around the base of diseased tree stumps. They are usually yellow or light brown but may have a grey, green or pinkish tinge to them. The gills, which may extend into the stalk, are white and darken with age to yellow.

Armillaria lives as a saprophyte in dead wood, spreading through the surrounding soil by a mass of black rhizomorphs (characteristic bootlace-like straps). These rhizomorphs can infect a new host; the infection shows initially as a stain and then develops into a soft brown rot. As the fungus withdraws nutrients from the host, the remaining wood is turned into a soft mass of stringy wood fibres mixed with white flakes. Fortunately it spreads relatively slowly, tending to kill a few woody plants each year. This allows a breathing space for steps to be taken to destroy it. The basidiospores of the fruiting bodies can also infect new hosts.

Armillaria is not easily killed. Any infected plants should be removed, together with their whole root system. The chemical treatments available have not proved to be very successful and infected plants have no chance of survival. As much soil as possible should be excavated from the site and disposed of away from your garden. No woody plants should be planted on the site for at least one year. If the source of the infection is not on your land, it is possible to establish a cordon using plastic sheeting, but this must be buried to a depth of at least 60cm (24in). The soil can also be soaked on a regular basis with a suitable fungicide, but this is not guaranteed to be successful.

Grey Mould Fungus (*Botrytis cinerea*) This exceptionally common disease affects a wide range of plants. A grey mould develops on the tissues of infected plants and matures to produce asexual spores, or conidia. These are transmitted by air and may persist in the soil or on dead plant material. The disease often attacks previously damaged tissue so the risk of infection can be reduced by good hygiene in the garden and the removal of dead peony leaves in the autumn. *Botrytis cinerea* is relatively easy to control with systemic fungicides.

Peony Grey Mould Blight or Peony Wilt (*Botrytis paeoniae*) Potentially the most dangerous disease for the peony grower, *Botrytis paeoniae* can devastate a collection of peonies in a relatively short period of time. The disease seems to vary in its virulence. In most seasons it seems to cause little damage and can be safely controlled by removing any infected material. However, in other years it can be quite devastating, slightly infected plants rapidly succumb and cannot be saved. Such an outbreak occurred in Britain during the 1960s and decimated a number of tree peony collections.

P. peregrina, as most species, is very disease resistant. The most likely cause of ill health is poor cultural conditions.

Botrytis paeoniae is a relatively common disease that causes soft brown areas to develop at the base of the leaves or shoots which then wilt and collapse. The infection progresses down the stem and along any other foliage and the buds turn black and rot. After a period of time a grey mould develops on the surface of the infected tissues and acts as a source of infection for other susceptible plants. If you only have one or two plants affected it is better to destroy them completely and remove the surrounding top soil, which should be removed from your garden and replaced with fresh. With any luck, this will prevent the disease from spreading. All other peonies and any lilies-of-the-valley (*Convallaria majalis*), an alternative host for *B. paeoniae*, should be sprayed with a systemic fungicide. It is good practice in the autumn to remove all dead peony leaves and burn them. The most dangerous time is when a collection is being started: any new plant may be infected and vigilance is essential. If you do not want to use fungicides, it is essential that any part of a plant infected with *Botrytis paeoniae* is removed immediately and destroyed by burning.

In the past the systemic fungicide Benlate would have been recommended for the control of *Botrytis*. However, during the last few years a number of pathogens have developed a tolerance to it and changes in safety legislation led to it being withdrawn from the market in 1995; it has also been implicated as the possible cause of a birth defect in babies. Fortunately there are several suitable alternatives, such as Bio Supercarb (which contains Carbendazim) and DOFF Plant Disease Control.

Leaf Blotch (*Cladosporium paeoniae*) This disease usually affects peonies after flowering. It starts as small reddish brown spots on the leaves, flowers and stems. On the upper surface of the leaves these develop into purplish brown blotches; the underside of the leaf will have corresponding dull brown blotches.

The disease can be controlled by the burning of infected plant material and removal of dead leaves at the end of the season. Further outbreaks can be prevented by spraying with a systemic fungicide or Bordeaux Mixture.

Peony Ringspot Virus A common and widespread virus, this causes irregular yellow rings or a mosaic on the leaves of peonies. Although it is disfiguring, peonies can usually tolerate the virus, but it makes sense to destroy infected plants before the disease is transmitted to others in your collection.

Peony Blotch (*Septoria paeoniae*) Common and widespread, this fungal pathogen causes greyish brown spots on the leaves and stems of peonies. The spots have a reddish margin and mature to produce black cup-shaped fruitbodies (*Pycnidia*). Attacks of this disease are not usually very serious. Damage is mainly cosmetic.

Verticillium Wilts Verticillium wilts are particularly devastating fungal diseases which affect a wide range of ornamental plants. The main symptoms are an initial wilting of the leaves, following by dark discoloration of the stem and, finally, the death of the infected plant. The pathogen is soil borne and attacks the host as a result of either underwatering, overwatering, root damage or nematode infection. The symptoms are caused by the blockage of the plants vascular system and the production of toxins by the fungus. Young tree peonies seem to be most vulnerable and, while spraying with a systemic fungicide may occasionally work, the plants will usually die once they are infected. Infected plants should be destroyed.

INSECTS AND OTHER PESTS

Chrysanthemum Eelworm (*Aphelenchoides ritzemabosi*) This widespread nematode infects a very wide range of ornamental plants. It is less of a threat than root knot nematode (below) but will stunt the growth of infected peonies. New plants should be checked carefully when they are purchased and any suspicious material avoided. Infected plants should be destroyed by burning or burying in a deep hole. Although *Aphelenchoides ritzemabosi* can be controlled by immersing infected plants in hot water, the temperature is critical and treatment is not recommended for the amateur gardener. Part of the problem with controlling this pest is the wide range of alternative hosts it may infest.

Swift Moth (*Hepialus* spp.) These white caterpillars, up to 6.5cm (2 ½in) long, with glossy brown heads are found in Europe. They are particularly common on newly cultivated land and feed underground on the shoot bases, roots, bulbs and rhizomes of a wide variety of plants, including peonies. The adult moths take to the wing at dusk during the summer months and are attracted to patches of weeds and herbaceous borders. During flight the females drop fertilized eggs which land on the ground and hatch after approximately fourteen days. The young caterpillars burrow into the soil and feed from autumn to winter, developing into pupae in the following spring.

A serious pest of lettuces and strawberries, the moths do not normally lay eggs on bare soil and control can be achieved by routine weeding and regular cultivation. Winter digging is particularly effective as the caterpillars are exposed to attack by predators. Peonies should be carefully checked when they are divided, and dusted with HCH or bromophos.

Ants: Common Black and Mound (*Lasius niger* and *Lasius flavus*) At first sight ants do not appear to cause any significant damage to peonies, although they find the nectar irresistible. However, it has been suggested that they may act as vector for the spores of *Botrytis*. By undermining the plant, large colonies may also cause damage to the roots. They are best controlled by using Ant Powder.

Root Knot or Root Gall Eelworm (*Meloidogyne* spp.) Peonies infected with this nematode have numerous thin stems and pale green leaves, show reduced vigour and rarely flower. It can be a very difficult pest to control and is most prevalent on light soils. If the plant is dug up, the thinner roots will be found to have distinctive galls up to 6mm (¼in) in diameter; on thicker roots the galls measure up to 13mm (½in) in diameter. Individual galls may be regular in shape but more frequently appear irregular due to the coalescence of several galls. The galls contain the female nematodes, while the surrounding soil is infested with their larvae. These larvae move through the soil and attack new hosts.

There are a number of chemicals that can be used to control these nematodes, but these are restricted to commercial nurseries. The best solution for the gardener is to burn the offending plant and grass over the area leaving it for a few years. On dry sandy soil, and in the absence of a suitable host, the eggs will die out within a few weeks. It is important to avoid contaminating other areas of the garden with eggs and larvae, as these can survive for several months in moist

conditions. Young seedlings should be potted up in new or sterilized pots using fresh sterile compost.

The risk of infection is reduced if commercial nurseries remove all of the fibrous roots when the plants are divided for sale. This is also said to produce more vigorous plants.

The Garden Symphylid (*Scutigerella immaculata*) These small white arthropods can be quite a serious problem in the USA, but are usually restricted to glasshouses in northern Europe. The adults measure approximately 6mm (¼in) long and, depending upon their age, have between 6 and 12 pairs of legs. Eggs are laid in the spring or autumn and hatch after 2–3 weeks to produce nymphs. Both the nymphs and the adults can cause severe damage to the root hairs of peony plants. Particularly common on soils that are rich in organic matter or have a high clay content, they can be controlled by using HCH dust or leaving the soil fallow, without any planting, for a couple of years.

CULTURAL PROBLEMS
Frost Damage A few species of peony, including *P. broteri* and *P. rhodia*, originate from Mediterranean countries and are easily damaged by frost. Other species

P. potanini, a variable shrub, spreads by stolons (see p.48).

may be extremely hardy when dormant but their young leaves are quickly damaged by late spring frosts. Frost damage usually occurs at the extremities of the leaflets, furthest away from the leaf stalk. The normal green tissue turns mid-brown, while the surface of the leaf loses its gloss. If the damage is slight the leaf will recover, but severe frost damage will kill the affected areas. Most of the damage is cosmetic and the plant will grow again next year. Vulnerable plants should be given protection at night when frost is expected. Large plants are best protected by hessian cloth supported on a cane frame, while smaller specimens can be completely encased with a glass or heavy plastic dome.

Certain hybrids, particularly those that have *P. wittmanniana* or *P. macrophylla* as a parent, can have their flowers spoiled by cold winds or late frost. The damage does not make itself apparent until the flower buds open, when the centre of the bloom will be found to have turned black. Unfortunately, there is very little that can be done to prevent this.

Waterlogging While peonies are very resilient plants, they cannot tolerate being grown on waterlogged soil. If water is allowed to stand for too long on an area planted with peonies, the plants will die. It is therefore best to avoid planting them in any location that has a very high water table.

The flowers of *P. wittmanniana* hybrids, such as 'Archangel' shown here, can suffer damage after late frosts.

5
THE PEONY SPECIES

If you were to ask the average person to describe a peony, the chances are that they would think of a substantial herbaceous plant with large double flowers. Few people realize that there are approximately forty peony species, many of which have beautiful and sometimes scented flowers, all of which are single. The actual number of species varies depending upon the authority consulted. To confuse the issue further, some botanists consider that certain peonies are subspecies, while others raise them to the level of a species.

Peonies have a long history and during the millions of years that they have existed a number of species have doubled the quantity of their chromosomes to become tetraploids. The basic number of chromosomes in a peony is 2n=10 (ie. diploid); in the tetraploid species this number is increased to 4n=20. This doubling up of the chromosomes tends to produce plants that are more adaptable and, therefore, better suited to a changing environment. Botanists work on the principle that if a plant is a tetraploid it probably evolved later than a similar diploid.

The greatest variability exists in the European species, with *P. mascula* divided into five subspecies and *P. officinalis* into four. In his article on the genus, published in 1941, H. N. Barber suggested that during the last ice age, the advancing ice cap drove the diploid species of peony into the peninsulas and islands of the Mediterranean. The tetraploids that arose from these surviving populations, such as *P. mascula* and *P. officinalis*, were more vigorous and adaptable than the diploids. As the ice retreated at the end of the ice age, the tetraploids were ideally suited to colonize the new territory that became available to them. The diploids (such as *P. rhodia* and *P. clusii*) could not compete with the tetraploids and remained restricted to the islands of the Mediterranean as the sea level rose. The Asian species, on the other hand, were not restricted in the same way and followed the retreating ice northwards when the climate improved. Consequently, these latter species, such as *P. lactiflora* and *P. anomala*, show less variability than their European relatives. The variation that is seen in *P. officinalis* and *P. mascula* makes it very difficult to classify them. Indeed, some botanists would include a number of other species (such as *P. mollis*) within these complexes.

The other problem results from the different interpretation that botanists in the former Soviet Union place upon the concept of the 'species'. Until recently most western botanists were unaware of a large mass of research that had been undertaken by their Soviet counterparts. As political barriers have fallen, this information has become available and is now being translated into English. One botanist in particular, L. M. Kemularia-Nathadze published an important scientific paper in 1961. In this she described a number of new species of peony which were considered to be endemic to the countries of the Caucasus region; at the present time only a few of these species are recognized by western botanists.

Until comparatively recently it was thought that there was only one species of tree peony, namely *P. suffruticosa*. This had been described in 1804 by a botanist called Andrews from a plant with double magenta flowers. During the following years almost every new introduction from China seems to have been given specific status, thus we have *P. papaveracea* (Andrews, 1807), *P. moutan* (Sims, 1808) and *P. arborea* (Donn, 1804) appearing in the literature. It was over a century before Sir Frederick Stern clarified the situation in his definitive monograph, *A study of the genus Paeonia* (1946). Stern came to the conclusion that all of these species were simply synonyms of *P. suffruticosa*.

In 1958 a Chinese botanist, Wen-Pei Fang described two new species of tree peony, *P. szechuanica* and *P. yunnanensis*. Both these species were overlooked by western scientists, presumably because the relevant scientific journals were unavailable outside China. The new peonies eventually came to light in 1992 when a team of botanists from the Chinese Academy of Forestry, led by Professor Hong Tao, announced two further species. Professor Hong Tao has suggested that the original *P. suffruticosa*, described by Andrews, was heterogeneous and that it should be split up into at least five species, namely *P. jishanensis*, *P. ostii*, *P. rockii*, *P. szechuanica* and *P. yananensis*. To these may now be added a sixth species *P. qiui*. This is a tree peony with red flowers, which has recently been described by Pei Yan-long and Hong De-yuan (1995). *P. rockii* has resulted from raising 'Rock's Variety' to the level of a species, while *P. jishanensis* is effectively Rehder's var. *spontanea* raised to specific status. The other four species are new to science.

The plant everyone knew as *P. suffruticosa* was based upon a rather mixed bag of wild, semi-wild and cultivated specimens that had been assembled by European explorers during the period 1897 to 1926. It is only very recently that foreign visitors have been able to travel more widely within China and thus gain access to the areas where tree peonies may still exist in the wild. To everyone's surprise it now appears that wild tree peonies may be far more common in China than was previously thought. Wild plants are still widely exploited for their use in traditional Chinese medicine, which clearly has implications for the preservation of these natural populations. The discovery of these new species appears to have made the name *P. suffruticosa* redundant and has consequently turned our terminology upside down.

Making the name *P. suffruticosa* redundant would leave us with the thorny question of where to place all of the hundreds of different cultivated varieties of tree peony. In the future it may be possible to unravel the ancestry of these plants but it is highly likely that the majority of them are hybrids of two or more wild species, whose origins go back many centuries. Some of these ancestral species may now be extinct, making it even more difficult to resolve the situation. I have therefore decided to retain the name as *P. × suffruticosa*

agg., more as a convenient pigeonhole than to suggest anything other than a loose relationship between these plants. The debate that is raging about these new species is not helped by the absence of any authentic specimens for other botanists to study.

The table opposite shows a formal classification of the genus *Paeonia*. This includes most of the recognized subspecies and varieties, together with the authors of their names and the date the name was published. If a species has an × after its generic name this indicates that the plant is considered to be a hybrid between two or more other species.

NOTES

It is common in gardening books to substitute simplified words of phrases for technical terms. This practice has been followed to some extent in this book. However, in the descriptions that follow, technical terms have been retained in many cases to avoid confusing the sometimes very subtle differences that distinguish one peony species from another. All technical terms used are explained in the glossary on page 152.

Where I have not been able to describe the species from living or preserved specimens I have had to rely on descriptions made by other authors. These are indicated by the intials of the author or authors at the end of the relevant passages (for example HT is Hong Tao et al and PH is Pei Yan-long & Hong De-yuan); further details can be found in the bibliography on page 153.

TREE PEONIES

P. delavayi AGM

P. delavayi originates from the Chinese provinces of Sichuan and Yunnan. It grows in shady moist areas of pine forest, in forest clearings and among scrub at altitudes of between 3,050 and 3,650m (10,000–12,000ft). It was first discovered by Pére Jean Marie Delavay in 1884. Delavay (1834–1895) was a missionary and botanist, who, during his very active life, sent an amazing total of 200,000 dried herbarium specimens to the Musée Nationale d'Histoire Naturelle in Paris.

P. delavayi eventually forms an imposing shrub up to 1.8m (6ft) high. The leaves are biternate, bronzy-purple when young turning to hairless, dark green above and blue-green below later in the year. The leaflets are deeply dissected; the lateral leaflets have five lobes with

BIOLOGICAL CLASSIFICATION OF THE GENUS *PAEONIA*

GENUS PAEONIA De Candolle (1818).

SECTION MOUTAN De Candolle (1824).
This section includes all of the tree peonies from eastern Asia, the name Moutan being the Chinese name for the tree peony. The section is further divided into two subsections dependent upon the presence or absence of a disc below the flowers. This disc forms a conspicuous leathery sheath around the fruit in the subsection Vaginatae. The sheath is absent in the subsection Delavayanae, which includes the species *P. delavayi*, *P. lutea* and *P. potanini*.

Subsection Vaginatae F.C. Stern (1946).
P. jishanensis Hong Tao & W.Z. Zhao (1992).
P. ostii Hong Tao & J.X. Zhang (1992).
P. qiui Y.L. Pei & Hong De-yuan (1995).
P. rockii (Haw & Lauener) Hong Tao & J. J. Li (1992).
  ssp. *linyanshanii* Hong Tao & G.L. Osti (1994).
P. × suffruticosa agg. (Andrews) Status nov.
P. szechuanica Fang (1958).
P. yananensis Hong Tao & M.R. Li (1992).
P. yunnanensis Fang (1958).

Subsection Delavayanae F.C. Stern (1946).
P. delavayi Franchet (1886).
P. × lemoinei Rehder (1920).
P. lutea Delavay ex Franchet (1886).
  var. *ludlowii* F.C. Stern & G. Taylor (1953).
P. potanini Komarov (1921).
  var. *trollioides* (Stapf ex F.C. Stern) F.C. Stern (1943).

SECTION ONAEPIA Lindley (1839).
There are two species of peony endemic to north-western America, both are very distinctive and are placed in this separate Section. The name ONAEPIA in an anagram of the word *Paeonia*. *P. brownii* and *P. californica* are distinguished from those in the Section PAEON by having petals which are either shorter or approximately the same length as the sepals. In addition the seeds are cylindrical ovoid in shape, while the disc is reduced to fleshy lobes at the base of the carpels.
P. brownii Douglas Hooker (1829).
P. californica Nuttall ex Torrey and Gray (1838).

SECTION PAEON De Candolle (1824).
This section includes all the herbaceous peonies found in Europe, the Caucasus, the Middle East and Asia. It is split up into two subsections, the Foliolatae and the Dissectifoliae. In the Foliolatae the leaves are entire and undivided, as in *P. wittmanniana*, *P. mlokosewitschi*, *P. mascula* and *P. cambessedesii*. The other species are placed in the Subsection Dissectifoliae, whose leaves are dissected into segments. The Dissectifoliae includes species such as *P. anomala*, *P. clusii*, *P. officinalis*, *P. peregrina* and *P. tenuifolia*.

Subsection Foliolatae F.C. Stern (1946)
P. bakeri Lynch (1890).
P. broteri Boissier & Reuter (1842).
P. cambessedesii Willkomm (1880).
P. caucasica Schipczinsky (1937).
P. × chamaeleon Troitsky 1930 ex Grossg.
P. emodi Wallich ex Royle (1834).
  var. *glabrata* Hook. f. & Thoms. (1872).
P. kavachensis Aznavour (1917).
P. lactiflora Pallas (1776).
  var. *trichocarpa* (Bunge) F.C. Stern (1943).
P. macrophylla (Albow) Lomakin (1897).
P. mairei Léveillé (1915).
P. mascula (L.) Miller (1768).
  ssp. *mascula*.
  ssp. *arietina* (Anderson) Cullen & Heywood (1964).
    var. *orientalis* (Thiébaut) F.C. Stern (1943).
  ssp. *bodurii* N. Özhatay (1995).
  ssp. *hellenica* Tzanoudakis (1978).
    var. *hellenica* (Tzanoudakis) Stearn & Davis (1984).
    var. *icarica* (Tzanoudakis) Stearn & Davis (1984).
  ssp. *russi* (Bivona) Stearn & Davis (1984) ex Cullen & Heywood (1964).
    var. *reverchoni* Le Grand (1899).
    var. *leiocarpa* (Cosson) F.C. Stern (1943).
  ssp. *triternata* (Boissier) Stearn & Davis (1984).
P. mlokosewitschi Lomakin (1897).
P. obovata Maximowicz (1859).
  var. *willmottiae* (Stapf) F.C. Stern (1943).
P. turcica Davis & Cullen (1965).
P. wittmanniana Hartwiss ex Lindley (1846).
  var. *nudicarpa* Schipczinsky (1921).

Subsection Dissectifoliae F.C. Stern (1946).
P. anomala Linnaeus (1771).
   var. *intermedia* (Meyer) O. & B. Fedtschenko (1905).
P. clusii F.C. Stern & W.T. Stearn (1940).
P. coriacea Boissier (1838).
   var. *atlantica* (Cosson) F.C. Stern (1943).
P. japonica (Makino) Miyabe & Takeda (1910).
P. kesrouanensis J.M Thiébaut (1936).
P. mollis Anderson (1818).
P. officinalis Linnaeus (1753).
   ssp. *officinalis*
   ssp. *banatica* (Rochel) Soó (1945).

   ssp. *humilis* (Retzius) Cullen & Heywood (1964).
   ssp. *villosa* (Huth) Cullen & Heywood (1964).
P. parnassica Tzanoudakis (1978).
P. peregrina Miller (1768).
P. rhodia W.T. Stearn (1941).
P. × smouthii Van Houtte.
P. sterniana Fletcher (1959).
P. tenuifolia Linnaeus (1759).
P. veitchii Lynch (1909).
   var. *beresowskii* (Komarov) Schipczinsky (1921).
   var. *woodwardii* (Stapf & Cox) F.C. Stern (1943).

acuminate tips, the terminal leaflet has three lobes. All of these segments are further dissected to give the leaf a delicate fern-like appearance. The leaflets have entire or toothed margins. The flowers vary from blood-red to dark crimson, maroon or mahogany-red and may be up to 8cm (3in) across, with at least 12–16 petals. Each flower has five sub-orbicular green sepals and 8–12 leaf-like bracts, a unique feature among peony species. The numerous stamens have dark red filaments; the anthers may be yellow, orange or red. There are five large hairless carpels, which are conical and long-attenuated into a short, coiled stigma. Nectar is produced in large quantities. It is a diploid with 10 chromosomes. The variety 'Alba' has white flowers.

P. delavayi flowers from late spring to early summer. Readily available from nurseries, it is often sold as a 'tree peony'. This is somewhat misleading as it can never compare with the beauty of a Moutan tree peony. The majority of the plants available have been raised from seed, but selected cultivars can have very attractive blood-red flowers. Mature specimens frequently have in excess of two hundred flowers on a bush and the species has the added advantage of flowering over a long period. The attractive foliage has led to it being used by an increasing number of landscape gardeners. It is hardy to -20°C (-4°F).

This undemanding plant will grow happily in most situations, whether in the open or in the shade of deciduous trees, and in most good soils, whether acidic or alkaline. It grows rapidly and produces many lateral shoots. It will self seed when permitted, the resulting plants may have flowers varying from dull orange to various shades of red. The selected forms must be propagated vegetatively.

P. jishanensis

This peony was first discovered growing in Shensi province in China by William Purdom in 1910. It was initially treated as a variety of *P. suffruticosa* but has subsequently been described as an independent species by Professor Hong Tao and his team.

P. jishanensis is a deciduous shrub which grows to 1.2m (4ft) high. The reddish brown bark is covered with striations. The leaves are bipinnate, with three pinnae, each pinna having 15 round or ovate leaflets, 2.8–5.5cm (1–2¼in) long by 1.3–4.9cm (½–3in) wide. The tip is blunt-acute and the base rounded, cuneate or slightly heart-shaped. The leaflets have 1–5 lobes; the upper surface is hairless, the lower is sericeous but becomes hairless. The lateral leaflets are stalkless or nearly so and have a small tuft of hairs at their bases. The solitary flowers are white with a slightly reddish purple base. The anthers are yellow and the filaments dark purple with a white tip. There are five carpels which are covered by fine soft pale yellow hairs. The disc is dark purple with a toothed apex (HT).

P. jishanensis flowers from mid- to late spring. Its hardiness is unknown.

P. × lemoinei

This cross has produced some of the most striking of all tree peonies. The name *P. × lemoinei* was first coined by Rehder in 1920 to include hybrids between *P. lutea* and Moutan tree peonies (*P. × suffruticosa* agg.).

The Japanese have adopted their own names for a number of these varieties, such as 'Kinkaku', which is a synonym for 'Souvenir de Maxime Cornu'. If you are looking for one of the Lemoine hybrids it is often worth looking for the plant under its Japanese syn-onym. While some *P.* × *lemoinei* varieties may grow to 2m (6ft) tall, the majority are less vigorous and aver-age 1m (3ft).

They flower a few weeks later than Moutan tree peonies and are said to have better resistance to *Botry-tis*. Many of these hybrids suffer from nodding flowers, a characteristic inherited from their *P. lutea* parent. They are hardy to temperatures as low as -20°C (-4°F).

P. lutea

P. lutea is very similar to *P. delavayi*, indeed some botanists consider it to be a subspecies of the latter. However, *P. lutea* differs in a number of important respects: the flowers are bright yellow, there is no involucre of leaf-like bracts beneath the sepals and the carpels are short-attenuated to the stigma. It is also slightly more erect and has paler leaves. It was discov-ered in 1884 by Pére Delavay on Mount Hea Chan Men in Yunnan, China and is restricted to China, where it grows in spruce forests and on the edge of scrub in open pastures, at altitudes of between 3,300 and 4,000m (11,000–13,000ft).

A hairless shrub, which grows to a height of 1.5m (5ft) or more, it has leaves that are biternate and deeply dissected, with leaf stalks 8–14cm (3–5½in) long. Dark green above, glaucous below, the leaflets are 12–17cm

(5–7in) long by 0.6–1.1cm (¼–½in) wide, and are very similar to those of *P. delavayi*. The bright yellow flowers, up to 7.5cm (3in) across, have approximately 12 petals. There are 5–9 persistent bracts and sepals, these bracts are very narrow, sword-shaped and cuspidate at the base. The stamens have yellow anthers and filaments 1.2–1.5cm (½in) long. The carpels are hairless, conical and short-attenuated to a very short stigma, approxi-mately 1cm (½in) long. *P. lutea* is a diploid

It flowers from late spring to early summer. Slightly less hardy than *P. delavayi*, it will survive temperatures as low as -15°C (5°F). *P. lutea* is rarely grown although easy to raise from seed and apparently indifferent to soil type.

P. lutea var. ludlowii AGM A form of *P. lutea*, var. *ludlowii*, or the Tibetan peony, is more frequently cultivated than the type. This plant was found by the famous plant hunters Ludlow and Sheriff while on an expedition to south-eastern Tibet in 1936. In the wild it grows in large colonies among holly and oak forest on dry gravel terraces, at altitudes of between 3,000 and 3,400m (10,000–11,150ft).

P. lutea var. *ludlowii* eventually forms a broad spreading bush to 2.5m (8ft) high and as much as 4m (13ft) wide. The leaves are broader and less divided than in *P. lutea*, effectively trifoliate with a distinct lamina. The flowers are larger, more open and up to 13cm (5in) across. They have 7–9 sepals and bracts; the bracts are broader than in the type and dagger-shaped. There are usually four flowers to a stem and whereas the type has 3–4 carpels, var. *ludlowii* has only one or two. The mature follicles are sausage-shaped and very large, to 7.5cm (3in) long. They are pale green, slightly flushed with pink.

This is a highly ornamental shrub and worth growing when space permits, it flowers slightly earlier than *P. lutea*. The variety 'Anne Rosse' has flowers up to 10cm (4in) wide, with red-streaked, yellow petals.

P. ostii

This tree peony is native to the Shaanxi and Heenan provinces of China where it occurs at altitudes of between 1,100 and 1,400m (3,600–4,600ft). It was named in honour of the Italian scientist, Dr. Gian Osti.

P. lutea var. *ludlowii* is an extremely elegant shrub with light green foliage and lemon-yellow flowers.

With its lovely pale yellow flowers, *P. potanini trollioides* is the most attractive variety of this variable species.

P. ostii is an extremely attractive deciduous shrub which grows to a height of 1.5m (5ft). The bark is greyish brown. The annual branches are pale yellow-green and grow to 20cm (8in) long. They have a slight longitudinal groove.

The leaves are bipinnate, with three pinnae and up to 15 leaflets. The leaflets are entire, narrow ovate-lanceolate or narrow long ovate and have an acute tip and a cuneate or rounded base. The terminal leaflet has 1–3 lobes, the upper surface is sparsely hairy along the middle vein close to the base and hairless beneath. The lateral leaflets are more or less stalkless. The solitary flowers are single, 13–15cm (5–6in) across, and usually pure white but may have a hint of reddish purple at the petals bases. Flares are absent, although some plants may have pink veins. The stamens have purple filaments and pale yellow anthers. There are five hirsute-sericeous carpels, the disc and stigma are dark purple in colour (HT).

P. ostii flowers in mid-spring and is said to be very hardy. Only one nursery ('Oriental Leaves' in Scotland) currently offers it for purchase.

P. potanini

P. potanini was first discovered by Grigori Potanin and named after him by Komarov in 1921. E.H. Wilson had already collected specimens in Sichuan during 1904, but thought that it was a variety of *P. delavayi*. While it is certainly very similar to *P. delavayi*, it is much shorter and produces stolons; it also lacks the conspicuous involucre that accompanies the flowers of *P. delavayi*. *P. potanini* is native to the Sichuan and Yunnan provinces of China.

In cultivation this species can reach 1m (3ft), but it is usually shorter. The leaves are deeply divided, with oblong leaf segments which taper to acuminate tips. The majority of these segments are 0.5-1cm (¼–½in) wide but may be as much as 2cm (¾in). The nodding flowers are cup-shaped, maroon or reddish brown and approximately 5–6cm (2–2½in) across. There are 5–7 sepals and bracts. The stamen filaments are red and the anthers yellow. It is a diploid.

It flowers in the late spring. 'Alba' has white flowers, while var. *trollioides* is a form with pale yellow flowers.

P. qiui

This new species of tree peony is recorded from the Hubei province of China. It grows at altitudes of 1,650–2,010m

(5,400–6,600ft) on steep cliffs and among overhanging rocks. It can be distinguished from the similar *P. jishanensis* by the shape and arrangement of the leaflets.

P. qiui is a deciduous shrub, to 60–80cm (24–32in) high, with brownish grey longitudinally striated bark. The leaves are biternate with ovate or ovate-rounded leaflets, purple-red above, light green beneath and 6.5–8.2cm (2¾–3in) long by 5–6.5cm (2–2¼in) wide. The leaflets are usually entire with blunt-acute tips and rounded bases; the terminal leaflet is sometimes trifid. The single flowers are terminal, rose-pink and 8–12cm (3–5in) across. The stamen filaments are pink and the anthers yellow. The leathery-textured disc is deep purple. There are five carpels covered with white or pale yellow hairs (PH).

P. qiui flowers from mid- to late spring; its hardiness in cultivation is unknown.

P. rockii

P. rockii, better known as 'Rock's Variety' has almost achieved cult status as a collector's plant. It is particularly expensive to buy and is always in short supply. The first western botanist to have seen it was probably John Reginald Farrer (1880–1930) a well known explorer who related some of his exploits in his book *On the Eaves of the World* (1917). For some unknown reason Farrer did not collect any specimens of this peony and nothing was heard of it again until Dr. Josef Franz Rock (1884–1962) visited south-west Gansu province between 1925 and 1926. It is now known to occur in northern Sichuan, southern Gansu and southern Shaanxi provinces and is cultivated in Gansu and Qinghai.

Rock spent the winter of 1925–1926 at the 'Yamen of the Choni' lamasery, which was situated at a height of 2,600m (8,530ft) in an area of dense *Picea meyeri* forest. Growing in the central courtyard of the lamasery was a white tree peony with single flowers. Rock took photographs of it and collected its seed when it had ripened. This seed was ultimately distributed to botanical gardens in the British Isles, the United States of America, Canada and Sweden. Until very recently, all of the known specimens of this species outside China originated from this single collection of seed. Rock's visit was opportune as two years later, in 1928, the monks were killed and the lamasery destroyed by 'Mohammedans'.

At one time many botanists considered that *P. rockii* was the ancestral wild tree peony, from which all of the cultivated varieties were derived. F. C. Stern adhered to this belief and the description of *P. suffruticosa* in his monograph was based on a specimen of *P. rockii*, raised from seed sent to him by Dr. Rock. Rock also sent him a photograph of the original peony growing in the lamasery courtyard and this was published by Stern in the Journal of the Royal Horticultural Society (1939). Also illustrated in the article was Stern's own plant, now a very substantial shrub, in the garden of his former home at Highdown, West Sussex, England.

In 1990 Haw and Lauener described 'Rock's Variety' as a subspecies of *P. suffruticosa*. In 1992 the plant was given specific status by Hong Tao and Jia-jue Li. The majority of botanists seem to have agreed with this decision.

The woody stems of *P. rockii* are hairless and relatively weak, sometimes barely able to support the weight of the heavy flowers. It grows to approximately 2m (6ft) high. It has bipinnate leaves with lateral leaflets that are more or less ovate and coarsely toothed or lobed. They are 4.5–9cm (1¾–3½in) long by 3.2–5cm (1¼–2in) wide, with short stalks. The terminal leaflets are deeply incised into three lobes. The side lobes are entire and about 6cm (2½in) long by 2cm (¾in) wide, the terminal lobes, 8cm (3in) long by 3cm (1¼in) wide, are coarsely 3-toothed, the apex of the teeth being sharply acute. The leaflets are bright green above, glaucous below with a few long hairs along the veins.

This is the 'British' form of *P. rockii*. The 'American' form has less ruffled petals.

Opening from pale lilac-pink buds, the flowers are pure white with deep purple flares which fade at the base into a red margin. They measure up to 16cm (6in) across when fully open. There are ten concave petals, triangular-ovate or ovate-rounded, 6.5–9cm (2¼–3½) long by 4–8.5cm (1½–3¼in) wide and notched at the tip, with shallow rounded teeth along the edge. There are 7 sepals. The stamen filaments, approximately 3cm (1¼in) long, are white touched with purple in the centre, or magenta at the base fading to white at the top, or pure white; the anthers are yellow. When the flowers are young the carpels are completely encased in a thin, creamy white sheath which extends from the disc; this sheath has grooves radiating from the centre. Inside the sheath there are five pale green carpels with creamy white stigmata. This sheath is mentioned regularly in the description of the different tree peony varieties and may vary in colour. American examples of *P. rockii* are quite different, with fewer rounded petals, while those in the British Isles are more vigorous and have frilled petals. *P. rockii* is a diploid.

Authentic specimens are quite difficult to obtain. It has always been considered to be a difficult plant to graft, possibly due to it being less vigorous than the hybrid tree peonies. Wild seed is being imported by Phedar Nursery in England and divisions are available from Oriental Leaves in Scotland. Plants propagated by division are likely to be more vigorous than those obtained by grafting. It appears to be hardy to at least -20°C (-4°F).

P. rockii ssp. linyanshanii differs from the typical species in having lanceolate or narrowly-ovate leaflets with entire margins. It has been recorded from the Gansu and Hubei provinces of China and flowers from mid- to late spring.

P. × suffruticosa Aggregate

While it is technically redundant, I have retained this species name to cover all of the many varieties of Moutan tree peony. The original *P. suffruticosa* was described from a double tree peony imported by Sir Joseph Banks in 1789.

P. szechuanica

This species grows at altitudes of between 2,640 and 3,100m (8,660–10,170ft) on mountains in north-west-ern Sichuan province. It was first described in a Chinese scientific journal by Wen-Pei Fang in 1958, but the paper was never seen by western botanists. One of its diagnostic features is said to be the leathery cup-shaped disc that surrounds the lower half of the hairless carpels.

P. szechuanica grows to 1.5m (5ft) high and has black-grey bark. The bipinnate or tripinnate, papery leaves are alternate, 9–12cm (3½–5in) long, and there are 3–4 pairs to a branch. Their upper surface is dark green, the lower is pale green. The leaflets are ovate, obovate or oblong-ovate, with three lobes, further divided into three smaller lobes. Their tips are acuminate and their bases cuneate. The leaf stalk is 5–6cm (2–2½in) long, the terminal leaflet stalk is 0.5–0.7cm (¼in) long and the lateral leaflet stalk is 0.2–0.3cm (¹⁄₁₆–⅛in) long. The solitary flowers, 12–13cm (5in) across, are rose-pink or purple. The stamens have white filaments, 0.5–1.5cm (¼–½in) long, and yellow anthers, 0.7–0.8cm (¼–⅜in) long. There are 4–6 carpels, which are hairless and purple. They are cone-shaped, 1.2cm (½in) long with a short style and flat recurved stigma (FW).

The species is currently unavailable in the west. Its degree of hardiness is unknown.

P. yananensis

This rare species from Shaanxi province in China is a small deciduous shrub, which grows to a height of 40cm (16in). The bark is greyish with green annual branches. The leaves are bipinnate having up to 11 ovate-rounded or ovate leaflets, 2.5–7.5cm (1–3in) long by 1.9–8.3cm (½–3¼in) wide. They have blunt-acute tips and cuneate bases and are divided or lobed and toothed. Initially, the underside of the leaves is sericeous but it becomes hairless with age. The lateral leaflets are almost stalkless or have a very short stalk, typically 0.1–1.1cm (¹⁄₁₆–½in) long, with patches of long silky hairs that lie flat against the surface of the leaflet. The solitary flowers are pale purple-rose or white with purple-black flares. The stamen filaments, 0.7–1.1cm (¼–½in) long, are mainly purple in colour with a white tip and the anthers are yellow. The disc is deep purple with five hirsute-sericeous carpels. The stigmata are deep purple.

It flowers in late spring and its hardiness is unknown.

P. yunnanensis

Little is known of this tree peony. Wen-Pei Fang (1958) says that it is a shrub with white flowers tinged slightly

P. anomala, which is very similar to *P. veitchii*, has the widest distribution of any peony species.

with red. It grows to a height of 80cm (32in) and is characterized by yellow tomentose carpels and ovate or oblong-ovate leaflets. It may be a synonym for one of the previous species featured.

HERBACEOUS PEONIES

P. anomala

First described by Carl Linnaeus in 1771, this species is very similar to *P. veitchii* but can be distinguished by the presence of only one flower to a stem (*P. veitchii* has several). *P. anomala* has a very wide distribution, from the Ural Mountains in western Russia to the Kola Peninsula in the North, the Tien Shan Mountains in Kazakhstan and the western Gobi Desert in Mongolia. Its northern limit seems to be defined by the minimum winter temperature. It occupies a fairly wide range of habitats, including scrub on rocky hillsides, dry steppe grassland and coniferous forest.

P. anomala grows to 50cm (20in) high and has much divided, dark green leaves, which are glaucous beneath. It is characterized by the presence of fine hairs on all of the main veins of the upper side of the leaves, the rest of the plant is hairless. The leaves are biternate; the leaflets are pinnatisect with numerous long segments, which may be deeply 2- or 3-lobed and narrow-oblong in shape. The leaf segments are drawn out into a narrow tip and are 0.4–1.5cm (⅛–½in) wide. The solitary flowers, 7–9cm (3–3½in) wide, have undulating petals. The flowers of wild plants are usually magenta-red, cultivated varieties may range from bright red to crimson-rose. The stamens are approximately 1.5cm (½in) long with yellow filaments; there are 3–5 carpels. *P. anomala* is a diploid with 10 chromosomes.

P. anomala flowers from late spring to early summer. The leaves turn a pleasant shade of orange-brown in the autumn. Although it is easy to cultivate, it prefers deep sandy soil in a sunny position. It is hardy to at least -25°C (-13°F).

P. anomala var. intermedia differs from the type in possessing carpels that are covered with a dense tomentum. It has a widespread distribution from the Kola Peninsula across to the Altai Mountains in Siberia, and as far south as Turkistan, near the Afghan border. The flowers are bright red. *P. hybrida* is considered to be a hybrid of *P. anomala* and *P. tenuifolia*, although Lynch (1890) claimed to have seen the plant growing wild in the Caucasus and it has been reported as a wild species by other botanists. It is a very attractive plant with large deep crimson flowers and finely dissected foliage.

P. bakeri

This species is only known from gardens and was originally described from the Cambridge Botanic Gardens. All of the other plants in cultivation originated from there and although wild plants may yet be discovered, some botanists have questioned whether it really is a true species. The species was named after the British botanist, J. G. Baker (1834–1920) who wrote an early monograph about peonies in 1884.

P. bakeri grows to a height of 60cm (24in), the stems, undersides of the leaves, leaf stalks and carpels are pubescent. The leaves are biternate, the terminal set usually divided again into two or three segments. They are dark green and hairless above, glaucous and villous underneath, The leaflets are oval to ovate, 7–10cm (3–4) long and 3–6cm (1¼–2½in) wide, cuneate to truncated at the base and tapering to an acute tip. *P. bakeri* has Roseine Purple (68A) flowers, up to 11.5cm (4¾in) wide with red filaments and yellow anthers. It has three tomentose carpels. It is a tetraploid with 20 chromosomes.

It is easy to grow in the garden, flowering from late spring to early summer, and comes true from seed.

P. broteri

P. broteri is an endemic of Portugal and Spain. Its natural habitat is rocky ground with alkaline soil, at altitudes of between 910 and 1,830m (3,000–6,000ft).

Growing to at least 40cm (16in) high, it has hairless stems and glossy green leaves, frequently with undulating margins, that are also hairless above, glaucous beneath.

The lower leaves are biternate with 19–23 leaflets; the terminal leaflet and sometimes the laterals are deeply cut into 2 or 3 segments. The upper leaves are biternate with entire leaflets. The leaf segments are more or less stalkless (they have a very short petiole), elliptic to broadly elliptic with a cuneate base and an acute tip. The flowers, 8–10cm (3–4in) across, are solitary and crimson-red. The stamens are 2–2.5cm (¾–1in) long, with yellow filaments and anthers. There are 2–4 carpels, with a dense covering of white hairs. *P. broteri* is a diploid.

While *P. broteri* is a relatively easy peony to grow, it will only thrive if planted in a sunny position, such as at the bottom of a sunny wall, in well-drained soil. It requires protection from frost. It flowers from late spring to the early summer.

P. brownii

P. brownii is native to the mountains of northern California, Washington State, Oregon and Nevada where it occurs at altitudes of between 900–1,800m (2,950–5,900ft).

It has hairless stems with 5–8 fleshy biternate leaves per stem, with short leaf stalks, and grows to 45cm (18in) high. The hairless, dark green leaflets have a strong marginal nerve, the base abruptly contracted into a long leaflet stalk. They are deeply dissected into three segments, further divided into three or four lobes with rounded or toothed tips, drawn to a very short point. They are glaucous beneath. The flowers are dark maroon or bronze, approximately 3cm wide (1¼in) and never open completely. The stamen filaments are 0.4–0.6cm (⅛–¼in) long with yellow anthers. It has 2–5 carpels, which produce very large matt-brown seeds.

P. brownii flowers from early to mid-summer. It is hardy to -30°C (-21.5°F) but needs to be grown on extremely well-drained soil. Exhibiting epigeal germination, it produces two cotyledons before the juvenile leaflets appear.

P. californica

This is a peony for the gardener who likes a challenge! Native to central and southern California, *P. californica* is one of the few peonies to have adapted to growing in an arid environment, which it does by avoiding the worst extremes of heat, commencing growth with the autumn rains and dying back in the spring. It is found at altitudes ranging from sea level to 1,212m (4,000ft).

P. californica differs from *P. brownii* in possessing smaller, less dissected leaves with bifid or trifid leaflets. The leaves of *P. brownii* are also glaucous beneath. Another distinguishing feature is the presence of five carpels in *P. brownii*, as opposed to a maximum of three in *P. californica*.

In the wild it varies considerably in size, ranging from 35 to 75cm (14–30in) high. In cultivation it may attain 90cm (36in). The whole plant is hairless, with 7–12 biternate leaves, which are dark green above, slightly paler beneath. The leaflets have a cuneate base and are almost stalkless. They are deeply divided into many very narrow, oblong segments, each with two to three lobes. The tips of the lobes are acute or sometimes blunt. Inconspicuous flowers are produced from early to mid-spring. They are dark reddish-brown and rarely more than 2–3cm (¾–1½in) across. It has 2–3 yellowish green hairless carpels, reddish yellow stamen filaments, 0.6-0.9cm (¼–⅜in) long, with yellow anthers.

This species has little garden value as the tiny flowers are dull in colour. With care it can be grown outside, but it should be protected from frost and needs good drainage. It is considered to be hardy to -5°C (23°F) but requires a period of dormancy during the summer.

P. cambessedesii AGM

P. cambessedesii, or the Majorcan peony, is a native of the Balearic Islands of Majorca and Puerti Pollenza, where it grows on limestone cliffs, scree and rocky ground. It was named after Jaques Cambessedes, a botanist who bequeathed his herbarium to the Botanic Garden at Montpellier in southern France. The only species of peony to be listed in the IUCN *Red Data Book* (1978), its native habitat is endangered by hotel development and local goats, which are fond of its seed pods.

The stems of *P. cambessedesii* are hairless, with a strong reddish purple tinge, and grow to 60cm (24in) high. The leathery leaves are biternate, regularly spaced along the stem and become smaller towards the top, measuring up to 29cm (11in) long. The leaflets are entire, lanceolate to ovate and 4–17cm (1½–7in) long by 2–8cm (¾–3in) wide, with more or less acute tips and often wavy margins. Hairless and dark greyish green with impressed veins above, they are dark greenish purple beneath with raised veins and red leaf stalks. The red veins of the leaves are transparent when held against the light. *P. cambessedesii* is a diploid with 10 chromosomes.

P. cambessedesii starts to grow early in the spring and flowers in mid-spring. The single flowers vary from magenta to deep pink and the petals have darker veins. The colour fades quickly in bright sunshine. Measuring 6–10cm (2½–4in) across, the flowers have 10–12 petals, with wavy outer margins. There are four sepals. The stamen filaments are reddish purple, the anthers yellow and the stigmata purple. The flowers have 5–8 carpels, which are hairless and deep reddish purple, becoming slightly recurved when mature.

Quite readily available and easy to grow from seed, *P. cambessedesii* is one of the most beautiful herbaceous peonies and well worth growing. Considered by some gardeners to be hardy to -10°C (14°F), it does not tolerate wet soil and has a habit of dying unless the growing conditions are ideal. Preferring a warm, well-drained spot, it requires some protection during the winter, so is best grown at the foot of a wall. Plants grown from seed are said to be hardier than those taken originally as divisions of wild plants.

P. caucasica

Originally described by Schipczinsky in 1921, the status of this species has long been the subject of debate. While the majority of botanists in the former Soviet Union have always treated it as an independent species, western botanists, such as Busch (1901) and Stern (1946), have considered it to be a synonym of *P. mascula* ssp. *triternata*. *P. caucasica* differs from *P. mascula* ssp. *triternata* in having leaves that are flat, rather than concave with an undulating margin as seen in the latter species.

P. caucasica is an endemic of the Caucasus Mountains where it grows around forest margins, in meadows and in woodland clearings at altitudes from 900–2,000m (2,950–6,560ft).

P. caucasica is said to grow to a height of 1m (3ft) in the wild, although the specimens I have seen in cultivation are much smaller, reaching 50cm (20in). It is a robust plant with hairless stems, which are slightly glaucous and flushed with red. The leaves are biternate and divided into nine entire segments. The leaflets, dark green and sometimes glaucous above, light green below, are usually hairless, but may be pubescent beneath. They are oblong-obovate to oval or oval-elliptic, 2.5–11cm (1–4½) long by 1.8–8.5cm (¾–3½in) wide, with a cuneate base and a blunt or acute tip. The terminal leaflet tapers equally or unequally to the leaf stalk, and is typically somewhat decurrent. The leaf stalks and main veins of the leaflets are often flushed with red. Komarov's *Flora of the URSS* states that the flowers have been used to make a red dye in home weaving and for colouring paper. They are 3–5cm (1¼–2in) wide and magenta-red with red or violet filaments and yellow anthers. The stigmata are flesh-pink. It has five carpels which are covered by dense white tomentum.

Specimens of this plant have only recently become available in the west, little is known about its cultural requirements but it can expected to be very hardy.

P. × chamaeleon

This 'species' is thought to be a natural hybrid between two species, *P. mlokosewitschi* and *P. caucasica*. The plants in cultivation are somewhat variable which suggests that the cross may have occurred on several occasions. The Georgian scientist Kemularia-Nathadze considered that the 'species' was heterogeneous and split it up into three: *P. chamaeleon*, *P. troitsky* and *P. makaschvilii*. There seems to be little justification for

The flowers of *P. × chamaeleon* are very variable, but are usually creamy white with pinkish veins.

this; the differences only warrant that they be given varietal status within something that is in any case a somewhat artificial taxonomic creation.

Unusually for a hybrid, *P. × chamaeleon* does not show the same vigour as its parents, growing only 50cm (20in) high. The vegetative parts of the plant look somewhat like those of *P. mlokosewitschi*, but share characteristics of both parents. A very attractive plant and well worth growing, it produces flowers with varying degrees of pink pigmentation: some specimens have creamy yellow flowers with pink veins, while others have pinkish petals with darker veins, fading to creamy white with age. There are reddish pink stamen filaments, golden yellow anthers and red stigmata. The mature seeds are shiny blue-black and frequently mixed with vivid pinkish red infertile ovules.

P. × chamaeleon flowers in the late spring. The degree of hardiness is unknown, but should be high bearing in mind the climate of its native Georgia.

P. × chamaeleon sets fertile seed, but this cannot be guaranteed to produce the most desirable plant. Divisions are becoming more readily available but, if possible, see the parent plant in flower before making any purchases.

P. clusii

This extremely beautiful white-flowered peony is native to Crete and the island of Karpathos to the east of Crete. It occupies various habitats there such as *Pinus halepensis* forest, *Cupressus sempervirens* var. *horizontalis* forest (as does *P. rhodia* in Rhodes), *Pistachia lentiscus* maquis and dry calcareous river beds.

Formerly known as *P. cretica*, the name was subsequently found to have been used before for another species and was therefore considered to be invalid. W. T. Stearn renamed it as *P. clusii* in 1935, in honour of Charles de l'Escluse (or Clusius), the botanist who is credited with writing the first European Flora in the early sixteenth century.

P. clusii is a plant of small stature but spreading habit, and is at least 35cm (14in) high. The stems are hairless with a pink or purple tinge. The lower leaves are biternate with leaflets dissected into thirty or more segments, these are narrowly oblong to elliptic and taper to an acute or acuminate tip. The leaves are green above, glaucous and almost hairless beneath. It has relatively large loosely held, cup-shaped white flowers, 7–10cm (3–4in) across, sometimes flushed pink. There are 6–8 petals. The stamens are 2cm (¾in) long, the filaments

P. clusii is a delicate and beautiful diploid, endemic to the islands of Crete and Karpathos.

pink and the anthers orange-yellow. There are 2–4 carpels, which are hoary tomentose. According to Stearn and Davis, the flowers are clove-scented. It is a diploid with 10 chromosomes.

A very pretty plant, *P. clusii* flowers in mid-spring and can be obtained from a few European nurseries. It is best grown in an alpine house as it is not very hardy and needs protection if cultivated outdoors.

P. coriacea

P. coriacea is endemic to the Atlas Mountains of Morocco and southern Spain: Stern (1946) pointed out that Moroccan plants start to grow very early in the year and flower in April, while those in Spain flower later, in June. Its natural habitat is in rocky places, old stone walls, among scrub and Cedar forests at altitudes of between 1,220 and 1,830m (4,000–6,000ft). The species name *coriacea* is derived from a Latin word *coriaceus*, meaning leathery. Some botanists consider it to be a subspecies of *P. mascula*, but it has a larger number of leaflets and their texture is very different.

P. coriacea grows to 60cm (24in) high and has hairless stems and leaves. The lower leaves are biternate but some may be further divided, to give a total of 14–16 segments. The leaflets are green above, glaucous below, broadly elliptic or lanceolate to ovate, and have a cuneate to rounded base with an acute tip. The lateral leaflets are almost stalkless. The flowers, from 7 to 15cm (3–6in) wide, have rose-coloured obovate petals. The stamens are 2cm (¾in) long with red filaments, the anthers are yellow and there are two hairless carpels. It is a tetraploid with 20 chromosomes.

Requiring dry soil and a sunny position, it starts to grow early in the year and may need protection from late frosts.

A. P. Saunders crossed *P. coriacea* with *P. lactiflora* to produce a number of seedlings known collectively as the 'Lavender Strain'. The most beautiful of these is

'Lavender' is an extremely beautiful Saunders hybrid, the result of a cross between *P. coriacea* and *P. lactiflora*.

known simply as 'Lavender', its flowers are possibly the bluest of any herbaceous peony.

P. coriacea var. atlantica differs from *P. coriacea* in having larger leaflets with a pubescent lower surface and pubescent leaf stalks. It differs from *P. mascula* ssp. *russi* var. *reverchoni* in having 14–16 leaf segments, rather than nine.

P. coriacea var. atlantica grows on mountains in Algeria at altitudes from 1,300 to 1,900m (4,260–6,230ft).

P. emodi

Originating from the western Himalayas, this is an extremely beautiful white peony. It has been recorded from Kashmir in northern India, N. Pakistan and Afghanistan where it grows in forest clearings at altitudes of between 1,500 and 3,200m (5,000-10,500ft). It is the only peony known from this region and in some areas is said to grow in large colonies. The name emodi is derived from *Emodi Montes*, the Latin name for the

Himalayas. P. emodi can be distinguished from P. sterniana by the presence of more than one flower to a stem and the smaller number of carpels: 1–2 compared to 3–4 in P. sterniana.

P. emodi grows to 75cm (30in) and has hairless, light green stems. The base of the stems may be flushed red, together with a small area in the leaf axils. The lower leaves are biternate and divided into 20–30 segments. The leaflets are usually decurrent, entire or divided into two; the terminal leaflet is often divided into three segments. Leaflets and segments are elliptic, narrowing towards the stalk and to the acuminate tip. They measure 8–17cm (3–7in) long and vary between 1.5 and 6cm (½–2½in) wide. The upper surface of mature leaves is dark green and hairless except for a line of very small hairs along the veins. The lower surface is a lighter green and completely hairless.

P. emodi has large white flowers, 2–4 to a stem. They measure 8–12cm (3–5in) across and have obovate petals, 4.5cm (1¾in) long by 2.5cm (1in) wide. The stamen anthers and filaments are yellow; the latter 1.5–2cm (½–¾in) long. The single carpel (sometimes two) is covered with stiff yellow hairs. P. emodi is a diploid with 10 chromosomes.

Gardeners appear to have difficulty growing this species although it is known to tolerate temperatures as low as -20°C (-4°F) and grows happily in the herbaceous beds at the Royal Botanic Gardens Edinburgh. It starts to grow very early in the year and flowers in late spring, as do many peonies. In the wild, the species grows in dappled shade, so the best chances of success are achieved if it is planted on the edge of deciduous woodland. In the absence of this habitat, it could be planted among shrubs so as to provide some protection from early morning sunshine.

A. P. Saunders bred two hybrids of P. emodi: 'Early Windflower' (with P. veitchii) and 'Late Windflower' (P. veitchii var. beresowskii). These are sometimes sold as P. emodi, but both have smaller nodding flowers with light green leaves. 'Late Windflower' flowers approximately ten days later than 'Early Windflower' and has more deeply dissected foliage. They are considered to be easier to grow than the species.

P. emodi var. glabrata differs from P. emodi solely in possessing hairless carpels. It flowers at the same time as P. emodi.

P. japonica

This species is said to be widely distributed throughout the mountainous areas of Japan, where it is known as 'Yama-shakuyaku'. It grows in deciduous forests at altitudes of 950–1,300m (3,120–4,260ft). The species was first described by Miyabe and Takeda in 1910; the RHS Plant Finder treats it as a synonym of P. lactiflora. The original description says that it is very similar to P. obovata but can be distinguished by the flowers, which open less widely, have more concave petals and short stigmata.

P. kavachensis

The status of this species is uncertain, some botanists treat it as a synonym for P. mascula ssp. mascula. In the Flora Iranica (1969) Riedl considered that P. kavachensis could be found in the Caucasus, Anatolia, Syria, Lebanon, Kurdistan (Iraq) and Talish.

It grows to 70cm (28in) high. The lower leaves are biternate, the upper undivided. The leaflets are obovate-lanceolate to broadly lanceolate, 5–12cm (2–5in) long by 3–7cm (1¼–3in) wide. Hairless on both surfaces, they are dark green with the lower surface often glaucous. The solitary flowers are an intense red. There are 2–3 densely tomentose carpels.

A few nurseries sell specimens that are purported to be this plant but may well be P. mascula.

P. kesrouanensis

An endemic of Syria, Lebanon and Turkey. P. kesrouanensis was discovered during the 1930s by J. Thiébaut (1936) at Kesrouan in western Lebanon. It grows in Abies cilicica forest and maquis. P. kesrouanensis is very similar to P. mascula but has hairless carpels and a stigma approximately 7mm (¼in) long. The stigma is coiled at the extreme tip, which distinguishes it from the otherwise similar P. turcica, whose stigma is curved from close to the base.

P. kesrouanensis grows to 60cm (24in) high and has hairless stems. The leaves are biternate and divided into 14 leaflets, which are usually broadly elliptic, but may be oblong-ovate or ovate-oval, each measuring up to 10.3cm (4in) long by 5.6cm (2¼in) wide and blunt- or more or less acute-tipped. The leaves are dark green and hairless; underneath they are paler and nearly hairless with a purplish midrib and veins. Rose-coloured flowers up to 10cm (4in) wide, appear from mid- to late spring. They have yellow anthers and red filaments.

PLATE I
All flowers are shown at approximately ¼ size

P. officinalis ssp. *villosa*

P. officinalis ssp. *officinalis*

P. mascula ssp. *mascula*

P. mascula ssp. *arietina*

P. anomala

P. cambessedesii

P. veitchii

P. mlokosewitschi

P. wittmanniana

P. × smouthii

P. delavayi

There are 2–3 carpels with a long narrow crimson style.

This species does not appear to be in cultivation and its hardiness is unknown.

P. lactiflora

For over a century this peony was known as *P. albiflora*, having been so named by Pallas in 1788. Then it was discovered that Pallas had called the same plant *P. lactiflora* in 1776. Botanical convention required that the plant should be known by its earlier name, which caused great consternation and antipathy in horticultural circles. Commonly known as the Chinese peony, *P. lactiflora* is found naturally in Siberia, Heilongjiang, Inner Mongolia, China and Tibet. Its natural habitat is steppe grassland and scrub.

From the horticultural point of view, this is the most important species of herbaceous peony, being the source of thousands of different cultivated varieties. Over the years several other species and subspecies have been described, all of which are now considered to be synonyms of *P. lactiflora*. It was first imported into England from China in 1808 by R.Whitley, who ran a nursery in Fulham, London. The variety 'Whitleyi Major' is considered to be closest to the wild species.

Wild specimens of *P. lactiflora* have erect, hairless, light green stems which grow to a height of 60cm (24in). The leaves are biternate, with entire or lobed leaflets, elliptic to lanceolate with an acuminate tip. The upper surface is dark green and hairless, underneath is light green with small hairs along the veins. The base of the leaflets is cuneate; the margins are papillose and rough to the touch. The stems carry two or more white flowers, to 10cm (4in) across, which have yellow filaments and anthers. The flowers are fragrant and have 3–5 hairless carpels with pink stigmata. The variety *trichocarpa* has hairy carpels. *P. lactiflora* is a diploid with 10 chromosomes.

It flowers from early to midsummer, somewhat later than the other species. It and its cultivars are easy to grow and are happy in most well-drained soils. While it can tolerate temperatures as low as -30°C (-21.5°F), waterlogging during the winter will result in its death. Many of its cultivars have attractive autumn colouring.

P. macrophylla

P. macrophylla was first described by Nicolas Albow in 1895 as *P. wittmanniana* var. *macrophylla*. Its true status

has been debated for many years, a situation that has not been helped by its rarity in cultivation. It is native to a small area of the western Caucasus in Georgia, where it occurs in mountain forests at altitudes of 800–1,000m (2,625–3,280ft). This region of the world has been inaccessible for many years and it has been almost impossible for western botanists to obtain authentic specimens although seed is now becoming available. The following description is taken from published material and confirmed with herbarium specimens.

P. macrophylla is similar to *P. wittmanniana* but has massive leaves up to 25cm (10in) long by 15cm (6in) wide. They are biternate, with elliptic-lanceolate, oval, oval-rounded or sub-orbicular leaflets. The leaves are very shiny on the upper surface and have deeply depressed veins, giving them a distinctive blistered appearance. The upper surface is dark green and hairless; beneath is a similar colour, slightly glaucous with a few hairs on the main veins. The flowers, which open more widely than those of *P. wittmanniana*, to 7.5cm (3in) across, are yellow in bud, opening to white with a slight hint of yellow, the colour fading after a few days. Two to four hairless or pubescent carpels are produced. *P. macrophylla* flowers from mid- to late spring. Its fertile seeds are blue-black; the infertile ovules are vivid rose-red. (A peony that I purchased as this species is too young to flower as yet and therefore impossible to verify. It has red-tinted leaves and reddish brown stems and the whole plant turns a wonderful shade of reddish brown in the autumn. It matches the above in all respects other than colour.)

P. macrophylla is extremely rare in cultivation, although it is a striking plant and flowers early in the season. On sunny days, it is said to have a rather bitter scent, somewhat reminiscent of boxwood. Bearing in mind its native habitat this species should be extremely hardy.

P. mairei

This species was first described by Léveillé (1915) from a specimen collected in Yunnan by E. E. Maire in 1913. *P. mairei* is native to northern Yunnan and western Sichuan provinces in China. It grows in scrub and open woodland on steep mountainsides at altitudes of between 800 and 3,200m (2,625–10,500ft).

Although superficially similar to *P. lactiflora*, it has one flower to a stem, rather than several as in *P. lactiflora*. It grows to 60–100cm (24–40in) high and has hairless, erect or spreading stems. The leaves are biternate, sometimes with the lateral leaflets divided again. The leaflets are elliptic to obovate-elliptic, cuneate at the base and long-acuminate or caudate at the tip. They are 12–19cm (5–7in) long by 3–11cm (1¼–4½in) wide. Hairless with smooth edges, they are dark green above, paler below. The solitary flowers, 8–15cm (3–6in) across, are rose-pink with obovate to obovate-elliptic, round-tipped petals. The stamens are 2cm (¾in) long with red filaments and yellow anthers. The distinctive carpels have a cone-shaped lower part which tapers towards the tip and are usually covered with a distinctive tomentum of short silky yellow hairs, although this may be absent in some plants.

P. mairei flowers from late spring to early summer. It is hardy to -15°C (5°F) and prefers well-drained, humus-rich soil. However, from existing evidence it seems that P. mairei is not grown in gardens; neither seed nor plants appear to be available.

P. mascula

In medieval times P. mascula was known as the 'male peionie', as opposed to the 'female peionie', which was P. officinalis. It is a very variable species which has a wide distribution throughout southern Europe. It is eas-ily distinguished from P. officinalis by the degree to which the leaves are divided. There are five recognized subspecies of P. mascula, all of which are tetraploid with 20 chromosomes.

P. mascula ssp. mascula is the most wide-spread subspecies and was known for many years as P. corallina. It has been recorded from Armenia, Bulgaria, Cyprus, England (where it is probably naturalized), France, Germany, the Aegean and eastern Central Greece, northern Iran and Iraq, Italy, Sicily, Syria and Turkey. Many of its recorded locations are near former monasteries, where monks are thought to have culti-vated it to exploit its medicinal properties. It grows in a wide range of habitats including beech, oak, and pine forest and on rocky slopes, at altitudes of 50–2,200m (160–7,220ft).

The typical subspecies grows to 60–90cm (24–36in) high, and has a rather spreading habit when compared with the more erect P. officinalis. The leaves, which are hairless above and usually hairless beneath, are biter-nate, dark green above, slightly glaucous beneath. There are 9–21 leaflets, which vary in shape from

Wild plants of P. mascula ssp. arietina, which was previously given separate species status, have pinkish magenta flowers; cultivated flowers are often pale pink or dark red.

elliptic to obovate-elliptic and have a shortly-acumi-nate tip. The terminal leaflet is usually broadly elliptic. The flowers are usually magenta and measure 9–12cm (3½–5in) across, with 6–8 petals. The stamens have purple filaments and yellow anthers. It has 2–5 very large carpels, which are lightly tomentose and strongly reflexed when mature.

Flowering from mid- to late spring, it is easy to grow but prefers well-drained soil in a sunny position. It is hardy to -15°C (5°F). Although subspecies mascula is variable, it is good for autumn colour: the leaves of some plants turn apricot-yellow with pink veins; the stems and leaf stalks turn pinkish brown.

P. mascula ssp. arietina was formerly consid-ered to be a separate species: P. arietina. An extremely pretty plant, it has a very wide distribution, being recorded from Armenia, Crete, Greece, Italy, Syria, Turkey and Yugoslavia. It grows in similar habitats to subspecies mascula. Arietina means like a ram's horn.

Subspecies arietina grows to 45–75cm (18–30in) high and has sparsely villous stems. The lower leaves are biternate and divided into 12–15 leaflets, with at least one or more deeply divided. The leaflets are narrowly or broadly elliptic to oblong, 7.7–13.5cm (3–5in) long by

2.5–6.5cm (1–2¾in) wide, with more or less acute tips and cuneate bases. The leaves may be light or dark green, hairless above, glaucous below. The undersides and the leaf stalks are villous.

Wild plants usually have pinkish magenta flowers but there are many cultivars that produce flowers with pale pink or dark red petals. The blooms are 8–12cm (3–5in) across with obovate petals. The anthers are creamy yellow and the filaments red. The 2–3 carpels are strongly recurved when ripe and they are covered by a dense tomentum. The leaves turn to a pinkish shade of brown in the autumn.

It flowers from early to midsummer and is hardy to -15°C (5°F).

The peony described as *P. orientalis* by J. Thiébaut in 1936 is a very beautiful variety of ssp. *arietina* with wavy pink petals. The carpels are almost identical to those of ssp. *arietina*, but are less hairy. The leaves, leaf stalks and stems are hairless.

Subspecies *arietina* is probably the most attractive of the *mascula* group of peonies and is very variable. During the past hundred years there have been many named varieties (Barr's 1899 catalogue listed ten) but of these few are still available commercially.

'Mother of Pearl' has very large pale pink flowers, the yellow stamens impart a golden glow to the centre of the flower. One of the best cultivars of ssp. *arietina* and worth searching out.

'Northern Glory' is a very attractive plant with grey-green leaves and single magenta-carmine flowers. The centre of the petals is flushed with magenta. Very good autumn colouring.

'Purple Emperor' has single magenta-purple flowers with golden anthers and grey-green foliage.

'Rosy Gem' has flowers of bright rose-pink with golden yellow anthers.

P. mascula ssp. bodurii is a peony with white-flowers. It is endemic to western and central Turkey and it is found growing in rocky places and among *Quercus pubescens* coppiced woodland at altitudes of 400–700m (1,300–2,300ft).

Growing to a height of 80cm (32in), it has hairless, purple-tinted stems. The lower leaves are biternate with 7–11 leaflets. The leaves are hairless, greyish green

'Mother of Pearl' is one of the most desirable cultivars of *P. mascula* ssp. *arietina*.

above, glaucous beneath. The leaflets are broadly ellip-
tic-ovate, almost orbicular, and shortly-acuminate.
The terminal leaflet has a short stalk while the laterals
are almost stalkless. The white flowers, 11–12cm
(4½–5in) across, have 5–7 white petals with a hint of
purple at the base. The stamen filaments are dark purple and the anthers pink or yellow. There are 3–4
carpels with short, dense white tomentum (Ö & Ö).

Evidence suggests that *P. mascula* ssp. *boduri* is not in
cultivation and its hardiness is unknown.

P. mascula ssp. hellenica is found on Sicily,
the Greek islands of Evvoia and Andros, Attica and
the southern Peloponnese. It is usually found growing
in areas of schistose rock in moist soil shaded from
strong sunshine and is also frequently found growing
among bracken fronds in *Abies* forest, in areas of scrub
or on rocky slopes at altitudes from 400–850m
(1,300–2,700ft). It is very similar to *P. mascula* ssp.
bodurii but differs in having upper leaves that are
divided twice, rather than once.

P. mascula ssp. *hellenica* grows 30–60cm (12–24in)
high and has hairless stems. The leaves are biternate
with 9–21 leaflets. Hairless or pilose, they are greyish
green above and glaucous below. The leaflets are obovate or elliptic, shortly-acuminate and approximately
twice as long as they are broad. The leaf blade of the terminal leaflet is decurrent along the stalk. The distinctive white flowers are 10–13cm (4–5in) across with 5–7
slightly crinkled petals. The filaments are purplish red,
the anthers yellow and the style is 0.8–1cm (⅜–½in)
long. There are 1–5 (usually 3) carpels, which are covered with long hairs.

This subspecies starts growing early in the year and
flowers from mid- to late spring. It is not as hardy as the
other subspecies and should be given some protection
from late frosts.

P. mascula ssp. russi is known from the Greek
Ionian Islands, western Central Greece, Calabria in
Italy, Corsica, Sardinia and Sicily. Its typical habitat is
Quercus coccifera scrub on rocky hillsides in limestone
areas, but it may also be found in mountain forests and
occasionally in vineyards.

This plant was first named *P. russi* by A. de Bivona
Bernardi in 1816 in honour of the Abbé Joachimi Russo
from the monastery at Monte Casino. This name has

The flowers of many peonies close at night and during wet
weather. This is *P. mascula* ssp. *russi* growing at Kew.

caused considerable confusion with authors who refer
to it variously as *P. russii* and *P. russoi*. In 1964 Cullen
and Heywood reduced *P. russi* to the rank of a subspecies within *P. mascula*, erroneously calling it *P. mascula* ssp. *russii*. The name was not validly published until
1984 when Stearn and Davis described it in Latin as *P.
mascula* ssp. *russi*.

A shorter plant than *P. mascula* ssp. *mascula*, it reaches
45cm (18in) in height. The stems, which are sparsely
hairy and tinted purple, are tightly packed in mature
specimens forming a substantial clump. The leaves are
divided into 9–10 segments. The leaflets are hairless and
glossy dark green above. The underside is purplish green
and sparsely hairy. The leaflets vary from ovate to elliptic or elliptic-lanceolate and have acuminate tips; the
stalks and veins of the leaflets are tinted purple in most
specimens. The flowers are 7–12cm (3–5in) across and
have between 5 and 9 magenta purple petals (usually
6–8). The stamen filaments are usually white but may be
rose-pink. There are 2–3 carpels, covered with a soft
white tomentum. The stigma is purple.

P. mascula ssp. *russi* flowers in mid-spring and is one of
the first peonies to bloom. It is easy to grow although it
does prefer deep rich soil in a sunny position. It is hardy
to -15°C (5°F).

Subspecies *russi* var. *reverchoni* is found on the islands
of Sardinia and Corsica. It is similar to the type but has
light pink flowers with hairless carpels. The underside
of the leaves is tomentose.

Subspecies *russi* var. *leiocarpa* is also found on Corsica and was introduced into cultivation by Collingwood Ingram. It is easily mistaken for *P. cambessedesii* as it has red leaf stalks and veins, but it differs in a number of ways: the underside of the leaves is green with a few scattered hairs, as opposed to purple and hairless in *P. cambessedesii*; the upper surface is mid-green, rather than greyish green; finally there are only three carpels in var. *leiocarpa* (*P. cambessedesii* has 5–8). These are hairless, green and flushed slightly with red pigment.

P. mascula ssp. triternata has been known in the past as *P. corallina* and *P. daurica*. It was first described as *P. triternata* by Pallas in 1795, but the name was never published correctly and is now considered to be invalid. Stearn and Davis reduced it to subspecific status and gave it the name *triternata*. *P. mascula* ssp. *triternata* has been recorded from the Aegean islands of Samos and Lesbos and also occurs in Turkey, Romania, Krym and Ukraine. There has been much debate as to whether ssp. *triternata* and *P. caucasica* are synonymous; the outcome will clearly affect the perceived distribution of these two plants.

P. mascula ssp. *triternata* grows up to 60cm (24in) high and has hairless stems. The plant has distinctive leaves with upturned and undulating margins. The lower leaves are biternate with 9–11 leaflets, which are usually broadly elliptic to broadly ovate-elliptic or oblong-oval and distinctly rounded or truncate at the tip. They are hairless and dark green above, glaucous and sparsely white-hairy or almost hairless beneath, with a shallowly notched or shortly-apiculate tip. The flowers are relatively small – 7.5–9.5cm (3–3¼in) across (larger in cultivation) – with 5–8 oblong-oval to obovate or orbicular petals. They are rose-red, magenta or soft pink, with yellow stamen filaments and anthers. The stigmata are pink. It has 2–3 carpels, which are covered by a dense tomentum. The seeds are bluish black and the sterile ovules are bright, almost fluorescent, red. The leaves turn to a very pleasant orange-brown in the autumn.

P. mascula ssp. *triternata* flowers in late spring. Its hardiness is unknown.

P. mlokosewitschi AGM

Commonly known as 'Molly the Witch', this species has primrose-yellow flowers and is probably one of the

'Molly the Witch' (*P. mlokosewitschi*) has gorgeous yellow flowers and makes a good border plant.

most beautiful plants that can be grown in the garden. It originates from the Caucasus and was named after G. Mlokosiewicz, who discovered it in 1900. The correct spelling of the name is *P. mlokosewitschi* although it is often spelt as *P. mlokosewitschii*.

A robust plant, *P. mlokosewitschi* can grow to 1m (3ft) in ideal conditions. The young stems are reddish green, eventually turning green with the area around the leaf axils flushed pink. The leaflets are more or less oval but may be oblong or obovate with an acute or sub-acute apex. The upper surface of the leaf is dark green or blue-green with a glaucous finish, the undersides are glaucous and sparsely hairy. The flowers measure 8–12cm (3–5in) across and have eight rounded petals. The stamen anthers and filaments are yellow, while the stigma is pinkish yellow. There are 2–3 densely tomentose carpels, which open wide when mature to show dark blue seeds and vivid pink unfertilized ovules. The leaves turn a wonderful shade of orange-brown, flushed with pink and purple, in the autumn. It is a diploid.

P. mlokosewitschi flowers from mid- to late spring. Individual plants seem to vary in their flowering time (which is typically ten days) and it would be possible to select plants to extend this flowering period. It is hardy to -20C (-4°F) and will grow happily in most well-drained soils. In Europe it grows steadily when established and will eventually form a large clump, up to 1m (3ft) across. Plants from wild-collected seed have pure yellow flowers but many that have been raised by nurseries have some pink colouring, suggesting that they are, in fact, hybrids. Demand for this plant always exceeds supply and it is, therefore, expensive and sometimes difficult to obtain. For reasons which are not clear, American gardeners have considerable difficulty in growing it.

The naturally occurring hybrid of *P. mlokosewitschi* with *P. caucasica* is called *P.* × *chamaeleon* (see page 54). Hybrids with this species are probably more common than was originally thought. 'Perle Rosé' is probably one of these hybrids.

P. mollis

There is considerable debate as to whether this should be considered an independent species. It is very vigorous, but sterile, which suggests that it may be a hybrid. Some authors now list it as a form of *P. officinalis*. It is not known to occur in the wild.

P. mollis is a very distinctive plant with stalkless leaflets and is unlikely to be mistaken for anything else. It is dwarf, growing to 45cm (18in) high, and the stems may be hairless or villous. The leaves are blue-green, hairless or glaucous above, paler beneath with long white hairs. Flowers, to 8cm (3in) across, in magenta-red or white, grow on very short stalks. There are 2 or 3 carpels, which are covered with dense white hairs. The seeds of *P. mollis* are ovoid, slightly glossy and dark blue-black. It is a tetraploid.

Readily available, it is very easy to grow, flowers in late spring and is hardy to -20°C (-4°F).

P. obovata (var. alba AGM)

This extremely widespread species, whose name is derived from the shape of the terminal leaflet, is native to China, Japan, Korea and Siberia. *P. obovata* was introduced into cultivation by E. H. Wilson in 1900.

It grows to a height of 60cm (24in) and has the unusual feature (among peonies) of having leaves that continue to grow in size after the plant has flowered. The stems are hairless and tinted pinkish brown, the colour extending as far as the main veins of the leaflets. The lower leaves are biternate, unequal, with an obovate terminal leaflet and oval or oblong lateral leaflets. The leaves reach a maximum size of 14.5cm (6in) long by 8.5cm (3¼in) wide when the plant is fruiting. The 7–9 thin papery leaflets are dark green, sometimes purple-flushed, and hairless above, glaucous below with a sparse covering of hairs. They are cuneate at the base and

shortly-acuminate at the tip. The flowers are up to 7cm (3in) across and range from white to rosy-purple; they are occasionally creamy white. The carpels are hairless.

Flowering from mid-spring to early summer, the majority of plants in cultivation have white flowers and are referred to as *P. obovata* var. *alba*. It is a tetraploid and hardy to -20C (-4°F).

P. obovata var. willmottiae is a very distinctive and highly desirable plant, native to the Sichuan province of China. It is more robust than the type and grows to 55cm (22in) high. The stems are purple, as are the undersides of the leaves and the leaf stalks. The upper surface of the leaves is glaucous, beneath they are villous, especially along the veins. The flowers are large, up to 10.5cm (4¼in) across, and white with golden anthers and pinkish red filaments. It is a tetraploid and hardy to -20C (-4°F).

The single red form of *P. officinalis* has been widely used in peony hybridization. It is less vigorous than 'Rubra Plena'.

While both *P. obovata* and *P. obovata* var. *willmottiae* are very attractive plants, they are considered to be a challenge to grow. The latter died out in cultivation and had to be re-introduced. They are best planted in well-drained loam, in a site where they are protected from early morning sun. The healthiest plants seem to grow in light shade beneath trees and shrubs.

P. officinalis

P. officinalis has been cultivated in Europe for hundreds of years, indeed the word '*officinalis*' is Latin for used in medicine. The majority of wild plants of this species have single magenta flowers, quite different from the better known 'Rubra Plena', whose blooms are double and a very deep cardinal-red. The species is currently divided into four subspecies, including two that were formerly treated as species in their own right; all are tetraploid. Some botanists would include *P. mollis* and *P. clusii* in the *P. officinalis* aggregate; however, I do not feel that this can be justified in view of the very different character of these plants.

P. officinalis ssp. officinalis is usually found growing wild in southern Europe. It has a wide distribution and occurs in most of the countries to the north and east of the Mediterranean. It has been recorded from France, Italy, Switzerland, Hungary, Albania and eastern Serbia.

Subspecies *officinalis* grows to a height of 35–60cm (14–24in). It is sparsely villous on the stems when young, becoming hairless as the plant matures. The lower leaves are biternate, deeply cut into 14–35 narrow-elliptic or narrow-oblong segments, 7–11.5cm (3–4¾in) long by 1.2–3.3cm (½–1¼in) wide. The leaf stalks are pale green with a slight furrow on the upper surface. The terminal leaflet has a long stalk, 5–11cm (2–4½in) long but the leaf segments are stalkless or have a short stalk (to 2cm/¾in long). The segments have a caudate base and may be divided into as many as three lobes each with an acuminate or, occasionally, notched apex. The upper surface is dark green and hairless, the lower paler and pilose, but may be hairless in cultivated specimens. The flowers are magenta-rose or deep red, 9–13cm (3½–5in) across with widely spreading obovate petals. There are 2–3 carpels which are covered with thick brown tomentum. The ovoid seeds are shiny and dark brown.

P. officinalis ssp. *villosa* (page 66) makes a good candidate for a rock garden. In the correct location it will self seed.

The single red form of this plant has been widely used by American breeders to produce improved hybrids with extremely decorative vivid red flowers.

P. officinalis ssp. *officinalis* flowers from late spring to early summer. It is hardy to -25°C (-12.5°F) and is easy to grow and happy in most soils. In spring the young shoots are an attractive shade of red, turning to green as the leaves develop.

P. officinalis ssp. banatica is restricted to a limited geographical area in eastern Europe: parts of Hungary, Romania and Serbia. Its name originates from the Banat region where it was first discovered. The diagnostic feature is the division of the terminal leaflet into two or three lobes; the lateral leaflets are entire. There are 12–15 leaf segments. They are dark green and hairless above, glaucous and hairless or villous beneath. The leaflets are narrow to broadly elliptic, 4.3–11cm (1½–4½in) long, with an acuminate apex. The carpels are tomentose.

P. officinalis ssp. humilis was formerly considered to be a species its own right (*P. humilis*). This subspecies is a dwarf form of *P. officinalis* growing to 40cm (16in) high. It is endemic to Spain and southern France. The leaves are smaller and less deeply divided than the typical species (to one third of their length) with broader segments and blunt tips. The stems and leaf stalks are hairy, while the underside of the leaves varies from being villous to tomentose. The carpels are hairless. It has magenta flowers, blooms from late spring to early summer and is suitable for a rock garden.

P. officinalis **ssp.** *villosa* was formerly known as a variety of *P. humilis*. The 'Saint Loup Peony', it occurs naturally in south-eastern France and the centre of Italy. While very similar to the previous subspecies it can be easily distinguished by the tomentose carpels. The leaf stalks and the underside of the leaflets are similarly hairy. *P. officinalis* ssp. *villosa* produces magenta flowers from late spring to early summer. It makes a very good subject for a rock garden and in·the right conditions will self seed.

P. officinalis cultivars At one time there were dozens of cultivated varieties of *P. officinalis*, but many of these lost favour when the Chinese peony, *P. lactiflora* was introduced. The Parisien nurseryman, Charles Verdier, is said to have listed more than fifty varieties in the 1850s. Many other nurseries, including those of Vilmorin and Barr, list them until they cease to appear in the 1930s. It is quite possible that many of these remain, unrecognized, in old gardens.

The following varieties should be available:

'Alba Plena' is slightly less vigorous than 'Rubra Plena'. It has double flowers which open with a hint of flesh-pink. This colour quickly fades to leave pure white blooms, with slightly enlarged outer petals. The petals are arranged in rosettes around the carpels, with small narrow sword-shaped petaloids on the outside. The carpels are tomentose with pinkish brown stigmata.

'Anemoniflora Rosea' AGM is short growing with vivid Tyrian-purple flowers and yellow-edged similarly coloured staminodes. It is a striking plant, eminently suitable for growing in a rock garden.

'China Rose' is an extremely attractive plant with single salmon-pink flowers and orange stamens.

'Crimson Globe' has single garnet-red flowers with crimson and golden staminodes.

'Lize van Veen' is a wonderful plant with rather flat flowers that have very large wavy petaloids. The double flowers open to deep pink but quickly fade to blush. The guard petals are large and well rounded with magenta-rose veins on the outside. The pink colour eventually fades to leave an almost white flower with touches of pink in the shadows. Very beautiful.

'Mutabilis Plena' bears vivid, almost fluorescent, pink double flowers with enlarged guard petals. It flowers very early and has shiny green leaves.

'Rosea Plena' AGM has vivid pink double flowers with irregularly toothed petaloids in the centre, becoming narrower towards the edge. The guard petals are nicely rounded. The carpels are pale green and tomentose with pink stigmata. The flowers fade in bright sunlight to almost white, touched with pink at the base.

'Rosea Superba Plena' is similar to 'Rosea Plena' but the central petaloids, which are broad becoming narrower towards the base with toothed tips, are built up into a large raised mound. The colour lasts better and has a nice warm glow. The guard petals are rounded. The carpels are green with dark red stigmata.

'Rubra' is a rather delicate plant when compared to its more robust double cousin. The flowers are deep cardinal-red, touched slightly with magenta. This may be the form known as 'Sabini' by Anderson (1818). Another variety with single garnet-red flowers is 'James Crawford Weguelin'.

'Rubra Plena' AGM is robust with large globe-shaped deep cardinal-red flowers which fade with age to deep crimson with a hint of purple. The petals are arranged in a series of rosettes around the carpels. The heavy flowers require support to prevent them from collapsing on the ground; if this is done they will last considerably longer. 'Rubra Plena' tolerates abuse and is known as

The flowers of *P. peregrina* range from vermilion to ruby red. Most of the cultivated varieties were collected by Peter Barr.

'The Memorial Day Peony' in the USA. It is extremely vigorous and it has even been suggested that this peony is a hybrid between *P. peregrina* and *P. officinalis*.

P. parnassica

P. parnassica originates from the mountains of southern Greece, where it grows in forest clearings and meadows. Formerly considered to be a variant of *P. arietina*, Tzanoudakis raised it to the status of an independent species in 1977.

A distinctive plant, *P. parnassica* grows to 65cm (26in) high and has hirsute stems. The terminal leaflet is usually entire, but the lateral leaflets may be entire or divided into two or three lobes. The leaflets are obovate to narrowly elliptic in shape and acute or shortly-acuminate. They may taper towards the leaf stalk.

When young, the upper leaf surfaces are purplish green, turning to light grey-green as they mature. The underside is greyish green and covered with soft slender hairs. The flowers are dark maroon-red and 8–12cm (3–5in) wide, with yellow anthers and purple stamen filaments. The carpels are tomentose and have a distinctive spirally wound style. It is a diploid.

As is the case with so many of the Mediterranean species, *P. parnassica* starts to grow very early in the year and it flowers in the late spring. It is a challenge to grow as it is not very hardy and has proved to be difficult to establish in British gardens. The main problem for gardeners seems to be caused by the high rainfall of north-western Europe: if the soil is excessively wet in the spring and summer, the crown will rot. New shoots may appear during the following spring but the plant will eventually succumb and die.

P. peregrina

The 'Red Peony of Constantinople' was introduced into Austria from Istanbul in 1583 but is native to Albania, Bulgaria, Greece, Romania, Serbia and Turkey. To confuse matters it has been known in the past as *P. femina Byzantica*, *P. lobata* and *P. decora*. The species can be readily distinguished from *P. officinalis* by its dark green notched leaflets.

The flowers of this species are a striking ruby-red, quite different from that of any other peony. This is due to the presence of a pigment called cyanidin, which occurs in minute concentrations in other species but is usually masked by the scarlet pigment peonidin. In *P.*

P. peregrina 'Fire King' has striking flowers that are a particularly vivid, shiny red.

peregrina the pigments are present in approximately equal concentrations, together with the yellow pigment flavone and it is this combination that produces the brilliant colouring.

P. peregrina grows to a height of 50cm (20in). The stems are hairless and green with a few red stripes. The leaves are biternate with 15–18 segments, often divided into 2–3 lobes. The leaflets are notched at the tip, shiny dark green and 5.5–11cm (2¼–4½in) long by 1.4–4.6cm (½–1¾in) wide. They are hairless above, glaucous and hairless or slightly villous beneath. The bright glowing ruby-red flowers, 7–12cm (3–5in) across, have strongly concave petals that are oblong-ovate to sub-orbicular in shape. The stamen filaments are 2–2.5cm (¾–1in) long and pink or red, and the anthers are yellow. The 3–4 carpels of this species are rather short, slightly recurved and covered with long white hairs. The leaves turn yellow in the autumn with red tints; the inner surface of the sepals becomes bright orange-red. It is a tetraploid with 20 chromosomes.

P. peregrina flowers from mid- to late spring. Hardy to -20C (-4°F), it grows well in most soils and is perfectly suited to rock gardens. The flowers are seen at their best when grown in partial shade.

P. peregrina cultivars In 1899 Barr & Sons catalogue listed seven varieties of this species, only a few of which still survive:

'Fire King' has incredibly shiny scarlet-red petals.

'Otto Froebel' (syn. 'Sunshine') is the mostly widely available and grows to 80cm (32in). It has satiny vermilion-red flowers, which seem to almost glow in sunshine, and dark green leaves. It has been widely used by American breeders to produce a number of exciting hybrids with vivid red and coral-pink flowers.

'Sunbeam' has glowing orange-red globe-shaped flowers.

P. rhodia

P. rhodia is a beautiful peony with dark foliage and white flowers. An endemic of the Greek island of Rhodes, its natural habitat is *Cupressus sempervirens* var. *horizontalis* forest and phrygana. The species is found at altitudes of 350–630m (1,150–2,070ft), on limestone soil.

The stems of *P. rhodia* are reddish brown, hairless and grow to a height of 35cm (14in). The leaves are dark green above and slightly paler beneath; hairless on both surfaces. They are dissected into 9–29 segments. The terminal leaflet is deeply divided to the base into three segments; the lateral leaflets are divided into two and are entire or divided into 3–4 lobes. Oblong-elliptic to lanceolate with an acute or acuminate tip, they are stalkless (sessile) or have a short stalk. They are 7–13cm (3–5in) long by 2–7cm (¾–3in) wide. The flowers, which are about 8cm (3in) across, have 6–8 petals and stamens with yellow anthers and red filaments. There are 2–5 tomentose carpels. It is a diploid.

P. rhodia is a peony that likes to take risks! It starts to grow in early to mid-winter and is consequently extremely vulnerable to frost damage. However, this species has been grown outside for several years at the Royal Botanic Garden Edinburgh and it is considered to be hardy to -15°C (5°F) when dormant. In its natural habitat, it flowers from February to April and by the end of May the foliage has completely withered away. While it may be a difficult species to grow, *P. rhodia* rewards persistence.

P. × smouthii

This 'species' is probably a hybrid between *P. tenuifolia* and *P. lactiflora* and has been known since at least 1843. It is thought to have been named after a Monsieur Smout, a chemist from Malines. The American breeder, Professor A. P. Saunders crossed both of these species and produced a plant that looked remarkably like *P. × smouthii*. It has finely divided, dark green leaves, grows to 45cm (18in) high and is a diploid. The crimson flowers measure about 8cm (3in) across and have a sweet fragrance. They appear from mid- to late spring. It is hardy to -20°C (-4°F).

P. sterniana

P. sterniana was discovered by Ludlow and Taylor in 1938, growing in the Tsangpo Valley in East Tibet. It looks quite similar to *P. emodi* but has only one flower to a stem (*P. emodi* also has flower buds that arise from the leaf axils).

In the wild *P. sterniana* grows to a height of 90cm (36in), but the only plant that is known in cultivation is much shorter and attains 45cm (18in). The alternate leaves have leaf stalks approximately 30cm (12in) long. They are hairless, biternate, deeply-divided and mid- to dark green above, glaucous below. The leaflets, 10–16cm (4–6in) long by 1-2.3cm (½–1in) wide, are narrowly elliptic or narrowly oblong-elliptic with an acute or acuminate tip. The single pure white flowers measure 5–8cm (2–3in) across and have four lanceolate sepals; the exterior sepals are leaf-like and longer than the petals. The flowers, which are much smaller than those of *P. emodi*, have white stamen filaments and pale yellow anthers. The 3–4 hairless carpels are pale green when immature with creamy white stigmas. When mature the capsules turn bright red; the enclosed seeds are indigo-blue.

P. sterniana flowers in mid-spring, a few weeks before *P. emodi*. This species has nice foliage and would make a

Originating from eastern Tibet, *P. sterniana* is an extremely rare species in cultivation and is not commercially available at the present time.

good garden plant, but at the present time it is not available commercially. It is known to be hardy to at least -11.5C (11°F).

P. tenuifolia

This very distinctive peony has finely dissected, glossy dark green leaves. Sometimes known as the 'Fringed' or 'Adonis peony', it occurs naturally in Romania, Ukraine and Hungary. During the past century a number of new species have been described from the former USSR including *P. biebersteiniana*, *P. carthalinica* and *P. lithophila*. All of these appear to be variants of *P. tenuifolia*. It is difficult to come to a definitive conclusion without the benefit of being able to study authentic specimens.

In the wild *P. tenuifolia* varies considerably from a dwarf 20cm (8in) high to a more robust plant attaining 60cm (24in) or more. In cultivation it usually grows to approximately 50cm (20in). In the spring the emerging shoots look like miniature shaving brushes. The leaflets are tripinnately lobed into numerous linear segments, 0.75–2cm (¼–¾in) wide, with a subacute or blunt apex. They are hairless above, very shiny or glaucous beneath. The flowers of wild plants are a deep cardinal-red and measure 6–8cm (2½–3in) across. They can have very short stems and appear to sit on top of the foliage. The stamen filaments and anthers are yellow and there are 2–3 tomentose carpels. It is a diploid.

Flowering in late spring, it is hardy to at least -25°C (-12.5°F). Available from specialist nurseries, the most common variety is the double form 'Plena'. There is also a white form, 'Alba', but this is very rare and expensive. 'Rosea' has pale pink blooms.

P. turcica

This species is endemic to the Caria and Lycia regions of south-western Turkey. Its natural habitat is *Pinus nigra* forest at altitudes of between 1,500 and 1,800m (5,000–5,900ft). It is very similar to *P. kesrouanensis* which grows in the Gâvur Daglari region of Turkey. The leaves of *P. kesrouanensis* are broader at the base, the style and stigma are longer and the style is curved at the extreme tip, rather than close to the base as in *P. turcica*.

P. turcica grows to 60cm (24in) high and has hairless, slightly glaucous, stems. There are 5–6 leaves per stem; the lower ones are biternate with 9–11 leaflets, which are elliptic or ovate-elliptic and measure 9–14cm (3½–5½in) long by 5–7cm (2–3in) wide. The terminal leaflet has a stalk, while the lateral leaflets are more or less stalkless. The leaf and leaflet stalks and the main veins of the leaves are reddish purple. The upper surface of the leaves is hairless and green, and may have a glaucous bloom, the underside is glaucous and pilose. The flowers are magenta-rose with 2–5 hairless carpels. The style is 0.2cm (¹⁄₁₆in) long with a distinctive stigma 0.25cm (¹⁄₁₆in) wide. The stigma is upturned halfway along its length with a wavy margin, similar to a cock's comb. It flowers in mid-spring.

P. veitchii

P. veitchii looks very similar to *P. anomala* but has several flowers to a stem, rather than one. It was first introduced into Europe in 1907 by E. H. Wilson, and was grown by the Veitch nursery in Chelsea, London. Native to the Chinese provinces of Gansu, Shensi and Sichuan, its natural habitat is subalpine meadows and scrubby grassland at altitudes of 2,400–3,000m (7,900–9,850ft).

P. veitchii grows to a height of 60cm (24in). It has bronzy green biternate leaves, which turn dark green as the plant matures. They are deeply cut, into 8–9 oblong-elliptic segments which are drawn out into long tapering tips and measure 5–15cm (2–6in) long by 0.5–2cm (¼–¾in) wide. Beneath they are pale green with a line of small hairs along the veins, or glaucous without any hairs. *P. veitchii* normally has two or more flowers to a stem. They are held erect but nodding slightly and are 5–9cm (2–3½in) across. Their colour has been called 'peony purple', but varies in shade. There is a form with white flowers known as 'Alba'. The petals are obovate-cuneate, truncate or notched at the tip. The stamens, up to 1.7cm (½in) long, have pink filaments and yellow anthers. The 2–4 carpels, short and abruptly tapered at the base, are dark green, flushed with red when mature. They are densely tomentose with pale yellow hairs. *P. veitchii* has wonderful autumn colour, with orange-brown foliage and bright red sepals. It is a diploid and has blue-black seeds.

There has been much debate about the status of a plant called *P. beresowskii*, first described by Komarov in 1921. The flowers can be various shades of pink or cream, the petals are said to be more deeply notched at the tip and it has cream stigmata. While there are definitely differences with *P. veitchii*, these do not seem to be sufficient to separate them into two species. The plants I have seen all appear to be *P. veitchii* and I follow F. C. Stern in considering it a variety of *P. veitchii*.

P. veitchii is easy to grow in the garden. Its small stature makes it a perfect subject for a rock garden. This species commences growth fairly late in the season, but then develops quickly and flowers in the early summer. Plants grown from seed will produce flowers of various shades of magenta. *P. veitchii* is hardy to -20°C (-4°F).

P. veitchii var. woodwardii is a smaller plant and only grows to a height of 30cm (12in). It occurs naturally in the Gansu and north-west Sichuan provinces of China.

P. wittmanniana

P. wittmanniana was discovered by Count M. Worontzoff near Abkhazia and named after a Mr. Wittman, a Russian who was exploring the Caucasus Mountains at the time. *P. wittmanniana* has been recorded from Azerbaydzhan, Georgia, northern Iran and Turkey. In the wild it grows in alpine pastures, beech woods and on rocky hillsides at altitudes of up to 1,700m (5,580ft). It occurs in two forms, one with tomentose carpels (also known as *P. tomentosa*) and the other, var. *nudicarpa*, with hairless carpels (also known as *P. steveniana*).

P. wittmanniana is a statuesque peony which can grow to 1m (3ft) high with stems up to 2cm (¾in) in diameter. They are hairless and green with some red flushing; the leaf stalks are sparsely hairy. The young leaves are bronze-green, maturing to dark glossy green, hairless above and scattered with long white hairs beneath. The leaflets are broadly-ovate or broadly-elliptic, cuneate or sometimes truncate at the base. The tips of the leaflets are acute to acuminate. Although not as large as the leaves of *P. macrophylla*, the leaflets of this species may measure as much as 17cm (7in) long by 11cm (4½in) wide. The bowl-shaped flowers, 10–12cm (4–5in) wide, are pale yellow or creamy white and somewhat hidden by the leaves. The sepals are hairy on the outside, particularly along the veins. It is a tetraploid.

A very underrated species, *P. wittmanniana* flowers from mid- to late spring. It is hardy to -15°C (5°F) and makes a good specimen plant for the larger garden but may be too large for small gardens. In the last few years seed has been collected from the wild so it can be expected to become more readily available.

The French breeders, Victor and Emile Lemoine produced some very desirable hybrids between this species and *P. lactiflora*. These are 'Avant Garde', 'Le Printemps', 'Mai Fleuri' and 'Messagere'. Another hybrid which may occasionally be found is 'Russi Major', the result of a cross with *P. mascula* ssp. *russi*. This has very large pink flowers, with a hint of mauve, but is not considered to be one of Lemoine's best plants.

6

CULTIVARS OF PAEONIA LACTIFLORA & HYBRIDS

The majority of plant genera have one or two species that outshine the rest or which have proved to be particularly valuable for breeding. Among roses the obvious candidate is *Rosa chinensis* (introduced in 1770), which gave rise to many of the modern hybrid roses. *Camellia japonica* (1739) has spawned hundreds of cultivars, some very similar to one another, and one peony in particular has been largely responsible for the success of these flamboyant 'roses without thorns': the Chinese peony, *P. lactiflora*.

Prior to the introduction of this species, European gardeners were limited to the restricted palette of colours that were available from *P. officinalis*. The other species such as *P. mascula* and *P. peregrina* were hardly exploited. *P. lactiflora* introduced the potential of a much wider range of subtle colours and, its greatest gift of all, fragrance. *P. lactiflora* also exhibited a capacity for doubling which was absent in most of the other herbaceous members of the genus.

Wild specimens of *P. lactiflora* are thought to have reached Europe during the mid-seventeenth century. The stimulus for plant breeders seems to have been the introduction from China of 'improved' varieties such as 'Fragrans' (1805), which had small reddish pink flowers, 'Whitleyi' (1808), a single white, and 'Humei' (1810), a double variety with watermelon-pink flowers.

INFLUENTIAL BREEDERS

The French led the way in peony breeding. One of the first to become interested in the potential of the genus was Nicolas Lemon (1787–?) who lived in Porte St. Denis near Paris. As well as growing a wide range of other plants, Lemon produced a number of new varieties from *P. officinalis*, such as 'Anemonifolia Alba',

and 'Edulis Superba' from *P. lactiflora*. These were all given descriptive Latin names, as was the trend in the early eighteenth century. 'Edulis Superba' remains one of the most popular peonies today.

The person who can be credited with starting the craze for herbaceous peonies was probably the Comte de Cussy an amateur gardener who imported peonies from China and subsequently produced his own varieties of *P. lactiflora*. His collection was inherited by Jacques Calot (?–1875) in about 1850. Calot succeeded in producing more than twenty new varieties, many of which are still widely grown and bear comparison with the more recent varieties. These include 'Duchesse de Nemours', 'Reine Hortense', 'Madame Crousse' and 'Philomèle'. In 1872, Calot's collection was bought by Felix Crousse (1840–1925), of Nancy, France. Crousse produced some outstanding plants, such as 'Felix Crousse', 'Monsieur Jules Elie', 'Asa Gray' and 'Avalanche'.

In 1849 Crousse's nursery and collection of peonies was purchased by Victor Lemoine (1823–1911). Lemoine is one of the most significant figures in the history of the peony cultivation but also raised numerous improved varieties of *Syringa* and *Delphinium*. The most famous of his *P. lactiflora* hybrids are 'Sarah Bernhardt', 'Le Cygne', 'Primevère' and 'Solange'. Victor and his son, Emile (1862–1942), continued to breed peonies and were responsible for 'Le Printemps', 'Mai Fleuri' and 'Avant Garde', all of which are hybrids between *P. lactiflora* and *P. wittmanniana*. This was not the limit of their achievement for in the late 1890s they succeeded in crossing a Moutan tree peony with *P. lutea*. The resulting hybrids (now known collectively as *P. × lemoinei*) caused a sensation with previously unseen

PLATE II

P. 'Angelo Cobb Freeborn'

P. 'Carol'

P. 'Edulis Superba'

P. 'Mister Ed'

P. 'Kelway's Scented Rose'

All flowers are shown at approximately ¼ size

P. 'June Rose'

P. 'Bunker Hill'

P. 'Albert Crousse'

P. 'Monsieur Jules Elie'

P. 'Charlie's White'

P. 'Bridal Gown'

shades of yellow and red. These tree peonies are described in Chapter 7.

Another famous French breeder was Auguste Dessert (1859–1929). Dessert was born and spent most of his life in Chenonceaux, a village in the Loire valley famous for its sixteenth century chateau. Working with his grandfather, Etienne Mechin, who was already famous as a collector and breeder of peonies, Dessert introduced a total of 41 named varieties including 'Adolphe Rousseau', 'Germaine Bigot', 'Laura Dessert' and 'Tourangelle'. He also introduced one with Doriat and two with his grandfather.

While the French dominated peony breeding in the eighteenth century there was also a single English company which was particularly successful. Kelways Nursery of Langport in Somerset was established by James Kelway (1815–1899), who produced his first varieties of *P. lactiflora* in 1863. Kelway's pioneering work was continued by his son William (1839–?) and subsequently his grandson, James (1871–1952). By 1884 the family had been responsible for introducing 100 new varieties; this figure had increased to 294 by 1904. By the turn of the century, Kelway's had become one of the largest nurseries in the world and employed about 400 staff. Their seed catalogue at this time was extensive, but the business suffered a dramatic decline with the demise of the large country estates after the First World War. Their last new peony was produced in 1939.

Many of the Kelway's peonies are still available and a large number of them are listed below. Some of the most significant are 'Lady Alexandra Duff', 'Baroness Schroeder' and 'Kelway's Glorious', varieties that are still widely grown throughout the world. The company also adopted the term 'Imperial peony' for the Japanese form of flower.

It is possible that William Kelway was the first breeder to intentionally cross *P. lactiflora* with another species. Several people, notably A. P. Saunders in *The Manual of the American Peony Society* questioned whether Kelway actually achieved this but the following is an extract taken from a letter written by William Kelway on 6th June 1890 to Mr. George Paul:

'I procured some of each of the species, and set to work in the following year hybridising. I got a plant of *corallina* (this is now known as *P. mascula* ssp. *mascula*), which my father's sister, an old lady of eighty-four, had found on Steep

'Ellen Cowley', bred by Arthur Saunders, has extremely vivid coral-pink flowers and spreads by runners.

Holm, an island in the Bristol Channel. The leaves of this species are different from all others, being entire; the foliage of all others, I believe, is divided; the seeds which remain on the seed-pods of *corallina* after the pods are open, are very ornamental, and when the sun is shining on them they look like amethysts. It so happened that the woman from whom I got my first lot of Paeonies possessed the scented variety, and from this fact I attribute my success in getting so many highly scented kinds.'

In the 1920s the production of most new varieties passed to breeders in the United States of America. The Klehm family have been prominent members of the American Peony Society since its inception in 1903. Charles C. Klehm (1867–1957) was the first member of the family to become interested in peonies and raised many seedlings which were subsequently named by his son. Carl G. Klehm (1916–1973) concentrated on raising varieties of *P. lactiflora* and produced a range of plants which he called 'Estate peonies'. The nursery, in Champaign, Illinois, grew large quantities of peonies for cut flowers and this greatly influenced their breeding program. Carl's most successful peonies have been 'Charlie's' White', 'Dinner Plate' and 'Emma Klehm'. His son Roy followed the family trade and has earned an enviable reputation as a breeder of hybrid peonies. He has continued the work of earlier breeders, such as Lyman Cousins, Orville Fay, William Krekler and Sam Wissing, and registered their best varieties as they have matured. Roy has also raised many of his own peonies including the striking coral hybrid 'Pink Hawaiian Coral' and the lactifloras 'Cheddar Charm', 'Chiffon Parfait' and 'Reine Supreme'. While the majority of peony breeders during this century have concentrated on raising hybrids, Roy and his father have shown that there is still considerable potential remaining in *P. lactiflora*.

Few individuals can have had as much impact upon the destiny of the peony as Professor Arthur Percy Saunders (1869–1953). Born in Canada, he spent most of his career teaching chemistry at Hamilton College in Clinton, USA and only became interested in peonies later in life. Few people can ever have achieved so much during their retirement!

Saunders began growing peonies in 1900 and started producing new varieties of *P. lactiflora* in 1905. He began collecting other species in 1913, when Lemoine sent him a specimen of *P. lutea*, and subsequently went on to undertake an extensive breeding program. He was meticulous in his maintenance of records and this has been of great benefit to those who have emulated his work. Saunders' research has had a major impact upon the subsequent breeding of herbaceous peonies. The results of his experiments are described in the APS publication, *The Peonies* (Wister, 1995).

The hybrids Saunders produced extended the flowering period for herbaceous peonies by at least three weeks and introduced new colours such as salmon, coral

'Moonrise' is a Saunders hybrid with flowers of the palest yellow shade.

PLATE III All flowers are shown at approximately ¼ size

P. 'Helen Hayes'

P. 'Emma Klehm'

P. 'Mischief'

P. 'Pink Lemonade'

P. 'Lotus Queen'

P. 'Claire Dubois'

P. 'Festiva Maxima'

P. 'Elsa Sass'

and pale lilac. There is little doubt that his work did more to advance peonies as garden plants than that of any other person in the twentieth century. Sadly, many of his hybrids are difficult to obtain: a situation likely to continue until peonies can be micropropagated. Four of the most beautiful Saunders hybrids are 'Defender', 'Ellen Cowley', 'Lavender' and 'Moonrise'.

Another influential breeder was Lyman Glasscock (1875–1952) who introduced 'Burma Ruby' and 'Salmon Glow'. He discovered that by building soil up around the crown of *P. officinalis* 'Rubra', he could delay its flowering by one month. This allowed him to use its pollen to pollinate the later flowering varieties of *P. lactiflora*. His work was continued by his daughter Elizabeth Falk who moved her father's peonies to her own home when he died. She continued to select the best of his seedlings for registration and introduced the popular 'Scarlet O'Hara'.

William Krekler (1900–) was far from methodical in his approach to breeding and he produced some wonderful plants. He started by gathering over 800 varieties of peony and collected their pollen in a kettle. The pollen was mixed together with his finger before being dabbed on to the stigmas of promising peonies. No one can doubt that his technique worked as he eventually registered a total of 381 new varieties.

In more recent years Don Hollingsworth (1928–) has introduced some interesting new plants such as 'Cherry Ruffles', a semi-double hybrid with crimson-red flowers, and 'Delaware Chief', which has fully double flowers. These plants fill an important gap; previously double red hybrids were relatively rare. Don Hollingsworth was also one of the first people in America to duplicate the work of Toichi Itoh (see p.143) and successfully produce intersectional hybrid peonies.

There are many other peony breeders but unfortunately it is not possible to include them all in the space available.

The raising of new varieties requires a long commitment: most peonies take 4–5 years before they are of flowering size. If the plant is worth propagating it may take a further 10–15 years before there will be enough material to sell. So peonies are not the best way of making a quick buck! Breeders occasionally register new varieties and then withdraw them when they find that their seedling has not lived up to expectation.

A visit to a typical garden centre in the British Isles reveals that, at the very most, only ten to fifteen herbaceous peony varieties are commonly available. These are almost invariably *P. lactiflora* varieties, but the range is increasing every year. The most popular are 'Bowl of Beauty', 'Duchesse de Nemours', 'Felix Crousse', 'Inspecteur Lavergne', 'Festiva Maxima', 'Lady Alexandra Duff', 'Karl Rosenfield' and 'Sarah Bernhardt'. However, American hybrids are starting to become available and these tend to flower approximately one month earlier than those derived from *P. lactiflora*. During the past forty years American breeders have introduced a number of peonies with coral-pink flowers. It is unfortunate that these do not seem to grow as well in the British Isles, where winters are wetter than in the United States. In France, plants bred by French growers tend to prevail, although there are an increasing number which have originated from America. *The Plant Finder* (RHS), which is published annually, provides an up-to-date list of the varieties that are commercially available in the British Isles.

NOTE The height stated is the maximum that is likely to be attained. Plants grown on moist soil are taller than those raised on drier soil in hotter climates. When two names are given in brackets the first usually refers to the breeder, the latter to the person who registered the variety.

The plates (II–XI) illustrate flowers that have been taken from plants at varying states of maturity, so they do not accurately reflect the relative size of the flowers in different varieties.

Abalone Pearl (Krekler, 1978)
Attractive single lactiflora with flesh-pink flowers. The stamens have very long pale yellow filaments and gold anthers. The carpels are hirsute with purple stigmata. This variety has a very conspicuous purple stigmoidal disc. Early season. 70cm (28in).

Admiral Harwood (Kelway, 1909)
Japanese lactiflora with white guard petals, flushed pink, and lemon-coloured petaloids with brown tips. Early to midseason.

Adolphe Rousseau (Dessert-Mechin, 1890)
Semi-double lactiflora with very large garnet-red flowers and dark red-tinged foliage. Free flowering but some

people consider it to have an unpleasant scent. Early to midseason. 95cm (38in).

Afterglow (Kelway)
Fully double lactiflora, whose deep rose-pink petals fade at the tips in bright sunshine. In the centre is a mass of golden anthers, surrounding pale green carpels with cream stigmata. May occasionally produce single flowers as side buds. Free flowering, good fragrance. Late season. 1.2m (4ft).

A. F. W. Hayward (Kelway, 1901)
Double lactiflora with intense carmine-red petals. The inner petals are narrow with a bright yellow base. The carpels are tomentose with bright red styles and stigmata. Midseason. 90cm (36in).

A la Mode (Roy Klehm, 1981)
Single lactiflora with shiny, pure white flowers and golden yellow stamens. The edge of the petals is slightly serrated. Often four flower buds to each strong stem. Musk-like fragrance. Early season. 85cm (34in).

'America' is probably the best single red peony. It was awarded a Gold Medal by the APS in 1992.

Albert Crousse (Crousse, 1893)
Very double lactiflora bearing fragrant, salmon-pink, globe-shaped flowers with flecks of carmine-red in the centre. The petals become progressively smaller towards the centre of the flower; those in the extreme centre are so tiny that they leave a depression in the middle of the bloom. The carpels are vestigial and the stamens absent. Very free flowering. Late season. 95cm (38in).

Alice Graemes (Kelway)
Very striking single lactiflora with deep magenta-pink flowers and a large mass of golden stamens. The carpels are hairless, light green with pale pink stigmata. Slightly fragrant with strong wiry stems. Mid- to late season. 1.1ft (3½ft).

Alice Harding (Lemoine, 1922)
Double lactiflora with rounded, flesh-pink guard petals surrounding a centre of incurved and irregular creamy

white petals. Vigorous and reasonably free flowering, but a somewhat untidy flower. Sweetly fragrant. Shares its name with the tree peony 'Alice Harding' which was introduced by Lemoine in 1936. Lemoine considered this variety to have been his best introduction but it rarely does well in the USA. Midseason. Medium height.

Alstead (Auten, 1939)
Japanese-form peony with purple guard petals and a large mass of crinkled, pink-streaked, golden yellow staminodes. The carpels are pale green with pinkish yellow stigmata. Free flowering. Midseason. 70cm (28in).

Ama-No-Sode (Japan)
Japanese lactiflora with large lilac-rose guard petals fading to pale rose at their edges. The flowers may be up to 22cm (9in) across with a very large centre of yellow petaloids with pink tips. Free flowering and vigorous with slight fragrance. Midseason. 1.1m (3½ft).

America (Rudolph, 1976) GM
Single hybrid ('Burma Ruby' × unknown)with very large brilliant scarlet flowers touched with magenta. The petals have a satin sheen and the foliage remains green throughout the season. The carpels are yellow-green with white stigmata and surrounded by a tight bunch of stamens. Slightly fragrant. Probably the best single red. Early to midseason. 90cm (36in).

Angelo Cobb Freeborn (Freeborn, 1943)
Double hybrid (P. lactiflora × P. officinalis) whose enlarged guard petals surround an attractive centre of soft coral-red petals, darkening with age. It has a long flowering period from early to midseason. 90cm (36in).

Anna Pavlova (Kelway)
Double lactiflora whose flowers open to rich rose-pink but fade to a pale pink. The outer petals are very large, the inner staminodes much smaller, being almost Japanese in character, and blush-pink with a golden centre. The carpels are purple with pink styles and stigmata. Fragrant. Midseason. 85cm (34in).

Ann Berry Cousins (Cousins-Roy Klehm, 1972)
Single to semi-double hybrid with large slightly notched, salmon-pink guard petals surrounding golden yellow, semi-functional stamens. In the very centre of the flower are a few small salmon-pink carpelodes. It has nice buds. 'Salmon Dream' (p.121) is a better plant. Early season. 70–75cm (28–30in).

Annisquam (Thurlows-Stranger, 1951)
Globe-shaped double with large, well rounded pink petals. Very symmetrical with a slight fragrance. Makes a good cut flower and retains its colour well. Midseason. 80cm (32in).

Antwerpen (Origin unknown)
Japanese lactiflora with wavy, coral-pink guard petals, darkening towards the centre where a large mass of bright creamy yellow staminodes have gold edges and tips. The carpels are very pale green and have pale pink stigmata. Slightly fragrant. Midseason. 80cm (32in).

Arabian Prince (Kelway)
Semi-double lactiflora with magenta-crimson flowers opening from maroon-purple buds. It has a small number of stamens in the centre with an additional ring surrounding the inner petals. The carpels are very small and creamy green with magenta styles. They may develop into carpelodes or be entirely absent. Free flowering. Late season. 1m (3ft).

Archangel (Saunders, 1950)
Single hybrid (P. lactiflora × P. macrophylla) with white flowers held erect and well clear of the foliage. Creamy white petals surround a large mass of golden anthers with very long filaments, which are pale yellow at the top and purple at the base. The carpels are furrowed, tomentose and greyish green with purple stigmata. Clearly macrophylla in character. Vigorous and robust with massive glossy leaves and a somewhat spreading habit. Early season. 80cm (32in), spread 100cm (40in) or more.

Argentine (Lemoine, 1924)
Creamy white, globe-shaped flowers with a pleasant scent. Midseason. 70cm (28in).

Armance Dessert (Doriat, 1929)
Double, blush-white flowers with very larger outer petals and smaller inner ones. Free flowering, with a slight fragrance. Makes a good cut flower. Mid- to very late season. 90cm (36in).

Artist, syn. 'Romeo' (Kelway)
Attractive double lactiflora with deep rose-pink guard petals and a paler flamboyant heart. The central petals become smaller towards the centre, becoming deeply toothed and with a hint of yellow at the base. Slightly fragrant. Mid- to late season. 83cm (33in).

Asa Gray (Crousse, 1886)
Double, deep rose-pink flowers are covered with small pink dots; the guard petals are salmon- and flesh-pink. Occasionally the petals that are in the central crown have a crimson edge. Strong fragrance. Late midseason. 85cm (34in).

Athena (Saunders, 1955)
Hybrid with beautiful single, ivory-coloured flowers. The petals are narrow with large and diffuse rose-pink flares. The cup-shaped blooms have a large ball of very pale, gold-tipped stamens. The green tomentose carpels have pink stigmata. The result of a quadruple cross

'Avant Garde' has pink flowers with magenta veins, colouring that is rare among *P. wittmanniana* hybrids.

between *P. lactiflora*, *P. macrophylla*, *P. mlokosewitschi* and *P. officinalis*. Early season. Dwarf, to 60cm (24in).

Audrey (Saunders, 1938)
Semi-double hybrid (*P. lactiflora* × *P. macrophylla*) with fragrant, bright pink flowers, fading to light pink with age. Glossy leaved and compact. Early season. 70cm (28in).

Auguste Dessert (Dessert, 1920)
Double or sometimes semi-double lactiflora with well rounded, deep pink petals, edged by a narrow border of silver. Additional petals grow from the centre, surrounded by a ring of golden yellow stamens. Free flowering with good autumn colouring. Late to midseason. 75cm (30in).

Augustin d'Hour (Calot, 1867)
Old lactiflora variety, quite widely grown in Britain as 'Général MacMahon' (or 'Marechal MacMahon'). It has very large deep red, bomb-shaped flowers with enlarged guard petals and a large mass of narrow inner petals. The petals in the extreme centre are minuscule. Free flowering. Late season. 90cm (36in).

Auten's 1816 (Auten)
This seedling was never named by the breeder. It has extremely large double or bomb-shaped flowers with densely packed, dark crimson petals. Stamens are absent and the carpels are green with elongated purple styles. The very dark cardinal-red buds look very like those of 'Rubra Plena' until they open. Early season. Potentially 75cm (30in), but the weight of the flower makes even these strong stems drop to the ground.

Avalanche, syn 'Albatre' (Crousse, 1886)
Double lactiflora with globe-shaped, blush-white flowers and a slightly pink centre. Some of its petals may be edged with carmine-red. Fragrant. Mid- to late season. 90cm (36in).

Avant Garde (Lemoine, 1907)
Vigorous hybrid (*P. lactiflora* × *P. wittmanniana*) with large single pink flowers marked with magenta veins. The flowers are held nicely erect on stiff dark red stems. The edges of the petals are slightly ruffled and suffused with magenta. The stamens have golden anthers and very long filaments, which are purple at the base and

white towards the top. The carpels are tomentose with narrow erect dark red stigmata. Glossy, light green leaves. An old variety but well worth growing. Early season. 1.1m (3½ft).

Bahram (Kelway)

The guard petals of this double lactiflora are vivid magenta on the inside, paler on the outside. The staminodes are pale pink, deeper at the tips. The cream and pink carpels are green at the base with cream styles and pink stigmata. Mid- to late season. Tall.

Ballerina (Kelway)

Double lactiflora with blush-lilac-pink flowers, which gradually fade to white in strong sunshine. White petaloids and purple carpels and styles. Good autumn tints. Early to midseason. 90cm (36in).

Ballerina (Saunders, 1941)

Double hybrid between *P. lactiflora* 'Lady Alexandra Duff' and *P. wittmanniana*. This has bomb-shaped, greenish yellow flowers, tinted with pink, eventually fading to white. The outer petals are broad and incurved. Early to midseason. 90cm (36in).

Barbara (Polish origin)

Bright pink Japanese flower with a distinct touch of lavender. Nice rounded guard petals and numerous wavy, forked staminodes. The flowers are held erect on strong stems. Late season. 80cm (32in).

Baroness Schroeder (Kelway, 1889)

Highly regarded double lactiflora with very large white, globe-shaped flowers, tinted slightly with pale flesh-pink. This pink coloration disappears as the petals open to leave a pure snow-white bloom. Vigorous and free flowering and good for cutting. Fragrant. Mid- to late season. 90cm (36in).

Barrington Belle (Carl G. Klehm, 1971)

Very distinctive anemone or Japanese-type lactiflora with deep red guard petals and a mass of wavy, golden-edged deep red or pink staminodes. Free flowering with long stems. Midseason. 85cm (34in).

Barrymore (Kelway)

Japanese lactiflora whose buds open to form very pale blush-pink flowers with a golden centre. Narrow staminodes are pale yellow. Late midseason. 85cm (34in).

Beatrice Kelway (Kelway, 1905)

Japanese lactiflora with very large, vivid rose-pink guard petals surrounding rose-pink central petaloids that have fawn and gold tips. Vigorous and tall with a long flowering period. Mid- to late season. 1m (3ft).

Belle Center (Mains, 1956)

Semi-double hybrid bearing shallow cup-shaped blooms with mahogany-red petals and bright yellow stamens. The petals have a velvety exterior when young; the shorter inner petals are crinkled. Almost identical to 'Buckeye Belle' (p.85) but flowers a fortnight later. Early season. 75cm (30in).

Bethcar (Kelway, 1926)

Single peony with slightly wavy, deep cherry-rose petals, which are distinctly concave. Quite pretty with a solid mound of yellow stamens and green carpels with magenta stigmata. Upright. Mid- to late season. 1m (3ft).

Betty Groff (Krekler, 1958)

Japanese lactiflora with light pink guard petals becoming paler towards an almost white centre. The pale yellow staminodes are tipped with pink. Free flowering. Narrow habit. Midseason. 90cm (36in).

Big Ben (Auten, 1943)

Stunning bomb-shaped, deep red lactiflora, with inner petals surrounded by a ring of narrow, thread-like petals. The pale green carpels have red-tipped stigmata. A good cut flower, fragrant. Early season. 75cm (30in).

Black Monarch (Glasscock, 1939)

Very double hybrid (*P. officinalis* × *P. lactiflora*) with dark red (53A) flowers, a similar colour to those of 'Buckeye Belle'. Stamens are absent and the carpels are greenish yellow with a long tapering magenta style. The colour appears much brighter in sunshine. Early season. 78cm (31in).

Blaze (Orville Fay, 1973)

Single hybrid peony ('Bravura' × 'Bravura') with two to three rows of bright red petals and yellow stamens. Robust. Early season. 75cm (30in).

PLATE IV All flowers are shown at approximately ¼ size

P. 'Instituteur Doriat'

P. 'Orpen'

P. 'Bluebird'

P. 'Crimson Glory'

P. 'Butter Bowl'

P. 'Jan van Leeuwen'

P. 'Honey Gold'

P. 'Calypso'

P. 'Barbara'

P. 'Gleam of Light'

P. 'Bowl of Beauty'

P. 'Break of Day'

P. 'Fair Rosamond'

Bluebird (Kelway)
Semi-double lactiflora with violet-coloured flowers, which are said to appear almost blue in a certain light. Very small flowers with narrow petaloids in the centre. Free flowering. Midseason. 93cm (37in).

Blush Queen (Hoogendoorn, 1949)
Double lactiflora whose flowers open pale pink but fade to creamy white. Small golden stamens are mixed with successive layers of inner petals. The carpels are very small or developed into white carpelodes. The central petals can be streaked with carmine-red. Free flowering with a slight fragrance. Early season. 90cm (36in).

Bowl of Beauty (Hoogendoorn, 1949) AGM
Extremely popular Japanese lactiflora with large Fuchsine-rose, rounded guard petals surrounding a mass of upright, pale creamy yellow staminodes with wavy forked tips. The carpels are pale pink with magenta styles. The base of the staminodes is golden yellow. Widely available. Mid- to late season. 90cm (36in).

Bowl of Cream (Carl G. Klehm) GM
Creamy white, double lactiflora with bowl-shaped flowers, to 20cm (8in) across, and curly central petals. The outer petals are quite large; the inner smaller and hiding the bright yellow stamens. Carpels are light green with ivory-coloured stigmata. Dark green foliage. Midseason. 80cm (32in) or more.

Break of Day (Murawska, 1947)
Japanese lactiflora. The large purple, nicely rounded guard petals have a deep red centre when young, fading to magenta. The staminodes are wavy, dark red with yellow-edged tips, fading to magenta with age. Long hairless, purplish green carpels have vivid purple elongated styles. Midseason. 85cm (34in).

Bridal Gown (Carl G. Klehm, 1981)
Pretty, bomb-shaped lactiflora with very large guard petals and a tight ball of central petals. Pure white flowers with a hint of cream in the centre measure up to 15cm (6in) across. Very good for cutting. Midseason. 75cm (30in).

Bridal Veil (Kelway)
Japanese lactiflora with large lilac-pink guard petals

'Bright Knight' is a single red hybrid peony with glowing flowers of a rich blood-red shade.

and long, creamy white, forked staminodes, which are pale yellow at their base. Pale green carpels. Mid- to late season. 90cm (36in).

Bright Knight (Glasscock, 1939)
Hybrid bearing large blood-red flowers, tinted with magenta, fading eventually to crimson-red. The relatively narrow petals have a white stripe at the base, edged or suffused with violet. The carpels are light green with coral-pink stigmata. The anthers are yellow, the filaments white, tinted with pink at the base and yellow at the top. The disc is very pale pink. Strong stems. Early season. 95cm (38in).

Brightness (Glasscock, 1947)
Single hybrid (*P. lactiflora* × *P. officinalis*) with cup-shaped, vivid scarlet-red flowers. The blooms develop from nicely rounded buds, becoming tulip-shaped before opening fully. There are pale green carpels with cream stigmata, and yellow anthers and filaments. All of the flowers are held nicely erect on strong stems. A good specimen for the herbaceous border. Very early season. 65cm (26in).

Buckeye Belle (Mains, 1956)

Unusual semi-double hybrid with extremely dark red (53A), well rounded guard petals, which appear much lighter in sunshine. They are slightly crinkled and surround a mass of unusual staminodes: some of the filaments are very broad and petal-like with arrow-shaped anthers, others are almost functional with pale red ribbon-like filaments, a few are completely petaloid without any sign of anthers. The carpels are pale green and tomentose with red stigmata. Free flowering. Early season. 85cm (34in).

Bunker Hill (Hollis, 1906)

Semi-double to double lactiflora with rather open blooms and deep cherry-red petals. In the centre golden yellow stamens surround pinkish green, tomentose carpels with red styles and stigmata. Some of the outer stamens may be developed into small petals, supported on thin yellow stamen filaments. A vigorous, fragrant plant that makes a good cut flower. Midseason. 90cm (36in).

Burma Midnight (Roy Klehm, 1980)

Single, a seedling of 'Burma Ruby' with darker scarlet (60B) petals and stronger growing than its parent. It has pale green carpels, cream stigmata and small yellow stamens. No fragrance, strong stems. Midseason. 95cm (38in).

The single, bright red poppy-like flowers of 'Burma Ruby' are fragrant. It is a parent of award-winning 'America'.

Burma Ruby (Glasscock, 1951) GM

Hybrid (*P. lactiflora* × *P. officinalis* 'Sunbeam') with single, bright red flowers. The petals have a hint of purple and surround a large mass of yellow stamens. When this variety was first introduced it created quite a stir and was used extensively for breeding. It is has now been somewhat eclipsed by its descendants. Fragrant. Early season. 70cm (28in).

Burning Light (Kelway)

Double lactiflora with bright cherry-red flowers. Mid- to late season. Tall.

Butch (Krekler)

Robust variety, prettier than the name suggests, with large semi-double, reddish pink flowers whose petals have a slightly silvered edge. A few yellow stamens. Very fragrant. Midseason. To 90cm (36in).

Bu-Te (Wassenburg, 1954) GM

Japanese lactiflora with pure white flowers and a small centre of pale yellow staminodes. The outer ten petals are large and slightly ruffled, the inner five are much smaller and slightly serrated, turned slightly inwards towards the centre of the flower. The carpels are green with yellow stigmata. A very pretty flower. Erect habit. Late midseason. To 1.1m (3½ft).

Butter Bowl (Rosenfield, 1955)

Japanese lactiflora with large pale pink guard petals surrounding a mass of broad canary-yellow petaloids. Vigorous, free flowering, fragrant. Midseason. To 90cm (36in).

Calypso (Andrews, 1925)

Japanese lactiflora with amaranth-pink guard petals, a large centre of dark rose and gold-tipped petaloids. Fragrant. Mid- to late season. 95cm (38in).

Candeur (Dessert, 1920)

Double, globe-shaped, delicate pink flowers turning white and flecked with carmine in the centre. Vigorous, tall growing. Late midseason. 95cm (38in).

Cardinal's Robe (Saunders, 1940)

Single hybrid (*P. lactiflora* × *P. peregrina*) with rigid, bright scarlet-red petals and large stamens with golden anthers and filaments. Pale green carpels are pilose and have pale pink stigmata. Early season. 90cm (36in).

Carina (Saunders, 1944)

Multi-petalled, semi-double hybrid (*P. lactiflora* × *P. peregrina*) with bright scarlet-red flowers and small stamens, pale green carpels and magenta stigmata. This variety has conspicuous red disc lobes and deeply dissected foliage. Early season. 70cm (28)in.

Carmen (Lemoine, 1898)

Double lactiflora with bright cherry-rose flowers. Fragrant. Mid- to late season. 83cm (33in).

Carol (Bockstoce, 1955)

Semi-double, deep crimson flowers with very large petals arranged in a neat rosette. Both stamens and carpels are absent, the latter developed into wavy petals. The flowers are very heavy and need support. Good as a show flower but not particularly for the garden due to its sprawling habit. Slightly fragrant. Early season. 70cm (28in).

Cascade (Kelway)

Double lactiflora with a large dome of petals. Deep blush-pink buds open to form a flower with pale blush guard petals, surrounding a collar of very narrow white staminodes. In the centre is a large mass of tightly curled white petals with yellow bases. The carpels are green at the base, pink at the top with white styles. The flower fades to pure white in strong sunshine. Mid- to late season. 90cm (36in).

Cecilia Kelway (Kelway, 1912)

Double lactiflora bearing pale flesh-pink flowers turning to creamy white with carmine markings on the outside of the petals. Occasionally produces single flowers. Very fragrant. Mid- to late season. 95cm (38in).

Chalice (Saunders, 1929)

Single hybrid (*P. lactiflora* × *P. macrophylla*) with large cream-coloured flowers and long yellow stamens. It has large glossy dark green leaves and is fertile. Very early season. 1.2m (4ft).

Champlain (Freeborn, 1950)

Robust plant with very large single, white or flesh-pink flowers and a substantial pompom of stamens. It has pale yellow filaments, large pointed yellow anthers and petaloid stigmata. The disc has pink-tipped vertical teeth which surround the base of the large green carpels. Glossy dark green leaves. 75cm (30in).

Charlie's White (Carl G. Klehm, 1951)

Lactiflora with very large bomb-shaped, pure white flowers illuminated by a golden glow at the base of the petals. Vigorous and slightly fragrant, one of the best peonies for cutting. Early season. 120cm (48in).

Charm (Franklin, 1931)

Japanese lactiflora with satiny, dark mahogany-red guard petals surrounding a mass of pale yellow-edged, red petaloids. Fragrant. Late season. 85cm (34in).

Cheddar Charm (Roy Klehm, 1985)

Very beautiful double lactiflora with anemone-form flowers. A double row of white overlapping guard petals surround a very large mass of golden yellow staminodes. Occasionally small white petals occur in the centre. Vigorous with a delicate scent. Midseason. 90cm (36in).

Cheddar Cheese (Carl G. Klehm, 1973)

Double lactiflora with large creamy white guard petals surrounding a ring of smaller petals, enclosing a mass of creamy yellow staminodes. The staminodes are deep yellow at the base fading towards their forked tips. Growing out of the centre of the staminodes is a tuft of creamy white carpelodes. Very fragrant. Midseason. To 1m (3ft).

Cheddar Gold (Roy Klehm)

Japanese lactiflora ('Charlie's White' × 'Alice Harding') with large white, well rounded guard petals surrounding a large mass of yellow staminodes. Similar to 'Cheddar Charm'. Very strong scent. Midseason. 75cm (30in).

Cheddar Supreme (Roy Klehm)

Japanese lactiflora whose satiny, milky white guard petals surround a small centre of golden staminodes. A few white petals may occasionally occur in the centre. Strong stems, fragrant. Midseason. 83cm (33in).

Cheddar Surprise (Roy Klehm, 1980)

Semi-double to double lactiflora with pure white outer

petals enclosing a ring of pale yellow petaloids and staminodes. From the centre of this erupts a tuft of curly pure white petals. Fragrant with strong stems. Midseason. 75cm (30in).

Cherry Hill (Thurlow, 1915)
Semi-double flowers with glossy, crimson-purple petals, just revealing the yellow stamens. The carpels have bright red stigmata. Dramatic, free flowering, fragrant. Very early season. 85cm (34in).

Cherry Royal (Wild, 1967)
Double lactiflora with deep magenta flowers. Each bloom has a very large number of petals forming a raised mound with a depression in the middle. Stamens absent. Midseason. 80cm (32in).

Cherry Ruffles (Hollingsworth, 1996)
Attractive semi-double hybrid (*P. officinalis* × *P. peregrina*) × *P. lactiflora*) with bright crimson-scarlet flowers. The stamens have golden anthers and pink filaments. The petals have a pale blotch on their reverse, close to the base. Carpels are tomentose with pale pink stigmata. The leaves are glossy green, deeply dissected and have curly margins. Strong stems, darker than 'America' and with long lasting colour. Midseason. 78cm (31in).

Chief Justice (Auten, 1941)
Semi-double hybrid (*P. lactiflora* × *P. officinalis*) with glossy deep cherry-red flowers. The stamens have somewhat weak, long red filaments and surround pale green carpels. Late-flowering for an officinalis hybrid. Late season. 85cm (34in).

Chiffon Parfait (Roy Klehm, 1981)
Fully double lactiflora ('Monsieur Jules Elie' × 'President Taft') with very full fluffy, ball-shaped flowers composed of numerous pale salmon-pink petals. Four flower buds to a stem without any stamens. Fragrant. Better than 'Sarah Bernhardt'. Very late season. 85cm (34in).

Chocolate Soldier (Auten, 1939)
(*P. lactiflora* × *P. officinalis*) The majority of dark red peonies still have a hint of purple in the flowers.

'Chocolate Soldier' can have single or Japanese form flowers on the same plant. The petals are deep reddish brown.

'Chocolate Soldier' is an exception and has very dark reddish brown flowers. Registered originally as a Japanese type hybrid, it frequently produces single and occasionally double flowers to confuse everybody! It has purple stamen filaments, yellow anthers and a distinctive bright pink disc. Tomentose creamy white carpels with red stigmata. Very early season. 70cm (28in).

Christine (Auten, 1945)
White Japanese with a large mass of gold-edged, pale yellow staminodes, thread-like at the base, broadening at the tip. The green carpels have creamy yellow stigmata. Vigorous, fragrant. Early season. 75cm (30in).

Christine Kelway (Kelway)
Very beautiful single lactiflora with nicely rounded, flesh-pink petals, fading to white in bright sunshine, and deep pink-purple carpels. Fragrant, one of the best singles. Midseason. 95cm (38in).

Circus Clown (Wild, 1970)
Large Japanese flower with deep magenta-pink guard petals. These surround a large mass of butter-yellow staminodes with wavy tips. A few of the centre staminodes may develop into narrow, pink-striped petals. The carpels are pale green with cream styles. Midseason. 90cm (36in)

Claire de Lune (White-Wild, 1954)
Beautiful single hybrid (a very rare cross between *P. lactiflora* 'Monsieur Jules Elie' and *P. mlokosewitschi*) with

pale yellow, cup-shaped flowers. Eleven to thirteen petals with slightly crinkled and well rounded edges. The filaments and the anthers are bright yellow. Large tomentose carpels have a red line down the inner surface and cream stigmata. Two buds on each dark red stem. Slightly fragrant. Very early season. 80cm (32in).

Claire Dubois (Crousse, 1886)
Double lactiflora with very pretty globe-shaped, rose-pink flowers. The colour fades towards the outer edge of the slightly serrated petals; the pink coloration has a hint of blue in it. Free flowering, excellent cut flowers. Dark green leaves. Late season. 95cm (38in).

Claudia (Saunders, 1944)
Single hybrid (*P. lactiflora* × *P. peregrina*) with vivid crimson flowers which eventually turn to pale salmon-pink. The petals are rather small for such a robust plant

'Comanche' is a vigorous peony with Japanese form flowers. The guard petals are vivid magenta.

and have a large white blotch at their base. Similar in colour to 'Ellen Cowley', but with single flowers. A ring of golden yellow stamens surrounds large pale green carpels with pink stigmata. The stamens have yellow filaments. Strong upright plant with thick stems and glossy green foliage. Early season. 95cm (38in).

Clemenceau (Dessert, 1920)
Double lactiflora bearing carmine-pink, globe-shaped flowers with a mass of small petals in the centre. The inner surface of the petals is a glowing rose-pink. Vigorous with a slight tea-rose fragrance. Very late midseason. Tall growing: 95cm (38in).

Comanche (Bigger, 1957)
Statuesque Japanese lactiflora with magenta guard petals and amber staminodes with wavy tips. The staminodes are surrounded by a ring of semi-functional stamens. The green carpels magenta-flushed and have purple stigmata. Leaves are dark green. Very vigorous, highly recommended. Midseason. 90cm (36in).

Commando (Glasscock, 1944)
Anemone-form hybrid (*P. lactiflora* × *P. officinalis*) with glossy, mahogany-red flowers, fading to deep claret-red. The pointed-tipped petaloids are in a large mound. The carpels are green with coral-pink stigmata. A good dark red peony with strong stems. Early season. 95cm (38in).

Cora Stubbs (Krekler)
Japanese lactiflora with pale magenta guard petals surrounding a large nicely rounded mass of creamy white and pale pink petaloids. Some of the petaloids have a pale yellow stripe down the centre. Vigorous with side buds. Midseason. 1.1m (3½ft).

Coral Charm (Wissing, 1964) GM
Semi-double hybrid with deep coral-pink buds opening to very large coral-peach flowers. This variety has introduced an important new colour to hybrid peonies, but is a bit too exotic for some tastes. Very vigorous. Early season. 90cm (36in).

Coral Fay (Fay, 1973)
Semi-double hybrid bearing deep crimson-red (57A) flowers with rather loose floppy petals that are glossy with a hint of coral-pink and have a pale stripe towards the base. The stamen filaments are yellow at the top and almost orange at the bottom, supporting yellow anthers. The carpels are pale green with pink stigmata; the disc is green with pale pink lobes. This variety has narrower foliage than usual, the result of hybridization with *P. tenuifolia*. A spreading plant which may need staking. Vigorous. Early season. 95cm (38in).

Coral 'n' Gold (Cousins-Roy Klehm, 1981)
Single or semi-double hybrid with coral-pink, cup-shaped flowers and a centre of golden stamens. Like a vigorous 'Otto Froebel'. Early season. 90cm (36in).

Coral Sunset (Wissing-Carl G. Klehm, 1981)
An unusual hybrid between 'Minnie Shaylor' and 'Otto Froebel', this has striking double apricot-coral flowers deepening to pink towards the petal edges. The colour ages to pale yellow. Early season. 80cm (32in).

Cornelia Shaylor (Shaylor, 1919)
Double lactiflora with large blush-pink, globe-shaped flowers and very large pale rose guard petals tinted green at the base. The flowers fade to white with age. Strong stems hold the flowers nicely erect. Midseason. 90cm (36in).

Couronne d'Or (Calot, 1873)
Vigorous double lactiflora with creamy white flowers. The central petals are pale pink, crinkled and slightly incurved and partially hiding a ring of bright yellow stamens. In the very centre is a tuft of short stamens and very small pale green carpels with ivory-coloured stigmata. Free flowering with a very strong, slightly unpleasant scent. Late season. Very tall, to 1.1m (3½ft).

Cream Delight (Reath, 1971)
Beautiful hybrid with large single, cream flowers (almost yellow) and glossy dark green leaves. Pale green tomentose carpels have pink stigmata. This variety has 3–4 side buds prolonging its flowering period. It is a fertile tetraploid with viable pollen and seed. Long season. 80cm (32in).

Crimson Glory (Sass, 1937)
Japanese lactiflora with ruby-red guard petals; the petaloids are salmon-pink at the base, pink above with a white line down the centre, the tips edged with gold. The carpels are green, flushed with purple at the top with purple stigmata. Free flowering and fragrant. Very late season. 1m (3ft).

Crusader (Glasscock, 1940)
Semi-double hybrid (*P. lactiflora* × *P. officinalis*) with five rows of scarlet-red petals, yellow anthers, pale pink filaments and green carpels with red stigmata. Strong stems, dark green foliage. Early season. 80cm (32in).

Cytherea (Saunders, 1953) GM
Popular semi-double hybrid (*P. lactiflora* × *P. peregrina*) with light crimson, cup-shaped flowers on strong upright stems. An unusual peony which spreads easily by runners to form a large clump. Highly regarded by the APS, and valued as a cut flower. Early season. Low growing to 60cm (24in).

Dad (Glasscock-Krekler, 1959)
Semi-double hybrid with cardinal-red flowers, turning slightly purple in sunshine and eventually fading to deep pink. It has a few pale yellow stamens and large

Only hybrids possess truly red flowers. This is the claret-red 'Dandy Dan'.

green carpels with pink stigmata. The petals are glossy and have a white strip on the underside. Robust plant with a spreading habit. Early season. 95cm (38in).

Dandy Dan (Auten, 1946)
Claret-red, semi-double hybrid with all of its outer petals the same size. In the centre a few stamens are petaloid, the rest in various stages of conversion to petals with dark pink filaments. The anthers are pale yellow with a red stripe down the centre, the carpels pale green with bright pink stigmata. Early season. Low growing to 63cm (25in).

Dauntless (Glasscock, 1944)
Single hybrid (P. lactiflora × P. officinalis) with very dark ruby-red flowers, approaching the colour of 'Chocolate Soldier'. Tomentose, very pale green carpels have cream stigmata edged with very pale pink. Yellow anthers and red filaments. Vigorous and tall growing but with only a few flowers. Early season. 90cm (36in).

David Kelway (Kelway, 1938)
Double, soft bright pink flowers with some golden stamens showing among the petals. Spicy fragrance. Mid- to late season. 90cm (36in).

Dawn Glow (Pehrson-Hollingsworth, 1986)
Very large hybrid of unknown origin, but descended from 'Silver Dawn' and originally distributed with a mixture of other seedlings known collectively as 'Silver Dawn F3'. Large glossy green leaves show its P. macrophylla parentage. The petals are large and creamy white with magenta flares. It has large tomentose carpels with red stigmata and a pink disc. Early season. 90cm (36in).

Dawn Pink (Sass, 1946)
Highly regarded single lactiflora with large china-rose petals and bright golden yellow stamens. The colour of the flowers lasts well but they are easily damaged by strong wind. The leaves are decurrent and medium green. The carpels are green with purple stigmata. One of the best single pink lactifloras. Early to midseason. 90cm (36in).

Daystar (Kelway)
Double, almost bomb-shaped lactiflora with deep magenta guard petals, which fade in sunlight. The broad pink staminodes fade to white at the tips and are pale yellow at the base. The carpels are purple and tomentose. The style and stigmata are magenta. Fragrant and very free flowering. A very pretty and under-rated variety. Mid- to late season. 95cm (38in).

Daystar (Saunders, 1949)
Hybrid peony (P. tenuifolia × P. mlokosewitschi) with single pale yellow flowers. It has red stems and very distinctive pointed leaves and is fertile. Saunders tried extremely hard to cross P. mlokosewitschi with other species, usually to no avail: this is one of his rarest achievements. Very early season. To 90cm (36in).

Defender (Saunders, 1929) AGM
Single hybrid (P. lactiflora × P. officinalis) with very large cup-shaped, dark crimson-red flowers. The base of the petals is white and the disc pink. There are golden anthers and yellow filaments with a hint of red. The carpels are furrowed and tomentose with bright pink stigmata. Glossy dark green leaves and nice flower buds. Early season. 1.1m (3½ft).

Delaware Chief (Hollingsworth, 1984)
This variety improves upon in its 'Rubra Plena' parent in every way. It is more robust, holds its flowers vertically on strong stems and has a spicy fragrance. The flowers are bomb-shaped with fully double, deep crimson flowers, fading to Tyrian-purple. The guard petals are well rounded and surround a large mass of petaloids. It is the

result of crossing *P. officinalis* 'Rubra Plena' with a red double variety of *P. lactiflora*. Stamens are completely absent in 'Delaware Chief'; the carpels are pale green with pink stigmata. Early midseason. 70cm (28in).

Denise (Lemoine, 1924)
Double lactiflora with very large white flowers, considered to be one of Lemoine's best. The petals are tinged with flesh-pink; there are usually crimson specks on the outer ones, although these may be quite faint. The flowers have a beautiful scent of roses. Late season. 80cm (32in).

Diana Drinkwater (Kelway)
Bright, bomb-shaped, rosy pink lactiflora with enlarged guard petals. Lighter petals are mixed with the others. Fragrant. Mid- to late season. Medium height.

Diana Parks (Bockstoce, 1942)
Hybrid (*P. lactiflora* × *P. officinalis*) with large double, cardinal-red flowers and pale green carpels with creamy white stigmata. The colour fades in strong sunshine to pale crimson. A beautiful plant with very fragrant flowers. Early season. 85cm (34in).

Dinner Plate (Carl G. Klehm, 1968) NGC
Double lactiflora with large shell-pink flowers; the larger outer petals have a paler edge. Pale yellow staminodes are mixed with the central petals; the carpelodes are very small and pale yellow. A very robust plant with thick stems. Dark green foliage, slight rose-fragrance. Late season. 85cm (34in).

Docteur H. Barnsby (Dessert, 1913)
Globe-shaped, double lactiflora with magenta-pink petals. Strong stems. Late season. 83cm (33in).

Dolorodell (Lins, 1942) GM
Large double, vivid pink flowers, to 20cm (8in) across. Vigorous plant, strong stems. Late season. 90cm (36in).

Doreen (Sass, 1949)
Japanese lactiflora with bright magenta-rose guard petals surrounding a large mass of frilly staminodes. These are very long and yellow, flushed-pink towards the top. The tips are crinkled and edged with pale yellow. The flowers are less symmetrical than is usual for a Japanese-form peony. The carpels are green, flushed with purple, and

have elongated vivid magenta stigmata. Light green foliage, slightly fragrant. Late season. 80cm (32in).

Do Tell (Auten, 1946)
Japanese lactiflora with orchid-pink, speckled guard petals, giving the general effect of rose-pink. The flowers are very variable, some have creamy white staminodes surrounded by pink and yellow, while others have creamy white staminodes with pink tips. The staminodes are bright yellow at their base. Midseason. 80cm (32in).

Douglas Brand (Tischler, 1972) GM
Fully double lactiflora with bright watermelon-red flowers on strong upright stems. The flowers are very symmetrical and may be up to 25cm (10in) across. Late midseason. 80cm (32in).

Dragon's Nest (Auten, 1933)
Vigorous Japanese variety with magenta guard petals. The wavy staminodes are golden yellow with pink stripes at the base; they grow broader with age. Green carpels with magenta stigmata. Midseason. 95cm (40in).

Dr. Alexander Fleming
Fully double lactiflora, a cross between 'Bunker Hill' and 'Sarah Bernhardt', with deep pink flowers, fading slightly towards the edges. The central petals may be curled into a ball, even when the flower is mature. These inner petals alternate with rings of golden stamens. Some flowers may be semi-double with green carpels

Several breeders rate 'Dawn Pink' as their favourite single.

and purple styles. Fuchsia-purple (67B) buds. Sweet fragrance, attracts bees. Midseason. Tall, to 1.1m (3½ft).

Dresden (Kelway)

Single lactiflora with ivory white flowers, developing from pink buds; the green carpels are tinted with red. The leaves are good for autumn colour. Early to late season. 85cm (34in).

Duc de Wellington (Calot, 1859)

Fully double, bomb-shaped, white flower with a creamy white centre, eventually fading to white. The flowers are said to be light sulphur-yellow if cut and allowed to open indoors. Very fragrant. Midseason. 90cm (36in).

Duchesse de Nemours,
syn. 'Mrs. Gwyn Lewis' (Calot, 1856) AGM

Double lactiflora whose creamy white, globe-shaped flowers are strongly tinted with yellow at the petal bases. The outer petals are very large, smaller towards the centre and mixed with narrow petaloids. A ring of large upturned petals surrounds a core of extremely narrow petaloids. If present, the carpels are purple with magenta stigmata. Strong sweet scent. Widely available, makes a good cut flower. Midseason. 80cm (32in).

Earlybird (Saunders, 1939)

Hybrid (*P. tenuifolia* × *P. veitchii*) with single nodding, bright crimson flowers and finely dissected olive-green foliage. Free flowering. Very early season (even before *P. tenuifolia*). 53cm (21in).

Early Glow (Hollingsworth, 1992)

Complex hybrid with cup-shaped, pale yellow flowers with obviously fluted petals. Long stamen filaments are pink at the base with gold anthers. Very large hirsute green carpels have intense red stigmata. It has a spreading habit and produces side buds which prolong the flowering period. Early season. 75cm (30in).

Early Scout (Auten, 1952)

Single hybrid ('Richard Carvel' × *P. tenuifolia*) with very dark crimson-red flowers. Dark green dissected foliage. Very early season. 53cm (21in).

Early Windflower (Saunders, 1939)

Very beautiful hybrid (*P. emodi* × *P. veitchii* var. bere-

sowskii) with single, white, nodding flowers borne on very long stems. The foliage is narrow and pale green. Flowers ten days before 'Late Windflower'. Early season. 90cm (36in).

Echo (Saunders, 1951)

Single F2 hybrid (*P. lactiflora* × *P. anomala*) with pale lavender-pink flowers. The filaments, stigmata and disc are crimson. The flowers are held erect and well above the foliage. Early season. 63cm (25in).

Edulis Superba (Lemon, 1824)

While this is one of the oldest lactiflora varieties it still remains one of the best. It has large guard petals and numerous notched, magenta-rose (66D) inner petals with silvered edges. These are surrounded by a collar of slightly paler, very narrow petaloids. The petals have pale yellow roots. The tomentose carpels are purple-green with tapering green styles. Mature plants have flowers with a well developed crown. Free flowering with a sweet rose-fragrance. It makes a good cut bloom. Early to midseason. 95cm (38in).

Ellen Cowley (Saunders, 1940)

Short-growing hybrid (*P. lactiflora* × *P. peregrina*) with extremely striking vivid pink semi-double flowers touched with a hint of orange or coral-pink. The petals are white at the base. There are a few yellow stamens and relatively large carpels with pink stigmata. One of the best Saunders hybrids. Foliage is dissected. Early season. 70cm (28in).

Elsa Sass (Sass, 1930) GM

Double lactiflora with perfectly formed camellia-shaped, white flowers with a hint of pale pink and yellow in the centre. Dark green foliage. Late season. 70cm (28in).

Emma (Stern)

Hybrid between *P. emodi* and *P. mascula* with single white flowers. Named by Sir F. C. Stern using the first two letters of each of the parents' names. Early season. 80cm (32in).

Emma Klehm (Carl G. Klehm, 1951)

Double lactiflora with a nice crinkled rosette of heather-pink (68B) petals; the colour is most intense in the depths of the flower, fading towards the slightly silvered edges. All

PLATE V

All flowers are shown at
approximately ¼ size

P. 'Emperor of India'

P. 'Joy of Life'

P. 'Queen Elizabeth'

P. 'Mistral'

P. 'Bethcar'

P. 'Nymphe'

the petals are a similar size. The flower has a slight depression in the centre. Carpels and stamens are completely absent. Compact. Very late season. To 80cm (32in).

Emperor of India (Kelway, 1901)
Japanese lactiflora whose deep purple guard petals surround purple staminodes. These are slightly curled and have golden yellow tips. Fragrant, free flowering. Mid- to very late season (it flowers into July). 90cm (36in).

Enchantment (Kelway)
Rose-pink double with slightly silvered petals. Fragrant. Midseason. 90cm (36in).

English Princess (Kelway)
Japanese lactiflora bearing saucer-shaped flowers with white-margined, blush-pink guard petals and broad snow-white petaloids, that narrow abruptly at the base. Green and cream carpels. Early season. 90cm (36in).

Etched Salmon (Cousins-Roy Klehm, 1981)
Fully double hybrid of unknown parentage. Salmon-pink flowers with enlarged guard petals surrounding a mass of petaloids with a few gold-edged carpelodes in the centre. There are no stamens or seeds. Fragrant, with strong stems. Early to midseason. 90cm (36in).

Evening Glow (Kelway)
Semi-double lactiflora with bright, silvered, cherry-carmine-red flowers. The carpels have developed into a tight bunch of petals, surrounded by a circle of yellow stamens. Fragrant. Midseason. 75cm (30in).

Evening World (Kelway, 1928)
Japanese lactiflora with coral-pink guard petals fading to white at the edges and a mass of blush-pink staminodes, aging creamy white and with a hint of gold at the base. The carpels are pale green, turning darker with age; the stigmata are creamy white. Free flowering. Mid- to very late season. 90cm (36in).

Eventide (Glasscock, 1945)
Hybrid (*P. lactiflora* × *P. peregrina* 'Sunbeam') with single rose-red, cup-shaped flowers with a white stripe down the petal centres. The colour fades towards the petal edges. It has greenish yellow filaments, golden anthers and green carpels with coral-pink stigmata.

The petals are shiny on the inside. Compact with dark green, slightly wavy leaves. Early season. 85cm (34in).

Fairbanks (Auten, 1945)
Japanese peony with numerous milky white staminodes; those in the centre are narrow and twisted, the outer ones are semi-functional and thread-like. The elongated carpels are pale green with cream stigmata. The guard petals are very large, opening pale pink and fading to milky white. Vigorous, but with rather weak stems. Very late season. To 95cm (38in).

Faire Rosamond (Kelway)
Japanese peony with yellowish pink (almost peach) guard petals and very long pale yellow staminodes. Mid- to late season. 90cm (36in).

Fairy's Petticoat (Carl G. Klehm)
Fully double lactiflora with extremely large blush-pink flowers and beautiful translucent petals. The heart of the flower has a golden glow. The colour fades to creamy white with patches of blush-pink on the innermost petals. Most of the petals are very large with just a few narrow petaloids mixed among them and a tuft of small petals in the centre. There are usually one or two functional pale green carpels; the remainder are developed into small petals (carpelodes). A very fragrant variety which makes a good cut flower. Early season. 80cm (32in).

Famie (Saunders-Krekler, 1955)
Orchid-pink anemone-form hybrid of unknown parentage. Large guard petals surround orchid-pink petaloids with a white line down the centre. Carpels are small, pale green with cream stigmata. Very pretty but may need staking. Early season. 80cm (32in).

Feather Top (Wild, 1970)
Unusual shaped Japanese peony with alternating layers of petals and staminodes. Magenta guard petals surround a ring of purple-streaked, buff staminodes with yellow tips. In the centre a ring of magenta petaloids surround a bunch of yellow staminodes; within this are a few pink carpelodes. Midseason. 90cm (36in).

Felix Crousse,
syn. 'Victor Hugo' (Crousse, 1881) AGM
Double lactiflora producing bright magenta-carmine,

globe-shaped flowers, with incurved petals surrounded by enlarged guard petals. The flowers are borne in clusters and have a sweet fragrance. The pink carpels are tomentose with purple stigmata. The anthers are yellow with short filaments. Mid- to late season. 75cm (30in).

Felix Supreme (Kriek, 1955)
Fully double lactiflora, like a larger version of 'Felix Crousse' with ruby-red flowers. Vigorous and strong growing, an excellent cut flower. Midseason. 1m (3ft).

Festiva Maxima (Miellez, 1851) AGM
A very old variety but still one of the best lactifloras. The double flowers open pale pink but quickly fade to creamy white at the edges with pink remaining in the inner recesses of the bloom. There may be red flecking. The base of the inner petals is yellow, imparting a golden glow to the centre of the flower. The very large guard petals surround smaller inner petals; the petals inside these are larger again, recurved and surrounding small narrow staminodes. The pale green carpels are extremely small with elongated cream styles. Very fragrant. Midseason. 1m (3ft).

Festiva Supreme (Roy Klehm, 1981)
Double lactiflora with large pearl-white flowers; a few of the central petals are flecked with carmine-red. There are no stamens. Fragrant, good for cutting. Midseason. 85cm (34in).

Firebelle (Mains, 1959)
Semi-double hybrid with bright scarlet-red flowers, long anthers and short yellow filaments. There are pale green carpels with pinkish magenta stigmata. Vigorous with strong stems, makes a good cut flower. Early season. 85cm (34in).

Firelight (Saunders, 1950)
Quadruple hybrid (*P. lactiflora* × (*P. officinalis* × (*P. mlokosewitschi* × *P. macrophylla*) with cup-shaped, single pale pink flowers that have unusual raspberry-red flares. It has long golden stamens and red stigmata. A very beautiful variety. Early season. 65cm (26in).

Flame (Glasscock, 1939)
A hybrid peony (*P. lactiflora* × *P. officinalis* 'Sunbeam') with single bright crimson flowers with a distinct hint of orange for added impact. Each petal has a white stripe

on the exterior, close to the base of the flower. The stamens are golden yellow with very long filaments; the carpels are green with crimson stigmata and styles. Compact and free flowering with foliage like that of *P. officinalis* foliage, it makes a good cut flower. Early season. 80cm (32in).

Florence Ellis (Nicholls, 1948)
Double lactiflora with rose-shaped flowers consisting of flesh-pink petals that fade to rose-pink on the outside as the flowers open. The outer petals are streaked with carmine on the outside; when young the inner petals are wrapped into a tight ball. Tall with strong stems and very large fragrant flowers. Midseason. 70cm (28in).

Fragrans, syn. 'Andre Lauries', 'George Cuvier' (Sir Joseph Banks, 1805)
One of the first varieties of *P. lactiflora* to be imported into Europe from China, this peony may be difficult to obtain. It has small double pale rose-pink flowers with erect central petals. Strongly scented and said to make a good cut flower. Late season.

Gardenia (Lins, 1955)
Very beautiful double lactiflora with gardenia-like large blush-white flowers. Small golden stamens are mixed with the central petals and the carpels are developed into petals. Some of the inner petals are streaked with pink. Sweetly fragrant with strong stems. Can be quite pink in wet years, the colour fades to milky white in strong sunshine. Dark leaves. Early midseason. 85cm (34in).

Garden Peace (Saunders, 1941)
Single hybrid resulting from a back cross (*P. lactiflora* × (*P. lactiflora* × *P. macrophylla*) with creamy white petals and extremely large glossy green leaves. The stamen filaments are pink with golden anthers and the carpels are green with a purple top and large purple stigmata. Bright pink disc lobes. Sparse foliage, may need staking. Several flower buds per stem mean a long flowering period. Fragrant. Early season. 90cm (36in).

Gay Paree (Auten, 1933)
Very striking anemone- or Japanese-form lactiflora with brilliant magenta guard petals. These surround a ring of toothed pale pink staminodes in the centre of which is a

PLATE VI All flowers are shown at approximately ¼ size

P. 'Charm'

P. 'Doreen'

P. 'Gloriana'

P. 'Paul M. Wild'

P. 'Lady Orchid'

P. 'My Pal Rudy'

P. 'Duchesse de Nemours'

P. 'Pink Parfait'

P. 'Gay Paree'

P. 'Dr. Alexander Fleming'

P. 'Albert Crousse'

P. 'Couronne d'Or'

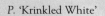

P. 'Alice Harding'

P. 'Krinkled White'

P. 'Cornelia Shaylor'

tuft of larger magenta petals. As the flower matures, the central petals grow taller, fading slightly and developing silvered margins. The central petals are absent from young flowers. The small outer staminodes fade to blush-pink. The carpels are yellowish green with salmon-pink stigmata. Very striking and flamboyant, good for making an impact. Late midseason. 1.1m (3½ft).

Gene Wild (Cooper, 1956)
Low-growing double lactiflora with soft pink flowers fading to creamy white with hints of rose-pink. The flowers often have streaks of red on the inner petals. The carpels are tiny or developed into petals, surrounded by a ring of golden yellow stamens. Midseason. To 55cm (22in).

Germaine Bigot (Dessert, 1902)
Semi-double lactiflora whose flowers open to flesh-pink with a hint of salmon and a paler centre. The colour fades in sunshine to creamy white with flecks of carmine-red in the centre. Some of the carpels are developed into a tight bunch of petals, surrounded by a ring of semi-functional golden yellow stamens, while the others are white with magenta styles. Large, fragrant flowers on low growing plants. Mid- to late season. 95cm (38in).

Gilbert Barthelot (Doriat, 1931)
Lactiflora with magenta-rose flowers whose short yellow stamens alternate with the inner petals. It starts as a semi-double with a depressed centre and a ball of unfurled petals, eventually developing into a fully double flower. The carpels are very small or completely absent. The petals are held nicely erect on older flowers. Fragrant. Midseason. 90cm (36in).

Gleam of Light (Kelway)
Japanese lactiflora with deep pink guard petals surrounding a centre of wavy narrow golden yellow staminodes. Free flowering and very fragrant. Mid- to late season. 95cm (38in).

Globe of Light (Kelway, 1928)
Japanese lactiflora whose vivid rose-pink petals fade to almost white at the edges. It has a good centre of golden yellow staminodes and green carpels. Vigorous and free flowering. Mid- to late season. 95cm (38in).

Gloire de Charles Gombault (Gombault, 1866)
Crown-shaped lactiflora with rather small flowers. The pale rose-pink guard petals are well differentiated; they surround a collar of salmon-apricot petals, within which is a mass of pale rose inner petals. The collar gradually fades to deep cream. Free flowering, perfumed. Midseason. 1m (3ft).

Gloriana (Kelway)
Double lactiflora with magenta-crimson flowers. Midseason. Medium height.

Glory Hallelujah (Carl G. Klehm)
Double lactiflora with large rose-pink flowers. Fragrant. Late season. 83cm (33in).

Glowing Raspberry Rose
(Cousins-Roy Klehm, 1981)
Bomb-shaped hybrid with a mass of raspberry-red petaloids surrounded by darker guard petals. The colour fades towards the edge of the petals, emphasizing the raspberry-red veins. Early season. 80cm (32in).

Golden Glow (Glasscock, 1935) GM
Single hybrid (*P. peregrina* 'Otto Froebel' × *P. lactiflora*) with glossy, slightly fluted, scarlet-orange petals and a bold centre of bright yellow stamens. Carpels pale green with cream or pink stigmata. Light green leaves with notched tips. Early season. 65cm (26in).

Goldilocks (Gilbertson, 1975)
Double hybrid ('Oriental Gold' × 'Claire de Lune') with flowers that are almost bomb-shaped, with light yellow guard petals, sulphur-yellow staminodes, and long pale yellow carpelodes. Slightly scented. Light green leaves. Early season. 70cm (28in).

Grandiflora (Richardson, 1883)
Double variety with flesh-pink flowers, tinted slightly yellow in the centre and fading to white in strong sunshine. Very large saucer-shaped flowers on rather weak stems. Very attractive, fragrant. Very late season. 95cm (38in).

Grandiflora Nivea Plena (Lemon, 1824)
Very early flowering double lactiflora with very large rose- or crown-type flowers. The outer guard petals are

large and pink, the inner smaller and curled into a ball. These open to pale yellow, often marked with carmine-red streaks, and eventually grow to form a raised tuft in the centre of the flower. Flower eventually fades to white. Sweet fragrance, free flowering but has rather weak stems; leaves are dark green. Very early season. Tall-growing.

Grover Cleveland (Terry, 1904)
Variety of P. lactiflora with very large double crimson flowers held erect on strong stems. Free flowering with a slight fragrance. Late midseason. 90cm (36in).

Halcyon (Saunders, 1948)
Occasionally a breeder will strike lucky with a cross and produce a plant as unique as 'Halcyon'. It is a single hybrid bearing very pale blush flowers with lavender flares at the base of the petals. The stamens have yellow anthers and red filaments; the tomentose carpels are light grey with red stigmata. One its parents was called 'Ozieri Alba' which Saunders had raised from seed. When he tried to discover its source he was disappointed to find that the nursery had lost the relevant records. Dark green foliage. Very early season. 60cm (24in).

Helen Hayes (Murawska, 1943)
Very double, bomb-type with magenta-rose (66B–66C) flowers. The stamens are vestigial and reduced to very small pink staminodes with yellow tips. No carpels. Rose fragrance. Mid- to late season. 88cm (35in).

Henri Potin (Doriat, 1924)
Japanese lactiflora with deep cherry-rose guard petals and a mass of golden yellow staminodes. Very fragrant. Late season. 85cm (34in).

Henry Bockstoce (Bockstoce, 1955)
Deep red, fully double hybrid with a depressed centre and large falling guard petals. Free flowering with very strong stems. Early season. 75cm (30in).

Heritage (Saunders, 1950)
Double hybrid (P. lactiflora × P. peregrina) with vivid scarlet-crimson-red flowers and light yellow stamens. Large lemon-yellow carpels. Slight fragrance. Early season. 90cm (36in).

Carpelodes are clearly visible in the centre of this flower of the hybrid 'Hit Parade'.

Hiawatha (Franklin, 1931)
Fully double, deep red flowers with glossy petals and strong stems. The stamens are mixed with the inner petals; the anthers are yellow, the filaments red and the carpels are rudimentary or absent. The colour of the flower fades on the outside and is deepest in the centre. Vigorous. Late season. 90cm (36in).

Highlight (Auten-Wild, 1952)
Very double lactiflora with velvety dark red flowers. The guard petals are striped white outside. The golden stamens form a small tuft in the centre of the flower with a few additional stamens scattered among the petals. The carpels are very small, white with pale pink stigmata. Late midseason. Medium height.

Hit Parade (Nicholls, 1965)
Extremely large Japanese with magenta-rose petals fading towards the edges. The outer staminodes are pale yellow, tapering at the tip. The inner ones are broader and pink with a yellow centre. The carpels are pale green with yellow stigmata, which are sometimes developed into long, pink carpelodes. Flowers are very variable in appearance. Midseason. Tall.

Honey Gold (Carl G. Klehm)
Double lactiflora with creamy white guard petals surrounding a large mass of wavy, pale yellow staminodes. The central staminodes are larger, fading to creamy white at the edges, or developed into wavy, distorted, creamy white petals. The petals are notched at the tip.

The carpels are very large, elongated and partially developed into carpelodes with pale reddish brown tips. A striking plant with side buds giving it a long flowering period. Fragrant. Midseason. 90cm (36in).

Honor (Saunders, 1941)

Single or semi-double hybrid (*P. lactiflora* × *P. peregrina* 'Otto Froebel') with deep Bengal-rose (75B fading to 75C) petals surrounding a nice centre of stamens. The anthers are pale yellow with very long greenish white filaments, the pale green carpels are tomentose with cream stigmata and there is a conspicuous white disc. Colour lasts well. Slight spicy fragrance. Light green leaves. Midseason. 90cm (36in).

Horizon (Saunders, 1943)

Hybrid (*P. lactiflora* × *P. officinalis*) with single flesh-pink (49B) flowers and slightly fluted petals the reverses of which are touched with magenta. Very long, slightly modified stamens with golden anthers and elongated filaments. The glabrous green carpels taper to a distinctive elongated style and have a pink stigmatal surface. The disc is pink. Very large plant which may need support. Early season. 1m (3ft).

Humei (Anderson, 1810)

Mainly of historical interest, 'Humei' was one of the first varieties of *P. lactiflora* to be imported into Europe from China. It has very large double, watermelon-red flowers and substantial leaves. It is said to have a strong spicy scent. Late season.

Illini Belle (Glasscock, 1941)

Pronounced Ill-li-ni, this is a semi-double hybrid (*P. lactiflora* × *P. officinalis*) with nicely symmetrical glossy ruby-red flowers (53B), purple stamen filaments and pale green carpels with pink stigmata. Needs staking. Pretty flower, but let down by poor foliage. Early season. 80cm (32in).

Illini Warrior (Glasscock-Falk, 1955)

Beautiful single to semi-double hybrid of unknown parentage with glossy tulip-shaped, deep cardinal-red flowers, nice stamens, green carpels and cream or salmon-pink stigmata. The petals have a paler line running down the centre. Vigorous and slightly fragrant. Early season; earlier than 'Red Velvet'. 1m (3ft).

Ingenieur Doriat (Doriat)

Double, carmine-pink petals with silvered edges gradually becoming smaller towards the centre of the flower with a tiny centre of yellow stamens. Fragrant. Midseason. 75cm (30in).

Inspecteur Lavergne (Doriat, 1924)

Very popular double lactiflora whose globe-shaped flowers have loosely-held bright crimson petals with paler edges. The guard petals are large and the central petals much smaller. The carpels may be developed into green carpelodes, which are flushed with magenta at the top. Fragrant. Mid- to late midseason. 78cm (31in).

Instituteur Doriat (Doriat, 1925)

Japanese lactiflora with large velvety carmine-red guard petals with white tips surrounding white-edged petaloids. Free flowering. Midseason. 90cm (36in).

Isani Gidui or Isani Jishi

('Smiling Lion' – Japanese, raised before 1928) Japanese lactiflora with a double ring of large milky white guard petals. These surround a spherical mass of narrow creamy yellow staminodes with deeper yellow edges. The carpels are pale green with orange tips and yellow bases. Extremely large flowers, much larger than those of 'Jan van Leeuwen', on a very vigorous plant. Midseason. 85cm (34in).

Isoline (Lemoine, 1916)

Double lactiflora with anemone-form flowers. The outer petals are creamy white, the inner form a canary yellow tuft with crimson-red spots. The flowers fade to creamy white with age, they are sometimes distorted and have an unpleasant scent. Midseason. 80cm (32in).

Ivory White Saucer (Cousins-Roy Klehm, 1981)

Single hybrid with saucer-shaped flowers and large rounded, ivory white petals. Very large carpels are green with creamy white stigmata and ringed by golden yellow stamens. Fragrant. Midseason. 85cm (34in).

James Kelway (Kelway, 1900)

Double lactiflora with very large blush-pink flowers streaked with magenta. The flowers fade to milky white with a golden glow in the heart of the bloom. Some of the inner petals are mixed with stamens, while the guard

petals are folded downwards. The anthers and filaments are golden yellow, the carpels pale pink with deep pink stigmata. Vigorous and tall, with very fragrant flowers, good for cutting. Midseason. 1m (3ft).

Janice (Saunders, 1939)
Single salmon-pink hybrid (*P. lactiflora* × *P. peregrina*) with a white centre, golden yellow anthers and yellow green carpels with cream stigmata. Slightly fragrant, strong stems. Midseason. 85cm (34in).

Jan van Leeuwen (Van Leeuwen, 1928)
Popular Japanese lactiflora with pure white guard petals surrounding a small centre of narrow, golden yellow staminodes. Carpels pale green with light yellow stigmata. Fragrant. A highly recommended variety with nice foliage but rather small flowers. Midseason. 90cm (36in).

Jean E. Bockstoce (Bockstoce, 1933)
P. lactiflora × *P. officinalis* hybrid with fully double,

The Saunders hybrid 'Honor' showing the white staminoidal disc at the base of the carpels.

claret-red flowers. All of the stamens are developed into petals. The carpels are pale green with a touch of purple on the stigmata. Strong stems. Early season. 85cm (34in).

John Howard Wigell (Wigell, 1942)
Double lactiflora with nice deep pink flowers and a coral-pink heart. The flower appears initially to be a semi-double with a ball of tightly furled petals in the centre but ultimately develops into a full double. Yellow stamens with short filaments are mixed with the inner petals. A further tuft of stamens is present in the centre with very small green carpels and pink stigmata. Early to midseason. 75cm (30in).

Joy of Life (Kelway, 1911)
Single to semi-double lactiflora with very large delicate

PLATE VII

All flowers are shown at
approximately ¼ size

P. 'John Howard Wigell'

P. 'Illini Warrior'

P. 'Zuzu'

P. 'Scarlet O'Hara'

P. 'Dresden'

P. 'White Wings'

blush-pink flowers, up to 25cm (10in) across, and translucent petals. A few of the central petals may be very deeply toothed. Very pretty; sweet fragrance. Mid- to very late season. 85cm (34in).

June Rose (Jones, 1938)

Cerise-pink, semi-double with flowers like huge roses. They open purplish pink but become deep pink (67A to 67C) in an extremely large, almost globular bloom. It retains its colour very well but the petals have slightly silvered edges. The stamens are mixed with the central petals and there are very small carpels with pointed, magenta stigmata. Dark green foliage, pleasant fragrance. Recommended. Midseason. 78cm (31in)

Kakoden (Japan)

Semi-double white lactiflora which was introduced from Japan by Louis Smirnow in 1955. The flowers open to show pale pink outer petals, before fading quickly to white. The inner petals are white with a pale yellow glow in the centre. The stamens are white, the carpels green. The herbaceous parent of the original 'Itoh' hybrids (see p.143). Midseason. 55cm (22in).

Kansas (Bigger, 1940) GM

Distinctive double lactiflora with deep fuchsia-purple (67B) flowers. The outer petals are conspicuously marbled on the outside, easily distinguishing it from other double reds. Stamens are mixed with the inner petals throughout the flower. The carpels are very small and green, with red stigmata. Vigorous with flowers held erect on strong stems. Midseason. 90cm (36in).

Karl Rosenfield (Rosenfield, 1908)

Double lactiflora with large globe-shaped bright crimson-red flowers. The inner petals are incurved and notched. Free flowering, a good cut flower. Mid- to late season. 78cm (31in).

Kelway's Brilliant, syn. 'Una Howard' (Kelway, 1928)

Japanese lactiflora bearing pure carmine-red guard petals and an unusual group of forked carmine-red staminodes, forming a flower within a flower. Mid- to late season. 90cm (36in).

Kelway's Fairy Queen (Kelway, 1927)

Very beautiful and underrated semi-double lactiflora

with very delicate coral-pink flowers; the petals fading slightly towards the edges. The flower starts as a single but then a large mass of twisted petals, ringed by golden yellow stamens, develops from the centre. The carpels are yellowish green with pink styles. Compact, very sweet fragrance. Mid- to late season. 78cm (31in).

Kelway's Glorious (Kelway, 1909)

Generally considered to be one of the best double white lactifloras, this has large creamy white flowers and a creamy yellow centre. The outer petals are soft, very large and turned downwards. Further large petals in the centre are turned upwards and surround a tuft of erect, very narrow petaloids. A few semi-functional stamens remain in the extreme heart of the flower, together with green carpels and purple stigmata. Some of the petals are streaked with carmine-red. Strong scent of roses, very free flowering. Mid- to late season. 1m (3ft).

Kelway's Majestic (Kelway, 1928)

Japanese lactiflora producing magenta-pink guard petals surrounding a large mass of long narrow staminodes. These are yellow at the base, fading to creamy yellow with pink stripes towards the broader middle and with pointed purple tips. Carpels are pale green with purple styles. Relatively long flowering period. Fragrant, with good autumn colour. Midseason. 1m (3ft).

Kelway's Scented Rose (Kelway)

Double, lilac-rose flowers with silvered petals. Very long flowering period, free flowering and very fragrant. Mid- to very late season. 90cm (36in).

Kelway's Supreme (Kelway, 1891)

Striking single or semi-double lactiflora with deep blush-pink flowers fading to white in strong sunshine, and with a small centre of yellow stamens. Strong growing and very fragrant, freely producing flowers on side shoots. Originally to be called 'Lady Alexandra Duff'. Very long flowering period (early June to mid-July). Mid- to very late season. 1m (3ft).

Kelway's Unique (Kelway, 1917)

Japanese lactiflora with bright rose-pink guard petals. The petaloids are creamy yellow with a deeper yellow base. The carpels are very deep purple with purple stigmata and styles. Free flowering. Mid- to late season. 1m (3ft).

PLATE VIII

P. 'Belle Center'

P. 'Wiesbaden'

P. 'Inspecteur Lavergne'

P. 'Kelway's Fairy Queen'

P. 'Argentine'

All flowers are shown at approximately ¼ size

P. 'Butch'

P. 'Kelway's Supreme'

P. 'Asa Gray'

P. 'Lois Kelsey'

P. 'Top Brass'

King of England (Kelway, 1901)

Japanese lactiflora bearing flowers with deep red guard petals and buff staminodes streaked with dark rose-pink. It can have either green or red stems, which suggests that there are actually two different varieties. Vigorous and tall. Midseason. 78cm (31in).

Krinkled White (Brand, 1928)

One of the best single lactifloras with large crinkled milky white petals. A small tuft of golden yellow stamens surrounds pale green carpels with cream stigmata. Early season. 78cm (31in).

La Fiancée (Dessert, 1902)

Crown-type lactiflora with creamy white petals touched with yellow at the base. The centre petals have a hint of red with a few stamens showing at the centre of the innermost ones. Vigorous. Midseason. 85cm (34in).

La France (Lemoine, 1901)

Double lactiflora with extremely large soft pink rose-type flowers, the outer petals flushed with red and often streaked with crimson. Free flowering and fragrant. Late season. 78cm (31in).

La Perle (Crousse, 1886)

Double, with large soft lavender-pink, globe-shaped flowers fading to creamy white. The darker centre is streaked with carmine-red. Very fragrant. Floriferous. Midseason. 78cm (31in).

Lady Alexandra Duff (Kelway, 1902) AGM

Very beautiful double lactiflora with lavender-pink outer petals and smaller white central petals. The tips of the petals in the extreme centre of the flower often have carmine blotches and stripes. The flowers are borne in clusters; they quickly fade to white in strong sunshine. The side flowers may be single or semi-double with golden stamens. A strongly fragrant variety with a long flowering period. Several similar plants masquerade as this variety. Midseason. 90cm (36in).

Lady in Pink (Krekler, 1977)

Vivid single hybrid whose china-rose flowers are stamped with a white mark at the base of the petals. The shape of the flowers is somewhat reminiscent of an iris when in bud. The stamens have golden anthers and long, pale yellow filaments. The carpels are pilose with pink stigmata. Ivory white disc. Inferior to 'Steve Nickel'. Very early season. 70cm (28in).

Lady Orchid (Bigger, 1942)

Fully double lactiflora with tightly packed soft lavender-pink petals. The outer petals fade almost to white in bright sunshine, while the central petaloids retain their deep pink colour. Carpels and stamens are absent; the petaloids are yellow at their base. Free flowering, slightly fragrant. Mid- to late season. 75cm (30in).

Largo (Vories, 1929)

Japanese lactiflora with rose-pink guard petals surrounding a centre of pink and gold staminodes. While some of the carpels are functional (green with pink tips) others are developed into rose-pink carpelodes. A good cut flower with strong stems. Midseason. 90cm (36in).

Late Windflower (Saunders, 1939)

Attractive hybrid between *P. emodi* and *P. veitchii* with single white nodding flowers. The leaves are narrow and pale green. Flowers ten days after 'Early Windflower'. Early season. 90cm (36in).

Laura Dessert (Dessert, 1913) AGM

Fully double lactiflora that has pink buds opening to pale pink, saucer shaped flowers, which fade to white at the edges. Stamens are absent but there is some yellow colouring at the base of the petals. Very strong rose fragrance. Early to midseason. 1m (3ft).

Lavender Strain (Saunders, 1939)

Originally a group of 7–8 hybrid clones between *P. lactiflora* and *P. coriacea*, only a few of which have survived, one of the most robust has been simply named as 'Lavender'. This is a very attractive peony with beautiful single lavender-coloured flowers. The foliage is similar to a vigorous specimen of *P. coriacea* and has leathery leaves with acuminate tips and wavy margins. The stigmata are tipped with red. 'Lavender' is a highly infertile triploid peony. Early season. 55cm (22in).

Le Cygne (Lemoine, 1907)

Double lactiflora with amber buds opening to milk-white flowers with a warmer heart. There are a few pale yellow staminodes and stamens in the slightly depressed centre; carpels are absent. Rather weak stems, fragrant. Early season. 69cm (27in).

Le Printemps (Lemoine, 1905)
Early flowering hybrid (*P. lactiflora* × *P. wittmanniana*) with 6–7-petalled, large single, creamy white flowers and yellow veining. The stamen filaments are white at the apex and purple at the base; the anthers are pale yellow. The carpels are green with purple stigmata. Makes a good cut flower. Early season. 80cm (32in).

Legion of Honor (Saunders, 1941)
Single hybrid (*P. lactiflora* × *P. officinalis*) with bright cherry-scarlet-red flowers and a nice ring of stamens. The anthers are yellow, the filaments cream. Tomentose carpels have bright pink stigmata. With light green foliage and wiry stems, it is spoilt by its poor shape and rather spindly growth. Early season. 70cm (28in).

L'Etincelante, syn. 'Silver Flare' (Dessert, 1905)
Single lactiflora with bowl-shaped, bright pink flowers and a centre of golden yellow stamens. The petal edges are lighter and almost silvered. Free flowering. Early to midseason. 1m (3ft).

Letitia, syn. 'Lady Beresford' (Kelway)
Single, cup-shaped, bright rose flowers, developing from deep rose-pink buds, but fading to almost white in strong sunshine. The petals have wavy edges and deeply notched tips. The stamen filaments and anthers are yellow, the carpels green flushed with purple and with bright pink stigmata. The carpels sit on a creamy white disc. Free flowering. Very early season. 78cm (31in).

Little Dorrit (Saunders, 1949)
Single hybrid (*P. officinalis* 'Rosea Plena' × *P. peregrina*) with rather unusual flowers, which are pink on the outside, bright salmon-pink on the inside, with white carpels and pink stigmata. Dwarf. Early season. 60cm (24in).

Little Red Gem (Reath, 1988)
Single hybrid with small red flowers. A very small plant which is suitable for a rock garden. Very early season. To 38cm (15in).

Lois Kelsey (Kelsey, 1934)
Very unusual but attractive semi-double lactiflora with creamy white flowers. The petals are very narrow with pointed, toothed tips or split into slender strips. Numerous purple carpels with magenta stigmata are surrounded by a ring of short golden stamens. Slightly fragrant. Midseason. 78cm (31in).

Lord Kitchener, formerly 'Balliol' (Kelway, 1907)
Single, maroon-red flowers are borne in clusters of 3–4 to a stem. There is a small centre of golden yellow stamens and the carpels are green-purple with purple stigmata. Very early to midseason. 90cm (36in).

Lorna Doone (Kelway)
Bomb-shaped double lactiflora with pink guard petals. From the top of the bomb erupts a mass of pale pink petals surrounded by a collar of creamy yellow petals. Fragrant. Mid- to very late season. 90cm (36in).

Lotus Queen (Murawska, 1947)
Attractive Japanese lactiflora with creamy white guard petals. The outer stamens are functional, those further inside are developed into narrow, creamy white staminodes with crinkled tips. The carpels are pale green with cream stigmata. Scented. Midseason. 83cm (33in).

Lovely Rose (Saunders, 1942)
Semi-double hybrid (*P. lactiflora* × *P. peregrina*) with carmine-rose flowers, pale green carpels and pink stigmata. The colour of the petals fades with age to pale pink with darker marbling. There are bold white blotches at the base of the interior of the petals. Free flowering. A wonderful plant. Early season. 75cm (30in).

Ludovica (Saunders, 1941)
Semi-double hybrid (*P. lactiflora* × *P. peregrina*) with crimson petals and conspicuous golden yellow stamen filaments. Cup-shaped flowers have four rows of petals and a white flare at the base of each petal. White carpels have bright pink stigmata. Very early season. 58cm (23in).

Lyric (Kelway, 1894)
Double lactiflora with lavender-blush guard petals; the inner petals are much smaller and creamy pink with a hint of yellow at the base. A pretty fragrant flower. Midseason. 90cm (36in).

Madame Auguste Dessert (Dessert, 1899)
Double cup-shaped flowers with rose-pink petals, flecked with carmine-red. Pink carpels in a depressed centre. Free flowering, fragrant, with strong stems. Midseason. 90cm (36in).

Madame Butterfly (Franklin, 1933)
Japanese peony with cyclamen-purple (74A) guard petals and forked magenta staminodes. The extreme tips of the staminodes have semi-functional anthers which produce a little pollen. The heart of the flower is yellow with small yellow carpels and magenta stigmata. In bright sunshine the staminodes fade to almost white with magenta tips. Midseason. 60cm (24in).

Madame Calot (Miellez, 1856)
Very double lactiflora, soft pink at first, opening to pale yellow with pink at the base, eventually turning to blush-pink, with pinkish green carpels and rose-pink stigmata. Very large flowers, very fragrant and free flowering. Late season. 75cm (30in).

Madame de Verneville (Crousse, 1885)
Double lactiflora with bomb-shaped flowers. The outer guard petals are pure white; the central petals start blush, turn sulphur-yellow and ultimately become pure white. Free flowering variety with fragrant flowers. Early season. 78cm (31in).

Madame Ducel (Mechin, 1880)
Double lactiflora with bomb-shaped flowers. The guard petals are lavender-pink and surround a large raised mound of smaller inner petals. At the base these are creamy white, further up they are flushed with lavender-pink; their roots are yellow. The top of the carpel is flattened, purple at the base and green at the top with magenta styles. Free flowering, with a sweet fragrance. Early to midseason. 60cm (24in).

Madame Edouard Doriat (Doriat, 1924)
Double, globe-shaped, creamy white to pure white flowers with a light carmine blotch at the centre. One flower per stem. Very fragrant. Late season. 1m (3ft).

Madame Emile Debatene (Dessert-Doriat, 1927)
Double rose-shaped flowers of warm pink (68B) with a silvery sheen and a centre of small curly petals. The

'Many Happy Returns' is an anemone-form flower with a centre composed entirely of petaloids.

majority of the stamens are mixed with the petals but there is also a tuft of very short golden stamens in the centre of the flower. Carpels are absent. Slight spicy fragrance, free flowering. Mid- to late season. 75cm (30in).

Madame Jules Dessert (Dessert, 1909)
Semi-double, rose-shaped, creamy white flowers with a hint of blush, fading to pure white and showing golden stamens. Very fragrant. Mid- to late season. 1m (3ft).

Madelon (Dessert, 1922)
Double lactiflora with large incurved guard petals and a globe-shaped mass of smaller inner petals. Rather small flowers: light pink with deeper pink heart, fading in sunlight with silvered edges. Fragrant. Late season. 90cm (36in).

Mademoiselle Lionie Calot,
syn. 'Monsieur Charles Leveque' (Calot, 1861)
Double, salmon-pink flowers with yellowish centres. The petals are ruffled and crinkled. Very free flowering but with weak stems, nevertheless making a good cut flower. Midseason. Medium height.

Madylone (Van Loon, 1966)
Fully double lactiflora bearing soft shell-pink flowers with nicely rounded guard petals and a tight centre of unfurling petals. Very similar to 'Mrs. Franklin D. Roosevelt'. Vigorous and robust, producing good cut flowers. Late season. 80cm (32in).

Mahogany (Glasscock, 1937)
Single hybrid ('Otto Froebel' × *P. lactiflora*) with shiny mahogany-red petals and large gold stamens; no pollen. Sweetly fragrant, makes a very good cut flower, light green foliage. Early season. 70cm (28in).

Mai Fleuri (Lemoine, 1905)
Vigorous hybrid (*P. lactiflora* × *P. wittmanniana*) which has large single white flowers slightly tinted with flesh-pink. The lower part of the petals has dark violet veins. Early season. 70cm (28in).

Many Happy Returns (Hollingsworth, 1990)
Anemone-form hybrid ('Good Cheer' × 'Nippon Splendour') with large rounded guard petals. Cardinal-red flowers have no stamens; they are replaced by similarly coloured petaloids. Three pale green carpels with tapered pink stigmata. Deeply dissected undulating foliage. Retains it colour well in bright sunlight. Strong stems, slight scent. Midseason. 75cm (30in).

Marie Crousse (Crousse, 1892)
Very large bomb-type flower with pale pink (almost salmon) petals and a slightly darker centre. The guard petals are very large. Fades to white in strong sunshine. Free flowering with a spicy fragrance. Midseason. 88cm (35in).

Marie Fischer (Fischer, 1973)
Single ivory white flowers suffused blush-pink. A very large mass of stamens have gold anthers and cream filaments with pink bases. The carpels are green, pilose, and have purple stigmata. Rigid stems and bright shiny green leaves. Very early season. 83cm (33in).

Marie Jaquin, syn. 'Bridesmaid', 'Water Lily' (Verdier)
Semi-double lactiflora with pale pink, cup-shaped flowers turning creamy white. This variety has glossy petals and a good centre of yellow stamens. Young plants have almost single flowers but as the plant matures the blooms become fully double. They are produced in clusters and have a very strong fragrance. Midseason. Medium height.

Marie Lemoine (Calot, 1869)
Double lactiflora with globe-shaped white flowers tinted lemon-yellow. The yellow stamens and staminodes are hidden by the petals but add further yellow colouring to the flower. Sweetly fragrant. A few of the petals may have flecks of red. A sweetly fragrant variety with very large flowers. Late Season. 78cm (31in).

Marietta Sisson (Sass, 1933)
Pretty globe-shaped double with magenta-rose flowers, the petals streaked with deeper magenta pigmentation. The flowers have deeply depressed centres with golden yellow stamens, within which are a further tuft of petals, surrounding yet more stamens. Opening semi-double, it has several concentric rings of petals and stamens when fully opened. Very fragrant. Early season. 80cm (32in).

Mary Brand (Brand, 1907)
Claret-red double with a few yellow stamens showing. Occasional longer stamens are scattered among the petals. This peony is a rich source of nectar and very attractive to bees. Relatively short growing. Midseason. To 70cm (28in).

Massasoit (White, 1954)
Crown-type lactiflora with bright purple-red petals. The inner petals have white streaks and surround a tight mass of purple staminodes. Pale green carpels have purple stigmata. Early season. 75cm (30in).

May Music (Saunders, 1973)
Single hybrid bearing flesh-pink flowers with dramatic magenta flares, long magenta filaments and pale yellow anthers. Pilose pale green anthers have magenta stigmata. Deep green leaves, inclined to have crooked stems. Vigorous. Early season. 90cm (36in).

May Treat (Krekler, 1978)
Semi-double hybrid with large coral-pink flowers, beautiful even when in bud, and yellow anthers and filaments. The petals are brushed with magenta on the outside; their bases have a greenish tinge on the inside. The green carpels have salmon-pink stigmata. Late season. 90cm (36in).

Messagère (Lemoine, 1909)
Hybrid between *P. lactiflora* and *P. wittmanniana*. Single cup-shaped, white flowers with cream and green tints. Early season. Tall growing.

PLATE IX

P. peregrina 'Otto Froebel'

P. 'Buckeye Belle'

P. 'Montezuma'

P. 'Postilion'

P. 'Legion of Honour'

P. 'Paladin'

P. 'Lovely Rose'

P. 'Flame'

P. 'Defender'

P. 'Rose Garland'

All flowers are shown at approximately ¼ size

Mischief (Auten, 1925)
Single, cup-shaped flowers of apple-blossom pink, flushed with magenta and fading to almost white with a hint of pink. They open very wide and are somewhat reminiscent of a magnolia flower. The inner petals are surrounded by a ring of short golden yellow stamens; the carpels are very small, green at the base and purple at the top, with purple styles and stigmata. Strong stems hold the flowers well above the foliage. Slight fragrance. Tall and vigorous. Late season. 1.2m (4ft) in ideal conditions.

Miss America (Mann-van Steen, 1936) GM
Extremely pretty semi-double lactiflora. Blush-pink buds open to form very large semi-double, pure white flowers with pale yellow at the base of the petals. The stamen filaments are yellow and the anthers buff. Carpels pale green, grooved with cream stigmata. Highly regarded and has been awarded the APS Gold Medal on two occasions (1956 and 1971). Only 'Nick Shaylor' has matched this achievement. Fragrant. Early season. 90cm (36in).

Miss Eckhart
(Roelof-Arendsveen van der Meer, 1928)
Very pretty semi-double to fully double. Reminiscent of a stick of candy floss, the fluffy magenta-pink flowers have streaks of magenta on the petals. The colour fades on the outermost petals, leaving a deeper pink heart. The buds are Roseine-purple (68A), fading to 68B with paler edges. Golden yellow stamens, some developed into pink staminodes. The carpels are pale green with magenta stigmata. Free flowering, musk fragrance. Midseason. 90cm (36in).

Mister Ed (Carl G. Klehm, 1980)
Very double flower with deep rose-pink outer petals, fading in the centre to creamy white, flushed with pink. The central staminodes are narrow and mixed with large petals; the extreme base of the petals and staminodes has a hint of yellow. The carpels are developed into small petals. A mutation of 'Monsieur Jules Elie'. Fragrant. Early season. 70cm (28in).

Mistral (Dessert, 1905)
Pretty single lactiflora with deeply toothed slightly silvered cherry-red petals. Has a small circle of golden yellow stamens with long filaments, green carpels and magenta stigmata. No fragrance but free flowering. Midseason. 75cm (30in).

Monsieur Jules Elie (Crousse, 1888) AGM
Very large double, crown-form lactiflora with large rose-pink guard petals, surrounding a raised mass of smaller incurved petals. These inner petals have a pale line running down the centre. Stamens are absent and the carpels are developed into narrow, twisted, yellow or pink petals. Fragrant, good cut flower but has rather weak stems. Retains its colour well in bright sunshine. Justifiably one of the most popular peonies, it is known as 'Fuji' in Japan. Early to midseason. 1.1m (3½ft).

Monsieur Krelage (Crousse, 1883)
Double lactiflora with large red flowers. Vigorous and free flowering. Midseason. Tall

Montezuma (Saunders, 1943)
Single or semi-double hybrid (*P. lactiflora* × *P. peregrina*) with beautiful buds and large dark scarlet (46A) flowers. The petals have slightly serrated tips and a broad white stripe on the outside. There are golden yellow anthers and filaments and greyish green carpels with salmon-pink stigmata. A very good early red hybrid with strong stems and scented flowers. Early season. 90cm (36in).

Moon over Barrington (Roy Klehm)
Attractive double lactiflora with well rounded, creamy white flowers. A few stamens poke out between the petals. Spicy fragrance, dark green foliage. Midseason. 65cm (26in).

Moonrise (Saunders, 1949)
Gorgeous F2 hybrid between *P. lactiflora* and *P. peregrina* with cream coloured buds opening to form creamy yellow single flowers with a large globular mass of golden yellow stamens. The carpels are green with cream stigmata. Well worth growing with nice light green leaves, noticeably undivided with 11–13 leaflets. Fragrant. Early season. 70cm (28in).

Moon River (Carl G. Klehm)
Fully double lactiflora with creamy white petals surrounded by blush-pink guard petals. Dark green leaves, slightly fragrant. Midseason. 70cm (28in).

PLATE X

All flowers are shown at approximately ¼ size

P. 'Carmen'

P. 'Madame Auguste Dessert'

P. 'Enchantment'

P. 'Grandiflora'

P. 'Cascade'

P. 'Candeur'

P. 'David Kelway'

P. 'Marie Crousse'

This is a young, just opening, flower of the hybrid 'Mrs. Franklin D. Roosevelt'.

Moonstone (Murawska, 1943) GM
Very attractive double lactiflora with large very symmetrical flowers, which open blush-pink, fading to white with pink outer petals. The flowers mature at different times so that there are likely to be a mixture of pink and white blooms at any one time. Midseason. 90cm (36in).

Mother's Choice (Glasscock, 1950) GM
Fully double lactiflora producing pure white flowers with a slightly warmer centre. White stamens and green carpels. Vigorous, with well held blooms on erect stems. Midseason. 90cm (36in).

Mr. G. F. Hemerik (Van Leeuwen, 1930)
Japanese-form flower with magenta-rose guard petals and a centre of creamy yellow crinkled staminodes. These staminodes continue to grow as the flower ages and develop wavy pale pink tips. This variety is difficult to mistake as

its leaves have distinctive crinkled margins. The carpels are very large, pale green with pink edged petaloid stigmata. Slightly fragrant. Late season. 75cm (30in).

Mrs. Edward Harding (Shaylor, 1918)
Unusual flower, opening semi-double, flesh-pink with magenta streaks on the outer petals, it eventually develops into a somewhat flat white double with a flesh-pink centre. The inner petals are narrow and wavy mixed with golden yellow stamens. The carpels are absent and developed into creamy white carpelodes. Low growing, slightly scented. Midseason. To 63cm (25in).

Mrs. Franklin D. Roosevelt (Franklin, 1932) GM
Fully double lactiflora with very beautiful and well shaped, light pink flowers, paler in the centre. The flowers open like a blush-pink water lily and eventually fade to almost white in bright sunshine. The carpelodes are yellow at their base. Free flowering and fragrant. Makes a good cut flower. One of the author's favourites. Midseason. 70cm (28in).

My Pal Rudy (Carl G. Klehm-Roy Klehm)
Fully double, rose-form flower with deep rose-pink petals. Strong stems, fragrant. Midseason. 93cm (37in).

Myrtle Gentry (Brand, 1925)
Double lactiflora with light pink flowers tinted with flesh- and salmon-pink. The colour is most intense in the centre. One of the nicest pale pink doubles. Very fragrant. Late season. 90cm (36in).

Nathalie (Saunders, 1939)
Very striking and unusual semi-double hybrid (*P. lactiflora* × *P. peregrina*) whose young flowers are deep pink. As they mature, the flowers open very widely, gradually fading until they are almost white. There is usually a mixture of deep pink and white flowers on any plant. The carpels are green with pink stigmata. Very beautiful, if slightly untidy. Early season. 60cm (24in).

Neon (Nicholls, 1941)
Japanese lactiflora with large, vivid pink guard petals surrounding a pompom of gold-tipped pink staminodes. The carpels are bright green with purple stigmata. Very large flowers which retain their colour well. Midseason. 1.1m (3½ft).

Nice Gal (Krekler, 1965)
Very striking semi-double with numerous symmetrical wavy, deep cerise-pink petals and a small centre of golden stamens. The petals have an occasional white stripe down the centre and have silvered edges. Carpels are absent and developed into carpelodes. Compact with dark green leaves, free flowering, fragrant. Late season. 55cm (22in).

Nick Shaylor (Allison, 1931) GM
Double lactiflora which opens blush-pink with a hint of yellow and fades to white with a blush centre. Streaks of carmine-red may occur on the reverse of the guard petals and on some of the central petals. Large flowers, no fragrance. Very late season. 85cm (34in).

Norma Volz (Volz, 1962) GM
Double lactiflora. Large white flowers have blush-pink and yellow tints. Some of the inner petals have carmine-red edges. Foliage dark green, stems stiff. Midseason. 90cm (36in).

Nosegay (Saunders, 1950)
Single hybrid (*P. mlokosewitschi* × *P. tenuifolia*) with shell-pink flowers, fading to white. The stamen filaments are red, the anthers yellow and the carpels pink. Deeply divided foliage. Early season. 70cm (28in).

Nova (Saunders, 1950)
F2 hybrid between *P. mlokosewitschi* and *P. macrophylla*. The flowers are single and pale yellow with a hint of green. The foliage is similar to that of *P. macrophylla* with massive glossy green leaves, slightly hairy beneath, particularly near the veins. Fertile. Very early season. 75cm (30in).

Nymphe (Dessert, 1913)
Pretty single lactiflora that produces cup-shaped, flesh-pink flowers. The stamens form a tight ball in the centre of the bloom and have yellow filaments; the carpels are green with magenta stigmata. Fragrant. Late season. 65cm (26in).

Opal Hamilton (Nicholls-Wild, 1957)
Japanese-shaped lactiflora with large soft lilac-pink guard petals. The central staminodes are very large, yellow and pink with toothed tips. The outer ones are thread-like, yellow with deep pink tips. The carpels are yellow-green with cream stigmata. Midseason. 90cm (36in).

Orpen (Kelway)
An extremely striking Japanese lactiflora with reddish purple guard petals and a large mass of very broad pointed staminodes, the tips of which are silvered and streaked with purple pigment. Fragrant. Late season. 85cm (34in).

Pageant (Saunders, 1941)
Triple hybrid (*P. officinalis* 'Rosea Plena' × (*P. lactiflora* × *P. macrophylla*)) with single rose-pink flowers and a large centre of light yellow stamens. Early season. 1m (3ft).

Paladin (Saunders, 1950)
Semi-double hybrid (*P. lactiflora* × *P. peregrina*) with bright carmine-red flowers. A pretty dwarf. Early season. 45cm (18in).

Paramount (Krekler, 1978)
Large single hybrid with rose-red (58B) flowers with a large white mark down the inner and outer surfaces of the petals. They have long yellow filaments, golden anthers and green carpels with pink stigmata. Strong growing with notched leaflets. Early season. 85cm (34in).

Pastel Elegance (Seidl, 1989)
Hybrid with double, light pastel salmon-pink flowers, the stamens scattered throughout the petals. The result of a cross between 'Salmon Dream' and 'Lemon Chiffon'. Midseason. 75cm (30in).

Patriot (Saunders, 1943)
Single hybrid (*P. lactiflora* × *P. macrophylla*) with bright blood-red flowers. The petals surround a large mass of yellow anthers with reddish orange filaments. Carpels are yellow green with crimson stigmata. The disc is very large and bright pink and white. Early season. 90cm (36in).

Paula Fay (Fay, 1968) GM
Semi-double, F2 hybrid with striking vivid pink flowers. When the flowers first open, the petals are crinkled; they have a rather waxy texture and a large white blotch at their base. The stamen anthers and filaments are yellow; the carpels green with salmon-pink stig-

mata. Light green foliage with nicely rounded leaflets. Vigorous, fragrant flowers. Early season. 88cm (35in).

Paul M. Wild (Wild, 1964)
Fully double lactiflora with large vivid ruby-red flowers. It has large rounded guard petals and no stamens or carpels; they are replaced with numerous small petals in the centre of the flower. Very beautiful, retains its colour for a long time. Midseason. 95cm (38in).

Peppermint (Nicholls-Wild, 1957)
Double lactiflora with flat rose-shaped blooms. These open blush-white with a hint of yellow in the centre and fade quickly to white in strong sunshine. The outer petals and some of the inner ones are streaked with carmine. Green carpels with purple stigmata, are surrounded by golden stamens. The central petals are much narrower. Some flowers have petals with toothed edges. Late midseason.

Peter Brand (Seit, 1937)
Fully double lactiflora with deep ruby-red flowers. Fragrant, good autumn colour. Midseason. 93cm (37in).

Petticoat Flounce (Roy Klehm, 1985)
Bomb-shaped lactiflora with very large blush outer guard petals. The inner collar consists of numerous forked creamy white staminodes, surmounted by a tuft of larger upward-pointing salmon-pink petaloids. The upper petals are occasionally streaked with carmine. A good cut flower. Early season. 85cm (34in).

Phillippe Rivoire (Rivière, 1911)
Fully double lactiflora with incurved satiny petals of dark crimson-red, occasionally almost black. Free flowering, with a scent of roses. Cup-shaped flowers held on wiry stems. Late season. 75cm (30in).

Philomèle, syn. 'Vadius' (Calot, 1861)
Anemone-form flower with lavender-pink guard petals surrounding a mass of buff and lavender petaloids. The central petals, which take some time to develop and may be absent in younger flowers, are larger and lavender-pink. There is a depressed centre of very narrow buff petaloids. The carpels are diminutive with magenta stigmata. Very beautiful, fragrant. Midseason. 75cm (30in).

Phyllis Kelway (Kelway, 1908)
Very large, rather flat, magenta-pink, semi-double lactiflora, fading to white in the middle with a touch of yellow at the centre. There are two sets of stamens: one surrounds the middle petals, the other forms a tuft in the centre. The very small yellow carpels have pink stigmata. Free flowering, slightly fragrant with abundant foliage. Stiff stems. Midseason. 80cm (32in).

Picotee (Saunders, 1949)
Single hybrid (*P. mascula* ssp. *russi* × *P. macrophylla*) with unusual picotee flowers. The rounded petals are white with a distinctive magenta rim. The magenta pigmentation may also occur in occasional spots over the petals. Filaments and stigmata are reddish purple. Compact with large leaves, it is more of a curiosity than a good garden plant. Early season. 45cm (18in).

Pillow Talk (Carl G. Klehm, 1974) GM
Double lactiflora with rose-pink petals, the colour deepest at the tips. The outer petals surround a ring of pale yellow staminodes, inside which is a ring of pink petals. The carpels have been reduced to a small number of tiny yellow petals. A very full and fluffy rose-shaped flower. Strong stems. Midseason. 80cm (32in).

Pink Angel (Christenson, 1948)
Single hybrid with broad, slightly fluted, blush-pink petals surrounding a large diffuse ball of stamens. The stamens have lavender filaments and yellow anthers. The carpels are yellowish white with a pink top; the stigmata are red. Derived in part from *P. wittmanniana*, the general impression is of a plant with pale lavender flowers. Very early season. 68cm (27in); spread to 100cm (40in) across.

Pink Cameo (Bigger, 1954)
Crown-shaped double with very large pink guard petals, surrounding stacked layers of smaller narrow petals. The inner petals are yellow at the extreme base and probably derived from stamens. Carpels pink with magenta styles. Glossy green leaves. Late midseason. 75cm (30in).

Pink Dawn (Kelway)
Single lactiflora that is bright carmine-rose becoming light pink. A vigorous plant with very large flowers.

PLATE XI
All flowers are shown at approximately ¼ size

P. 'Black Monarch'

P. 'Peter Brand'

P. 'Monsieur Krelage'

P. 'Augustin d'Hour'

P. 'Miss Eckhart'

P. 'Marie Lemoine'

P. 'Afterglow'

P. 'Madelon'

P. 'Felix Crousse'

P. 'Burning Light'

P. 'Grover Cleveland'

P. 'Phyllis Kelway'

P. 'Madame Edouard Doriat'

P. 'Pillow Talk'

P. 'Marietta Sisson'

P. 'Kelway's Glorious'

This variety was widely planted in old British gardens and should not be confused with the better 'Dawn Pink' raised by Sass. Midseason. 85cm (34in). See also Pink Princess.

Pink Formal (Nicholls-Wild & Son, 1953)
Fully double lactiflora bearing rose-type flowers with pale mauve-pink petals and a paler centre, fading to milky white with a pink heart. In young flowers the central petals are wrapped into a tight ball. Stamens and carpels absent. Late midseason. 90cm (36in).

Pink Hawaiian Coral (Roy Klehm, 1981)
Semi-double hybrid (*P. lactiflora* 'Charlie's White' × *P. peregrina* 'Otto Froebel') with rather small coral-pink petals, which fade to pink at the edges and have a very large white stripe on the outside. Two rows of guard petals surround numerous wavy staminodes. These vary from narrow semi-functional anthers to broader coral and white petaloids. The carpels start creamy white before turning green and have coral-pink stigmata. Fragrant. Early season. 90cm (36in).

Pink Lemonade (Carl G. Klehm, 1951)
Very dramatic bomb-shaped lactiflora with extremely large shell-pink guard petals. The centre is filled with a rounded mass of pale yellow staminodes, mixed with large pink staminodes and carpelodes. These give the impression that they are bursting out of the flower. Vigorous with fragrant flowers. Midseason. 90cm (36in).

Pink Parasol Surprise (Roy Klehm, 1988)
Bomb-shaped flower with light pink guard petals and creamy yellow staminodes, surrounding a mass of peach, pink, cream and yellow petals. Very fragrant flowers on a vigorous plant. Early season. 75cm (30in).

Pink Parfait (Carl G. Klehm, 1975)
Fully double lactiflora producing large bright pink flowers with silvered petal edges. The petals gradually reduce in size from the enlarged guard petals. The stamens and carpels are absent and replaced with small pale pink petals, flushed yellow at the base. Slightly fragrant. Late season. 95cm (38in).

Pink Pom Pom (Freeborn, 1943)
Distinctive fully double hybrid (*P. lactiflora* × *P.*

officinalis). Rose-Bengal guard petals surround a pompom of spathulate orchid-pink inner petals with Rose-Bengal tips. A nice plant with yellow-green carpels. Midseason. 80cm (32in) .

Pink Princess, formerly 'Pink Dawn'
(Originator unknown)
Single lactiflora producing pale pink flowers with very long, slightly crinkled petals. The petals are speckled with pink pigmentation, almost as though they were airbrushed; they fade to white at the base. In strong sunshine the flowers turn mostly white with occasional patches of pink. A nice heart of golden yellow stamens with short yellow filaments. The mature carpels are purplish green with purple stigmata; pink carpelodes may be present in mature specimens. Strong stems and beautiful flowers. Midseason. 95cm (38in).

Postilion (Saunders, 1941)
Semi-double hybrid (*P. lactiflora* × *P. officinalis*) with enormous deep scarlet-red flowers with a hint of orange. The petals have an embossed central section. The stamen filaments are pink, the anthers golden yellow and the stigmata crimson. This variety may occasionally exhibit the characteristic of having a flower within a flower. A tuft of distorted petals grows among the carpels, within this are further stamens and carpels. Robust with extremely large leaves and strongly scented flowers. Highly recommended. Early season. 90cm (36in).

Pottsii (Potts, 1821)
Very early variety with double crimson-red flowers. Introduced by John Potts. Not listed by any nursery. Midseason.

Prairie Afire (Brand, 1932)
Japanese lactiflora with deep pink guard petals surrounding a centre of erect bright red petaloids. Midseason. 80cm (32in).

Prairie Moon (Fay, 1959)
Without any doubt this is one of the most beautiful hybrid peonies. The single to semi-double pale yellow flowers have a good centre of yellow stamens and the green carpels have creamy white stigmata. The result of a cross between 'Archangel' and 'Laura Magnuson'. Early season. 80cm (32in).

President Poincaré (Kelway)

Single to semi-double lactiflora with bright ruby-red (59A) flowers (fading to 61A) and glossy petals. The stamens have long filaments, yellow at the top and red at the base, arranged in concentric rings around the petals. The anthers are yellow, the carpels purplish green with magenta stigmata. Slight spicy fragrance. Mid- to late season. 88cm (35in).

Primevère (Lemoine, 1907)

Anemone-type lactiflora producing blush-white flowers with a lemon-yellow petaloid centre, changing to ivory white with age. Free flowering, very fragrant. Midseason. 88cm (35in).

Princess Margaret (Murawska, 1960) NGC

Fully double lactiflora with very beautiful deep pink flowers. Named after HRH Princess Margaret. Early season. 75cm (30in).

Queen Elizabeth (Kelway)

Underrated single lactiflora with nicely rounded pale flesh-pink petals. The flowers are large with a pale mark down the centre of the petals. Vigorous and fragrant. Early season. 83cm (33in).

Queen of Sheba (Sass, 1937)

Deep magenta-pink double-flowered peony. The blooms have a warmer coloured centre and silvered petals margins. The guard petals are rather large and have distinctive square tips. The petals become progressively smaller towards the centre, alternating with several rings of stamens. In the extreme centre is a small tuft of stamens; carpels are absent. Mid- to late season. 80cm (32in).

Raspberry Charm (Wissing-Roy Klehm, 1985)

Semi-double hybrid bearing raspberry-red flowers with a centre of golden stamens. Reliable with strong stems. Early season. 1m (3ft).

Raspberry Ice (Carl G. Klehm, 1980)

Bomb-shaped flowers with purple-red guard petals surrounding a massive ball of twisted purple-red inner petals with paler edges. The carpels are green at the base, purple at the top with red styles. Large flowers on strong stems. Midseason. 90cm (36in).

Raspberry Sundae (Carl G. Klehm, 1968)

Few flowers can have been so aptly named. This bomb-shaped lactiflora has large pale pink guard petals surrounding a collar of pale yellow petals, topped with a mass of curly pale pink petals. The extreme centre is slightly depressed with a few very narrow pale yellow petaloids. Carpels are absent. Sweet fragrance. Midseason. 90cm (36in).

Red Charm (Glasscock, 1944) GM

Double hybrid (*P. lactiflora* × *P. officinalis* 'Rubra Plena') with deep red, ruffled petals. The guard petals are large, enclosing numerous narrow petals surmounted by a crown of broader petaloids. Stamens are completely absent; the carpels are large, green with almost non-existent stigmata. Long flowering period. Very early season. 90cm (36in).

Red Red Rose (Saunders, 1942)

Semi-double hybrid (*P. lactiflora* × *P. peregrina*) with very symmetrical intense blood-red flowers. The petals are stiff, the anthers golden yellow and the filaments red. Yellow-green carpels have purple stigmata. Very strong stems, particularly attractive when in bud. Midseason. 75cm (30in).

Red Velvet (Auten, 1945)

Beautiful ruby-red single with satin-textured petals. This variety has a large centre of golden stamens, surrounding pinkish green carpels with purple stigmata. Very similar to the better known 'Illini Warrior' but later and slightly more purple. One of the best single reds. Late season. 85cm (34in).

Reine de Mai (Arends)

Single hybrid (*P. peregrina* × *P. wittmanniana*) with flesh-pink flowers. Late season.

Reine Hortense, syn. 'President Taft' (Calot, 1857)

Very beautiful double lactiflora whose globe-shaped flowers have enlarged guard petals. The flowers are pale pink with patches of crimson along the edges of the uppermost petals. The bloom fades to white in strong sunshine. The carpels are developed into small white petals, surrounded by a small ring of short golden stamens; further stamens are scattered throughout the flower. Free flowering with good fragrance and grey-green foliage, makes a good cut flower. Midseason. 83cm (33in).

Reine Supreme (Roy Klehm, 1985)
Double bomb-shaped lactiflora with apple-blossom-pink flowers. The enlarged outer petals surround a tight mass of smaller inner petals. The petals have a shallow double notch at the tip and occasional red stripes. Very fragrant. Midseason. 85cm (34in).

Requiem (Saunders, 1941)
Dramatic plant with single creamy white flowers warmed by a hint of pink. One of the best of the Saunders' hybrids, resulting from a back cross (P. lactiflora × (P. lactiflora × P. macrophylla)). The stamens have very large anthers, the filaments are golden yellow at the top and pink below. The carpels are yellow-green with pink stigmata; the disc lobes are pink. Large, glossy dark green leaves, free flowering, spicy fragrance. Midseason. 93cm (37in).

Reward (Saunders, 1941)
Very early single hybrid (P. lactiflora × P. peregrina) with glossy ruby-red petals. The filaments are very short, pale yellow at the top and pink at the base. The anthers are yellow. The carpels are tomentose and have dark red stigmata. The disc is conspicuous and bright magenta. Slightly fragrant. Early season. 70cm (28in).

Robert W. Auten (Auten, 1948)
Semi-double hybrid (P. lactiflora × P. officinalis) bearing very dark red flowers with partly hidden yellow stamen filaments. Considered very beautiful. Early season. 75cm (30in).

Roselette (Saunders, 1950)
Triple hybrid (P. lactiflora × (P. officinalis × P. macrophylla)) with single cup-shaped flowers. A pretty, delicate flower with blush-pink petals and magenta veins. The colour fades in sunshine, leaving bold patches of magenta in the centre of almost white petals. Pale yellow-green filaments and golden anthers. Tomentose carpels with dark red stigmata. Light green foliage. Early season. 55cm (22in).

Rose Garland (Saunders, 1943)
Single hybrid (P. lactiflora × P. peregrina) with vivid china-rose flowers, with white patches at the base of the petals. Very much like a pink P. peregrina flower. The anthers are yellow and the filaments light apricot.

Carpels greyish green with bright pink stigmata. A beautiful plant. Early season. 85cm (34in).

Rose of Delight (Kelway, 1925)
Single, brilliant pink flowers fading to white in bright sunshine with a hint of pink in the centre of the petals. Large mass of semi-functional stamens, carpels and stigmata purple. Fragrant, free flowering. Early to midseason. 90cm (36in).

Rose Shaylor (Shaylor, 1920)
Double lactiflora bearing flowers that open light pink with rose-pink shading. The mature flowers become white with crimson splashes. Free flowering, mildly fragrant. Midseason. 70cm (28in).

Rosy Cheek (Saunders, 1943)
Very pretty single or semi-double hybrid (P. lactiflora × P. peregrina) with slightly fluted pink flowers. The stamens are long with red filaments and yellow anthers. The green carpels have very long styles; both styles and stigmata are bright red. Early season. 78cm (31in).

Royal Rose (Reath, 1980)
Unusual flower when opening with the petals formed into concentric triangles. A semi-double hybrid ('Paula Fay' × 'Moonrise') with Neyron Rose (55B/C) flowers, golden anthers and yellow filaments. The flowers are more double than 'Paula Fay'. Very large yellow-green carpels and salmon-pink stigmata. Early season. 85cm (34in).

Salmon Beauty (Glasscock-Auten, 1939)
Double hybrid (P. lactiflora × P. officinalis) bearing a large bomb-shaped flower with bright pink guard petals surrounding a mound of similarly coloured divided petaloids. Vigorous with flowers held on strong stems. Highly recommended. Midseason. 90cm (36in).

Salmon Chiffon (Rudolph-Roy Klehm, 1981)
Dramatic single hybrid with cup-shaped, salmon-pink flowers, flushed pink and gold. In bud the flowers are deep pink; after opening the outside of the petals is a deeper pink than the interior. With its slightly ruffled petals it is altogether a beautiful flower. There are golden anthers, yellow filaments, pale green carpels and bright pink stigmata. Bright green leaves. Early season. 85cm (34in).

'Salmon Dream' is a beautiful semi-double hybrid.

Salmon Dream (Reath, 1979)
This has to be one of the most beautiful flowers ever produced. It is a semi-double hybrid ('Paula Fay' × 'Moonrise') with pale salmon-pink flowers, opening almost coral-pink before fading slightly. The petals have a satin sheen and a slight white flare at the base. The anthers and filaments are yellow; the carpels are tomentose with salmon-pink stigmata. Nicely rounded plants with a good habit and attractive glossy green leaves. Strong erect stems. Midseason. 85cm (34in).

Salmon Glow (Glasscock, 1947)
Semi-double hybrid (*P. officinalis* 'Sunbeam' × *P. lactiflora*) with beautiful pale pink translucent petals and magenta edges. The flowers fade to an unusual creamy white with a salmon-pink heart. The areas of the petals that are shaded from the sun remain pink. In the centre, very large mint-green carpels have small yellow-green stigmata. A distinctive and very unusual peony with very large flowers. May lack vigour when grown in the UK. Early season. 85cm (34in).

Salmon Surprise (Cousins-Roy Klehm, 1981)
Single hybrid with salmon-pink petals and carpels surrounded by a ring of golden yellow anthers with long filaments. The prominent disc is bright pink. Flowers are supported by strong stems. Early season. 75cm (30in).

Sanctus (Saunders, 1955)
F3 hybrid (*P. lactiflora* × *P. officinalis*) with single white flowers and very long stamens. The filaments are white at the top, pinkish red at the base. Pale green carpels and crimson stigmata. Very early season. 78cm (31in).

Sarah Bernhardt (Dessert, 1895)
See Umbellata Rosea.

Sarah Bernhardt (Lemoine, 1906) AGM
Double lactiflora with very large fluffy apple-blossom-pink flowers, deeper in colour in the centre of the flower

fading towards the outside. The flowers retain their colour very well but eventually fade to near white in very bright sunshine. Some petals may have flecks of carmine. Carpels are usually absent or vestigial with magenta styles and stigmata. The stamens are golden yellow and mixed throughout the central petals. Fragrant, popular and a successful cut flower, but with very weak stems that can barely support the heavy flowers: a number of modern varieties are as good as if not better than 'Sarah Bernhardt'. Mid- to very late season. 95cm (38in). See also Umbellata Rosea.

Scarlet O'Hara (Glasscock-Falk, 1956)
(*P. lactiflora* × *P. officinalis*) Aptly named variety with vivid scarlet-red flowers, fading with age to crimson. Golden anthers and similarly coloured filaments; yellow or green carpels with salmon-pink stigmata. The pale pink disc is very conspicuous with numerous lobes. Very robust and vigorous with large, moderately fragrant flowers; the side buds enable it to flower over a long period. Best planted in groups for maximum effect. Early season. To 1.1m (3½ft).

Sea Shell (Sass, 1937) GM
Very beautiful single lactiflora with warm lilac-pink petals. Strong stems make this a good cut flower. Free flowering and vigorous. Midseason. 93cm (37in).

Shawnee Chief (Bigger, 1940)
Double lactiflora with dark red flowers. The outer three rings of petals are greatly enlarged with a centre of much smaller petals. Vigorous, a good cut flower. Late midseason. 90cm (36in).

Shirley Temple (Originator unknown)
Double lactiflora ('Festiva Maxima' × 'Mme. Edouard Doriat') with pink buds which open to blush-white and finally develop into extremely large creamy white flowers. The central petals are thread-like with yellow 'roots'. The carpels are very small with elongated magenta stigmata. Free flowering and slightly fragrant, the strong stems make it a good flower for cutting. Mid- to late season. 83cm (33in) or more.

Silver Dawn (F3 Mixture) (Laning)
This is a series of hybrid seedlings whose colours range from white to ivory, pink and coral. The flowers are sin-

gle with a tight centre of golden yellow stamens. Some of these seedlings have been selected and sold as distinct varieties. Early season. 70–80cm (28–32in).

Silver Shell (Wild, 1962)
Single white with a small boss of golden yellow stamens. Carpels green with cream stigmata. Makes a good cut flower, slight fragrant. Early midseason. 73cm (29in).

Snow Swan (Roy Klehm, 1987)
Extremely attractive single peony with rounded, slightly fluted, ivory white petals. The golden stamens form a compact tuft in the centre. A very pretty flower. Midseason. 85cm (34in).

Soft Salmon Saucer (Cousins-Roy Klehm, 1981)
Very pretty single peony bearing saucer-shaped flowers with soft salmon-pink petals whose colour deepens towards the centre. A ring of golden stamens surround green carpels with cerise-pink stigmata. Midseason. 85cm (34in).

Solange (Lemoine, 1907)
Double lactiflora with creamy flesh buds opening to creamy white, globe-shaped blooms tinted with amber. The centre is a dark shade of salmon-pink. Fragrant. Very beautiful, but the flowers do not always open well. Very late season. 85cm (34in).

Souvenir de A. Millet (Millet, 1924)
Fully double with deep Bengal-rose outer petals and carmine-rose inner petals which slowly turn to salmon-rose. All the petals have a slightly paler edge. Free flowering with a strong spicy fragrance. It has been suggested that there may be two forms of this variety; the one with darker flowers is considered to be the best. Mid- to late season. 63cm (25in).

Souvenir d'Haraucourt (Origin unknown)
Single lactiflora looking for all the world like the flower of a pink magnolia with massive rose-pink petals, sprinkled with carmine. The stamens are golden yellow. Midseason. 70cm (28in).

Souvenir de Louis Bigot (Dessert, 1913)
This lactiflora produces semi-double, globe-shaped flowers which are bright rose with carmine-red at the

base, changing to salmon-rose. The flowers have a spicy fragrance. Mid- to late season. 63cm (25in).

Starlight (Saunders, 1949)
Quadruple hybrid (*P. lactiflora*, *P. officinalis*, *P. macrophylla* and *P. mlokosewitschi*) bearing single ivory yellow flowers occasionally flushed with warmer tints and a cream and gold centre. Early season. 65cm (26in).

Steve Nickel (Krekler, 1980)
Single hybrid with wonderful single vivid china-rose flowers with clean white flares at the petal bases. Gold anthers have very long pale yellow filaments and the green pilose carpels have bright pink stigmata. Ivory disc lobes and dark green foliage. Early season. 90cm (36in).

Sunburst or Shaylor's Sunburst (Allison, 1931)
Japanese lactiflora with white guard petals tinted blush, fading to white surrounding yellow staminodes. Yellow-tipped carpels. Slightly fragrant, strong stems. Early season. 90cm (36in).

Sweet 16 (Carl G. Klehm, 1972)
Vigorous double lactiflora with large globular flowers. There are magenta, marbled guard petals, within which is a collar of narrow pale yellow staminodes with bright yellow roots. Above is a rounded mass of pale pink petals, mixed with narrow cream staminodes. The carpels (if present) are large, pale green and partly petaloid. Stamens are absent. Upright plant with slightly scented flowers. Midseason. 70cm (28in).

Sweetie (Krekler-Roy Klehm, 1977)
Japanese-flowered peony with outer petals flushed pink, while the inner staminodes are narrow, linear and creamy white. The centre of the flower is lightened by a hint of yellow. The stigmata are partly developed into carpelodes. They are much flattened and slightly twisted, pale green and edged with white. Fragrant. 45cm (18in).

Tango (Auten, 1956)
Single hybrid with cup-shaped, glossy orange-scarlet (R46B) flowers which have yellow anthers and red filaments. There are tomentose pale green carpels, pink stigmata and a pink disc. This is a pretty plant with unusual coloured flowers. Early season. 75cm (30in).

The Fawn (Wright)
Double lactiflora with pink flowers covered in darker pink speckles and streaks. The colour fades towards the edge of the petals. Midseason. 85cm (34in).

The Mighty Mo (Wild, 1950)
Double lactiflora bearing velvety carmine-red flowers with silvered edges. In the centre of the flower is a small mound of stamens, with a further ring of stamens hidden beneath the inner petals. The very small carpels are green with red stigmata. Free flowering, makes a good, long lasting, cut flower. Early season. 70cm (28in).

Thérèse (Dessert, 1904)
This variety opens initially as a semi-double saucer-shaped flower with magenta-rose petals and a ring of golden stamens surrounding a tight ball of unfurling inner petals. As the flower develops it becomes fully double with blush-white petals. The central petals are very small and irregular, surrounded by larger petals mixed with golden stamens. The outer petals remain flushed with magenta. All may be edged or streaked with carmine-red. There are white carpels and pink stigmata. This variety produces numerous side buds, fragrant. Midseason. 78cm (31in).

Tokio (Origin unknown but introduced by Dessert in 1910)
Japanese lactiflora with large cup-shaped, rose-pink guard petals surrounding a mass of large pale yellow staminodes. The staminodes have pink tips and buff edges. Carpels green with white base and pink tips. Vigorous and free flowering. Midseason. 1m (3ft).

Top Brass (Carl G. Klehm, 1968)
Very beautiful bomb-shaped lactiflora with large ivory white guard petals surrounding a mass of similarly coloured petaloids with a canary yellow collar, surmounted by a tuft of pink petals. The carpels are vestigial or developed into wavy carpelodes. Side buds extend the flowering season, vigorous. Midseason. To 1m (3ft).

Toro-no-maki (introduced by B.H. Farr before 1928)
Japanese lactiflora. Flowers have guard petals that are initially blush-pink but fade to pure white. The long staminodes are white, edged and tipped with gold with

a touch of pink on the inside of the tip. Carpels green-white with pink styles. Slightly fragrant. Midseason. 85cm (34in), but often shorter.

Torpilleur (Dessert, 1913)
Japanese lactiflora whose light crimson guard petals surround a mass of crimson staminodes tipped with yellow and pink. The carpels are green, pink at the base, with red stigmata. Vigorous and free flowering, slightly fragrant. Has a long flowering period. Midseason. 90cm (36in).

Tourangelle (Dessert, 1910)
Double flower of creamy white with a flesh-pink centre, flushed sulphur-yellow. Compact, slightly fragrant with weak stems which may need supporting. Prone to attack by thrips. Mid- to late season. 95cm (38in).

Tranquil Dove (Saunders)
Single hybrid with white petals edged lavender. The petals are slightly curled. The stamen filaments are magenta at the base fading to almost white higher up. The anthers are golden yellow. The pink carpels are tomentose with red stigmata. The flowers have a tendency to suffer from spots of intense lavender pigmentation, spoiling an otherwise pretty bloom. Glossy green foliage. Early season. 65cm (26in).

Triomphe de l'Exposition de Lille (Calot, 1865)
Double lactiflora with light shell-pink flowers speckled violet-rose. The guard petals gradually fade to white. Free flowering. Late season. 68cm (27in).

Umbellata Rosea (Dessert, 1895)
Originally called 'Sarah Bernhardt', this variety, which can still be found in older gardens under its original name, has fully double pink flowers with violet-rose guard petals. Free flowering. Early season. 80cm (32in).

Vivid Glow (Cousins-Roy Klehm)
Presumably a *P. macrophylla* sibling with very large leaves. Single rose-Bengal flowers with a white line on the reverse of the petals with yellow stamen filaments and green carpels with magenta stigmata. Early season. 100cm (40in).

Vogue (Hoogendoorn, 1949)
Double lactiflora with very large rose-pink flowers, to

35cm (14in) across. The reflexed petals have a silvery backing. Very free flowering, fragrant. Early season. 85cm (34in).

Walter Mains (Mains, 1956) GM
Japanese hybrid (*P. lactiflora* × *P. officinalis*) bearing large dark red guard petals surrounding a mound of golden-tipped red and white petaloids. Early season. 80cm (32in).

Westerner (Bigger, 1942) GM
Pretty Japanese lactiflora with orchid-pink guard petals surrounding a large mass of butter-yellow staminodes

'White Cap' is impressive for the contrast between the beetroot-red guard petals and the white staminodes. It could not be greater.

with wavy tips. Carpels pale green with purple stigmata. Strong stems. Midseason. 90cm (36in).

White Cap (Winchell, 1956) GM

Striking and rather expensive Japanese lactiflora with beetroot-red guard petals contrasting strongly with the creamy white staminodes. These staminodes fade to white with a hint of pink at the base; they are broad and toothed at the tip. The carpels are pale green with creamy yellow stigmata. Midseason. 80cm (32in).

White Innocence (Saunders, 1947)

Single hybrid (*P. emodi* × *P. lactiflora*) with small, but very beautiful, pure white flowers. The stamens form a tight ball around the pale green carpels. Free flowering with several flowers to a stem; produces a few seeds and needs staking. Very late season. To 1.5m (5ft).

White Wings (Hoogendoorn, 1949)

Single lactiflora with fluted petals surrounding a nice boss of deep yellow stamens with short filaments. The buds open with purple streaks on the outside, quickly fading to pure white. The petal margins are slightly serrated. The carpels are very pale green with magenta stigmata. Red stems, slightly fragrant. Late season. 83cm (33in).

Whitleyi Major, syn. 'Alba Grandiflora', 'The Bride' (Whitley, 1808) AGM

Many people consider this cultivated variety to be closest to the original wild plant of *P. lactiflora*. It has large single flowers which open blush-white but fade quickly to pure white. The stamens are yellow and the carpels green with white stigmata. The fragrant flowers are borne in clusters on slightly twisted stems. The leaves turn a vivid red in the autumn. Early season. 95cm (38in).

Whopper (Carl G. Klehm, 1980)

Bomb-shaped, double peony with enlarged pink guard petals surrounding a large mass of inner petals. The central petals are pink with a collar of flesh-pink petals. Pleasant scent, vigorous. Midseason. 85cm (34in).

Wiesbaden (Goos-Koenemann, 1911)

Very pretty double peony with a ring of magenta guard petals surrounding a mass of frilly pink petals. The guards are flushed magenta in the centre with parallel lines of pigmentation, fading towards the petal edges. The inner petals, which have a hint of flesh-pink, are mixed with concentric rings of stamens. Some of the stamens are developed into narrow pink petals with broad yellow filaments. The carpels are tiny, pale green with pink stigmata. Rose-scented. Early season. 80cm (32in).

Wilbur Wright (Kelway, 1909)

Single lactiflora with three rows of very dark crimson-maroon petals and a centre of yellow stamens. Probably the darkest single peony available. Mid- to late season. 1m (3ft).

William Gage (Krekler, 1975)

Hybrid peony with very large single, multi-petalled (a flower within a flower) flowers. Glossy currant-red buds open to crimson-scarlet – few peonies show such a dramatic change in colour. The carpels are green, flushed with pink towards the top and have pink stigmata. The filaments are purple-red. A central tuft of distorted petals hides a further group of stamens within the carpels. Robust with fragrant flowers. Early season. 83cm (33in).

Wilmington (Krekler)

Hybrid peony with single bright wine-red petals. The stamens have bright red filaments and yellow anthers. Fragrant, low growing with divided foliage. Early season. 40cm (16in).

Wind Chimes (Reath, 1984)

Single hybrid of *P. tenuifolia* (the other parent is unknown) with nodding deep lavender-pink flowers. The leaves are finely divided but broader than in *P. tenuifolia*. Very early season. 90cm (36in).

Zuzu (Krekler, 1955)

A semi-double lactiflora, initially with cup-shaped, very pale flesh-pink flowers, the large rounded petals on the outside becoming much narrower towards the centre. As the flower matures it loses its curved shape and flattens out, the colour fading to pure white. Gold stamens with very short filaments. Dark red carpels with paler stigmata. Pretty plant, slightly fragrant. Midseason. 85cm (34in).

7
TREE PEONIES

Few plants have approached the status that tree peonies hold in oriental art. The ancient Chinese called them *Hua Wang*: The King of Flowers, while the herbaceous peony was called *Hua Leang*: The King's Ministers. The most common Chinese name for the tree peony is Moutan (*Mow Tan*), a word thought to have been derived from Mütang, the mythical flower emperor. Other writers have suggested that the name means (more prosaically) 'male scarlet flower'.

As far as we know, the Moutan was first cultivated as an ornamental plant during the Sui Dynasty (AD581–618), a period of relative stability in China. Prior to this, it had only been used for medicinal purposes. During the following Tang Dynasty (AD618–906), the Moutan became extremely fashionable and was placed under the legal protection of the emperor. In Chinese art the Moutan represents the month of March and the season of spring. Summer is represented by the lotus flower, autumn by the chrysanthemum and winter by the plum.

The Ming Dynasty (AD1368–1644) and the Kang Hsi period (AD1662–1796) produced exquisite art which was widely copied when it reached Europe. Consequently many items of porcelain, fabrics or furniture of European origin are decorated with paintings and other representations of tree peonies. The Moutan was also eulogised in verse, painted on walls and printed on to silk. When the Imperial court was moved to Peking by the Emperor Yung-Lo (AD1360–1424), he ordered his courtiers to pay an annual pilgrimage to see the tree peonies flowering in the old Imperial Palace at Nanking.

The flowers of the Japanese tree peony 'Duchess of Marlborough' are a wonderful flesh-pink.

In about AD734 the tree peony reached Japan, where the Japanese called it the Boutan (later Botan). It was quickly adopted by them and given royal status, together with the cherry tree and lotus flower. The Japanese approached the breeding of the tree peony in a different way to the Chinese, and this is reflected in the more elegant and subtle blooms of their plants. Chinese tree peonies tend to have heavier blooms with numerous petals, Japanese ones are less double or more frequently semi-double. The traditional Japanese approach to growing tree peonies is also very different from that of the Chinese. They are treated with reverence and grown in a situation where they are isolated from other plants.

The first contact Europeans had with tree peonies was when the Dutch East India Company sent explorers from Canton to Peking in 1656. There they saw amazing flowers in white, yellow and red, which they described as being like those of roses, but without any thorns. A century later Sir Joseph Banks, who had seen paintings of these tree peonies, asked Alexander Duncan whether he could obtain them for the Royal Gardens at Kew (later the Royal Botanic Gardens). Banks had been instrumental in helping Duncan to obtain his post as a surgeon with the British East India Company. After much difficulty Duncan was able to send a plant to Banks in 1787, which arrived at Kew in 1789.

The new arrival (subsequently named 'Banksii') caused great interest but attempts to obtain other varieties proved to be almost impossible. It has been suggested that the Chinese resorted to many devious methods to prevent their tree peonies being shipped abroad. There were stories of the roots being boiled and the viable buds being cut out of the stems. However, the most likely reason for their inability to obtain plants was more prosaic. Although for much of the year the staff of the British East India Company were based at Canton, once the ships for Britain were despatched in February, the staff left for the cooler climes of Macao; all had gone by March. Shortly after they had left, the tree peonies arrived!

They were grown in northern China and transported to the southern parts of the country in the spring. The climate in the south was far too hot for the peonies to survive the summer and after flowering they were simply thrown away. It must have been very frustrating for the early collectors. The other major problem was that at this time it was very difficult for foreigners to travel into the interior of China.

There were many further attempts to import tree peonies into England, but by 1826 only five varieties had been successfully introduced, plus three that had been raised from their seed. In 1834 Robert Fortune, the great plant hunter, was sent to China by the Royal Horticultural Society. He made four trips to the country and soon discovered that each district had its own varieties of tree peony. In 1846 he returned to England with 25 different varieties. These were propagated by British nurseries and became generally available in the 1860s. Fortune's collection was by far the best to have reached Europe and a number of European nurserymen used his plants to raise their own varieties. Chinese tree peonies were most popular during the period from 1860–1890, after which time Japanese tree peonies became available and effectively superseded the Chinese.

It is difficult to tell how many varieties of tree peony were produced in Europe at the beginning of the twentieth century. Nurseries such as Kelways listed a large number, but whether the majority of these were renamed Chinese or Japanese plants is difficult to say. Interested gardeners have always found it difficult to resist the temptation to grow their own seedlings, but few of these plants were ever propagated. The great majority of the plants available in Europe today are imported from Japan or China. Tree peony growing in Japan is a 'cottage garden industry' with numerous small growers selling their grafts through large co-operatives.

Tree peonies are invariably propagated by grafting on to a *P. lactiflora* rootstock, a process which has been used by the Chinese since at least AD1000. It is quite common for young Japanese tree peonies to be supplied in pots with the top of the rootstock showing: the graft union between the rootstock and the scion (the piece of tree peony) must be planted below soil level if the plant is to thrive. After a period of time, the scion should produce its own roots and cease to be reliant upon the rootstock, which will eventually wither away. Once established, the tree peony should produce new shoots from below the ground, ultimately forming a low rounded bush. Tree peonies take a varying amount of time to become established after initial planting. A new plant may make slow growth for a number of years and will then suddenly grow substantially over a short period of time.

CHINESE TREE PEONIES
The old varieties of Chinese tree peony have one major fault: the flowers are often so double that they hang down among the foliage. Even the popular 'Chromatella' suffers from this imperfection. By comparison, the majority of Japanese varieties are semi-double, or if double have fewer petals than their Chinese equivalents; their stems are also stronger. This made the Japanese tree peonies far more popular in the West. Many of the older Chinese tree peony varieties are still available from the French nursery Pivoines Michel Rivière. They grow to a height of 3m (10ft) and flower in mid-spring.

Banksii
The first tree peony to be introduced into Europe, this was named after Sir Joseph Banks. It was planted in the Royal Gardens at Kew in 1789 and first flowered in 1793. By 1829 the original plant had grown to a height of 2.4m (8ft) and measured 3m (10ft) across. It survived until 1842, when it was destroyed during the construction of a new building. Joseph Sabine (1826) described it as having very double flowers. 'The petals are slightly tinged with blush, becoming nearly white at the edges, and marked at the base with purplish red.' This variety should still be available, it is free flowering and very hardy.

Bijou de Chusan
(Chinese, introduced by Fortune 1846)
Blush-white flowers with a rose-coloured centre.

Comtesse de Tuder (pre-1866)
Double, bomb-shaped flower with blush-pink petals. Enlarged and spreading guard petals surround the base of the flower. Very free flowering.

Duchesse de Morny (France)
Very large, double, bowl-shaped, pale pink flowers with a deeper centre. Free flowering.

Fragrans Maxima Plena (France)
Very double flowers with tightly packed flesh-pink petals. Fragrant.

Reine des Violettes (Chinese, introduced by Fortune)
Double, large and very full violet-coloured flowers.

Reine Elizabeth (Cas., before 1846)
This is a vigorous variety with very large double, bowl-shaped flowers. The petals are salmon-pink and slightly flushed with copper red pigmentation. 2m (6ft).

Triomphe de Van der Maelan (Van der Maelan, 1849)
Very regular double flower, bright pink with a deeper centre. Very free flowering.

RECENT CHINESE VARIETIES
With the notable exception of the plants introduced by Robert Fortune, the majority of Chinese tree peonies were raised by European nurseries during the latter part of the nineteenth century. A few new varieties appeared from China but in the main the Chinese managed to keep their tree peonies to themselves. Through most of the twentieth century there has been little interest in Chinese cultivated tree peonies and the creation of the People's Republic has made access to China extremely difficult. However, even during this political turmoil, Chinese gardeners have continued to raise new varieties and propagate the old. Recently, Chinese tree peonies have enjoyed something of a renaissance in the West, partly due to the labours of Kasha and David Furman of Cricket Hill Garden in Connecticut, USA.

During the last few years the Chinese have become aware of the economic potential of their flowers and are now actively promoting their export. The majority of peony production is centred around the town of Heze (formerly Caozhou) in Shandong Province. Tree peonies have been grown in this area of the Huan He Valley since 1550. The Chinese currently offer in excess of 480 varieties. The International Peony Festival is held in China every year from the 20th to 26th of April.

While the majority of the cultivars offered are still double, there are now a few single and semi-double varieties available. Many of these plants hold their flowers upright, thus rectifying one of the faults of the earliest introductions into Europe. The Chinese plants seem to be more vigorous than their Japanese relatives, with several varieties capable of reaching a height of 3m (10ft). One unusual peony, Dou Lu (Pea Green) has flowers that are light pea-green when they open, turning to white as they mature, but they droop down among the foliage.

Da Jin Fen (Gold Dusted Pink)
Semi-double light pink flowers with darker pink veins. Relatively small flowers on a low growing plant. Early season. To 1.2m (4ft).

Da Ye Hu Die (Great Winged Butterfly)
An amazing plant with both red and white flowers on the same bush. Some of the flowers may have red and white petals. Fragrant. Midseason. 1.2m (4ft).

Fen Dian Bai (Phoenix White)
Single, fragrant, pure white flowers. Thought to be a cultivar of *P. ostii.* Early season. To 3m (10ft).

Luoyang Hong (Luoyang Red)
Double red flowers, to 25cm (10in) wide, with perfectly placed petals and yellow centres. Midseason. To 3m (10ft).

Qing Long Wo Mo Chi
(Green Dragon Lying on a Chinese Inkstone)
Semi-double flowers with dark purple petals, turning to green at the base with very dark flares. Vigorous, flowers up to 25cm (10in) across. Fragrant. Midseason. 3m (10ft).

Sheng Dan Lu
(Taoist Stove Filled with the Pills of Immortality)
Semi- to fully double pink and pale red flowers up to 25cm (10in) across. Late season. To 3m (10ft).

Wu Long Peng Sheng
(Black Dragon Holds a Splendid Flower)
Double, globe-shaped flower with magenta-red petals. A few green petals in the centre of the flower. Fragrant. Late season. 3m (10ft).

Ying Luo Bao Zhu (Necklace with Precious Pearls)
Very double, coral-red flowers with silver edging. Late season. 1.2m (4ft).

Yao-huang (Yao's Family Yellow)
Very large, fully double creamy yellow flowers, to 25cm
(10in) across. Enlarged guard petals surround a raised
mass of petals. Midseason. To 3m (10ft).

Zhao Fen (Zhao's Family Pink)
Flowers varying from single to very double. Light flesh-
pink with incurved petals. Vigorous. Late season. To
2.4m (8ft).

Zhuang Yuan Hong (Number One Scholar's Red)
Semi-double to double magenta-pink flowers. Midseason. To 2.4m (8ft).

Zhu Sha Lei (Cinnabar Ramparts)
Semi-double, mid-pink flowers with darker pink flares
at the base of the crinkled petals. The flowers are fragrant, but rather small at 15cm (6in) across. Early season. 1.2m (4ft).

JAPANESE TREE PEONIES
There are hundreds of tree peony varieties available in
Japan, but to the western eye many look very similar,
particularly the double reds. Only a limited selection of
Japanese tree peonies have been exported to Europe
and America and it is rare for a western nursery to list
more than twenty or so varieties, but do not be put off
by this: they are usually the best. Many, such as 'Kamada
Fuji' and 'Godaishu', are widely available.

Attempts to make the correct translation of names
from the Japanese has caused considerable problems,
different spellings may be found and to make matters
worse there are two different ways of translating names;
for example the name 'lion' is very popular and may be
spelt as 'jisi' or 'jishi'. The definitive translations are
those in *The Peonies* (Wister, 1995) and *The Moutan or
Tree Peony* (Haworth-Booth, 1963).

Until comparatively recently the Japanese grafted
their tree peonies on to the roots of field-grown tree
peony seedlings. The problem with this technique was
that the rootstock was often more vigorous than the
grafted scion. Many of the plants that were imported
from Japan during the latter part of the nineteenth century ultimately died unless suckers were removed at an
early stage.

Japanese tree peonies do not grow as high as their
Chinese cousins, rarely exceeding 2m (6ft). They

flower for 2–3 weeks, although inclement weather may
shorten this, from mid- to late spring, depending on the
climate in which they are growing.

Asahi-no-sora (Sky at Sunrise)
Semi-double, light pink flowers with a reddish purple
sheath and stigmata. Low growing. Midseason. To
90cm (36in).

Azuma-kagami (Mirror of the East)
Semi-double, small dark carmine-crimson flowers with
a large centre of stamens. Dwarf growing and relatively
weak plant. Late midseason.

Banzai-mon (Gate of Cheers)
Semi-double, medium-sized, carmine-red flowers with
creamy white stripes on the outer edge of the outer
petals. Midseason.

Bifuku-mon (Beautiful Gate)
Beetroot-purple flowers with a warmer centre and black
flares. The filaments are also beetroot-purple, the
anthers pale yellow. The sheath is white.

Fuji-no-mine (Snow Clad Fuji)
Fragrant, semi-double white flowers with fringed edges
and some small petaloids in the centre. The lower part
of the stamen filaments and the stigmata are pale pink.
Free flowering. Early season. 1m (3ft).

Gessekai (Kingdom of the World or Moonworld)
Vigorous with large double, white flowers and very symmetrical fringed and crinkled petals.

Godaishu (Giant Globe)
Semi-double with large pure white flowers, almost
devoid of flares except for a hint of pink at the base of
the petals. The sheath is ivory white and remains intact
for a long time. The carpels are greyish green, tomentose and have ivory white stigmata. The sepals are pale
green, slightly striped with white marks. The foliage is
slightly tomentose.

Gunpo-den (Temple adorned with Many Flowers)
Semi-double tree peony producing bright purple flow-
ers. Both the stigmas and the sheath are reddish purple.
Midseason.

Haku-banriu (Many White Dragons)
Semi- to fully double bearing very large white flowers with wavy petaloids. The sheath is creamy white, the anthers golden yellow with white filaments. The leaves are very broad for a Japanese tree peony. Vigorous. Late season.

Hakuo-jisi
(King of White Lion or White Tailed Lion)
Double white flowers with very faint purple flares at the base of the petals and a nice centre of yellow stamens. The sheath is white. This is a vigorous plant with slightly glossy leaves which turn bright red in the autumn. Midseason.

Hana-kisoi (Floral Rivalry)
Very beautiful semi-double tree peony with deep cherry-blossom-pink flowers. Each petal has varying amounts of colour: some are almost white, others mainly pink. The flowers open from nice rose-shaped

'Hakuo-jisi' has white flowers with faint purple flares.

buds. Vigorous with bright green foliage, white sheath and stigmata.

Hinode-sekai (World of the Rising Sun)
Semi-double, carmine-red flowers, with crinkled petals and green exposed carpels. Dwarf plant. Late midseason.

Hino-tobira (Passage of The Sun)
Single carmine-red flowers with long narrow petals, showing a pronounced gap between each petal. The flowers have red carpels and a small number of yellow anthers. Relatively weak growing. Late midseason.

Hoki
Semi-double, large, very bright red flowers with well shaped blooms. Sheath red and globe-shaped. Vigorous with light green foliage. Midseason.

PLATE XII All flowers are shown at approximately ¼ size

P. 'Taisho-no-hokori'

P. 'Kaow'

Horakumon (Invitation to Abundant Pleasure)
Semi-double tree peony with beetroot-purple outer
petals and a warmer red centre. The sheath is white
with a hint of purple. The filaments are purple, the
anthers pale yellow. Yellowish green pilose carpels have
salmon-pink stigmata.

Howki (Charming Age)
Fully double, cardinal-red flowers with a hint of pink;
very similar to 'Kozan' but with more petals. Numerous
green carpels with purple stigmata. There are only a few
stamens, which have purple filaments. The sheath is
purple. Free flowering.

Impu-mon (Gate of Impu or Gate of Opulence)
Semi-double, carmine-red flowers that are medium-
sized with exposed pale green carpels. It has green leaf
stalks. Low growing.

Iwato-kagura (Sacred Dance of Iwato)
Double, medium-sized, crimson flowers with silver-

'Horakumon' has flowers of deepest beetroot-purple.

edged petals. The inner petals are asymmetric, crinkled
and serrated at the tips. Vigorous with large leaflets.
Midseason.

Jitsu-getsu-nishiki
(Sun and Moon Brocade or Finest Brocade)
Double, medium-sized, crimson-pink flowers. The
outer petals may have a thin white edging and a few vertical white stripes. Sheath red. Midseason.

Kagura-jishi (Sacred Lion Dance)
Double, carmine-red flowers with fringed petals which
fade at the edges after full bloom. The inner petals are
quite asymmetrical. Vigorous with long and wavy
leaflets. Midseason.

Kamada-fuji (Wisteria at Kamada)
Very large semi-double, magenta flowers. Considered
to be very beautiful. Well recommended.

Kamada-nishiki (Kamada Brocade)
Fully double, lilac-pink flowers darkening towards the centre of the flower. The edges of the petals fade as the flower becomes older.

Kaow or **Kao** (King of Flowers)
Dramatic variety with very large semi-double, cardinal-red flowers. The centre is a darker shade of red with a hint of purple at the base of the petals. The sheath is creamy white, speckled with magenta. The carpels are tomentose and have flesh-coloured stigmata. The stamen filaments are reddish purple. Although very dramatic, the flowers fade fairly quickly to a purplish pink. This is counterbalanced by the free flowering nature of the plant which produces a succession of deep red flowers. Leaf stalks are pink. Late midseason.

Kenrei-mon (Gate of Kenrei)
Semi-double, purple-red flowers and black-purple flares. The innermost petals are nicely ruffled. Rather sparse foliage. Midseason.

Koku-ryu-nishiki (Black Dragon Brocade)
Double, blackish purple flowers turning deep purple in strong sunshine. The petals are crinkled, a few have a white rim. Pale green carpels have salmon-pink stigmata. Dark blackish purple stamen filaments and yellow anthers.

Naniwa-nishiki (Naniwa Brocade)
Very free-flowering with medium-sized, semi-double, rosy pink flowers. The outer petals have an unusual creamy white edge, merging into the red with numerous stripes. The inner petals are much smaller than the outer. Vigorous. Midseason.

Niigata-otomenomai
Large semi-double flowers are pure white with diffuse flares of a magenta shade. The petals have ruffled tips. It may have ten or more yellowish green pilose carpels with yellow stigmata. This is a very pretty and desirable tree peony.

Rimpo (Bird of Rimpo)
Semi-double, maroon-red flowers with slightly ruffled petals. Cream carpels and stigmata enclosed by an ivory sheath. Fragrant.

Shin-tenchi (New Heaven and Earth)
Very large semi-double, orchid-pink flowers fading towards the outer edge of the petals. Red, arrow-shaped flares. Green carpels with purple stigmata.

Taisho-no-hokori (Pride of Taishow Dynasty)
Wonderful semi-double tree peony with deep strawberry-red flowers and mauve flares. The flowers may have an occasional white stripe.

Yachiyo-tsubaki (Eternal Camellias)
One of the best pink tree peonies with semi-double, phlox-pink flowers. The outside of the petals is slightly lighter, while on the inside their bases are tinted magenta. The pink colour is more intense in the veins. There are only a few stamens with yellow anthers and purple filaments. The carpels are green with magenta stigmata and a purple sheath. Very vigorous and free flowering. Slightly glaucous foliage.

Yae-zakura
(Very Double Cherry or Host of The Cherry Blossom)
Very large single or semi-double flowers of cherry-blossom-pink with magenta veins, concentrated at the base of the petals. Green carpels and red stigmata.

Yoyo-no-homare
(Glory of Many Generations or King of Peonies)
Semi-double, medium-sized, bright magenta-pink flowers with yellow anthers and a red sheath. Relatively weak growing plant with long leaf stalks and sparse foliage.

KELWAYS TREE PEONIES
While Kelways of Langport are best known for their herbaceous peonies, they have been selling tree peonies for over a century. Their old catalogues show that they were breeding and propagating their own varieties in the early 1900s. While a number of these varieties may still exist in British gardens, they are no longer available for sale. Kelways currently offer a number of Japanese cultivars, which have been known by their English synonyms for many years. They flower in mid-spring and attain a height of 1.5–2m (5–6ft).

Alice Palmer
Semi-double with narrow mauve petals, edged with white and streaked with reddish purple along the

centre. Pale purple sheath, greyish green carpels. White filaments flushed with magenta at the base. Red stigmata and golden stamens. Vigorous.

Cardinal Vaughan

Beautiful semi-double tree peony with deep purplish red flowers, fading to red, particularly in the centre. The inner petals are incurved, the outer have a slightly paler margin. The colour lasts well. The stigma and sheath are white. The sepals striped with reddish purple.

Duchess of Kent

Fully double, pinkish red flowers which have a darker red centre. The stamens remain hidden until the flowers are fully open from tulip-shaped buds. Free flowering and vigorous with the blooms held well above the foliage.

Duchess of Marlborough

Semi-double, lovely cherry-blossom-pink flowers. White sheath and stigmata. This is one of the very best Japanese tree peonies with wonderful ruffled petals. Vigorous.

Glory of Huish

Semi-double, brilliant crimson-red flowers with a bright golden centre. The petals form a very symmetrical saucer-shaped flower. Sheath red.

Lord Selborne

Semi-double, very pale blush-pink, cup-shaped flowers. The petals retain their colour and have slightly paler margins. Relatively small flowers with green carpels and pink stigmata. Red sheath.

Mischka

Beautiful single tree peony with violet petals, large purple flares and magenta veins. The colour fades towards the petal edges. The stigmata and the sheath, which persists for a long time, is dark red. The stamens have yellow anthers supported by violet filaments with a white top.

Mrs. Shirley Fry

Single or semi-double with pure white petals and a tight centre of golden yellow stamens.

Mrs. William Kelway

Semi-double, creamy white flowers with ruffled petals

'Raphael' has symmetrical deep flesh-pink flowers.

open from tulip-shaped buds. Has a few stamens and a creamy white sheath, one of the best white tree peonies.

Raphael

Semi-double, cup-shaped flowers with warm flesh-pink petals and silvered edges. The flowers often open on naked stems before the foliage develops. The stigmata and sheath are reddish purple. A very beautiful variety with a few golden anthers.

Superb

Semi-double with bright cherry-red flowers, slightly more pink than those of 'Glory of Huish'. Green carpels, red stigmata and a red sheath.

LEMOINE AND HENRY HYBRID TREE PEONIES

While Victor and Emile Lemoine are best known for their work with herbaceous peonies they were also the first to produce a successful cross between a Moutan tree peony (*P. × suffruticosa* Agg.) and *P. lutea*, thus producing the first yellow hybrid tree peonies. The new plants caused amazement when they were first shown. This cross was not as easy as it might appear as Moutan tree peonies flower approximately one month before *P. lutea*. To cross-pollinate the two species successfully required storing the pollen of the Moutan tree peony until the yellow peony flowered. The Lemoine's achievement was celebrated in 1920 when Rehder coined a new term for these hybrids: *P. × lemoinei*.

One of the most famous of the Lemoine hybrid tree peonies is 'Alice Harding' which was subsequently used by the Japanese breeder Toichi Itoh as one of the parents for his intersectional hybrids (see p.143). At approximately the same time as the Lemoines were working, Professor Louis Henry (1853–1903) achieved the same result, raising two varieties 'Mme. Louis Henry' and 'Souvenir de Maxime Cornu'. The latter was named (slightly tongue in cheek) after Monsieur Maxime Cornu, a famous horticulturist of the time, who had previously stated that *P. lutea* would never be successful as a garden plant. While the majority of lutea hybrids are relatively low-growing plants which seldom exceed a height of 90cm (36in), some may reach 1.5m (5ft). They flower in late spring.

Alice Harding, syn. 'Kinko' (Lemoine, 1935)
Double, ruffled, bright lemon-yellow flowers with yellow stamens. Unusually for a tree peony, this variety can be propagated by division. The flowers are somewhat hidden by the leaves. Low growing.

Chromatella, syn. 'Kinshi' (Lemoine, 1928)
Very double yellow flowers with carmine-rose edged petals. Said to be very vigorous but badly let down by the drooping flowers. Mildly fragrant. Originated as a sport of 'Souvenir de Maxime Cornu'.

L'Espérance, syn. 'Kintei' (Lemoine,1909)
Single or semi-double flowers of primrose-yellow with carmine-red flares and 8–10 carmine-edged petals. A very pretty flower with golden anthers and red filaments.

Madame Louis Henry (Henry, 1919)
(*P. lutea* × 'Reine Elizabeth') Rather loose semi-double pale yellow flowers are heavily flushed towards the outside with red. The smaller inner petals have dark red flares, the outer petals are larger and incurved. Large mass of golden stamens.

Sang-no-Lorrain (Lemoine, 1939)
Semi-double, glossy deep crimson-red flowers with a dark edge around the petals and dark red flares. The flowers are very fragrant. A vigorous hybrid between *P. delavayi* and a Moutan tree peony.

Souvenir de Maxime Cornu, syn. 'Kinkaku' (Henry, 1919)
(*P. lutea* × 'La Ville de St. Denis') This is a readily available plant with double, sulphur-yellow flowers, edged with buff and cerise-pink. The flowers can measure up to 25cm (10in) across but nod and have a tendency to be hidden by the foliage. Very popular, slightly perfumed.

SAUNDERS HYBRID TREE PEONIES

A. P. Saunders is probably best known for his famous line of yellow hybrid tree peonies, obtained in the main by crossing Japanese tree peonies with *P. lutea*. Saunders found the very double flowers of the typical tree peony unattractive and had a preference for single and semi-double varieties. The presence of stolons in a number of the members of this group suggests that he also used *P. potanini* in his hybridization work. Regrettably few of these hybrids are available from European nurseries but they can be obtained from the American suppliers listed on page 157. While some of these plants are outstanding, many are rather bland with somewhat muddy colours. Bearing in mind their high price, I recommend that potential buyers should see a flowering plant before taking the plunge and ordering.

Age of Gold (1948) GM
Semi-double, warm yellow flowers with ruffled petals, sometimes faintly edged with pink. The petals darken towards the centre of the flower and have small red flares. The anthers are golden yellow, the short filaments red. Numerous carpels with pink stigmata, are enclosed by a pale lilac sheath. Midseason. 1m (3ft).

Alhambra (1948)
Semi-double with ruffled golden yellow petals and dark red flares. Narrow twisted yellow petals may appear in the centre of the flower along with golden anthers and

yellow filaments. There are greyish green carpels and cream stigmata and sheath. One of the best yellow tree peonies. Midseason. 1.2m (4ft).

Amber Moon (1948)

Single, primrose-yellow flowers with pink-edged petals and small raspberry-red flares. The leaves are similar to those of P. lutea var. ludlowii. Golden anthers are on short red filaments. The carpels are green with yellow stigmata, enclosed by an ivory white sheath. Vigorous. Midseason, but may flower again in late summer. 1.2m (4ft).

Argosy (1928)

The first of the Saunders P. lutea hybrids, this has single flowers of bright lemon-yellow with 10–14 petals and pointed crimson flares at their base. Crimson filaments and cream stigmata are enclosed by a creamy white sheath. This variety has been illustrated in several books but is almost impossible to obtain. Midseason. 1.5m (5ft).

Black Panther (1948)

Rather untidy semi-double flowered peony producing ruffled mahogany-red flowers with distorted petals in the centre. There are bright yellow stamens with red filaments, red stigmata and a dark red sheath. Stoloniferous, spreading plant. Midseason. 1m (3ft).

Black Pirate (1935)

Semi-double, mahogany-red flowers with satin-textured petals and very dark red flares. Bright yellow stamens sit on dark red filaments and there are bright pink stigmata and a lilac sheath. Glossy broad foliage. Midseason. 1m (3ft).

Canary (1940)

A single P. lutea hybrid with very bright yellow flowers. The petals are broad and nicely rounded with small maroon flares. The anthers are golden yellow, supported by short dark red filaments. The stigmata and the sheath are cream. The leaves are slightly glossy and tinted red. Vigorous with the flowers held well above the foliage. Midseason. 1.2m (4ft).

Chinese Dragon (1950) GM

Semi-double, purplish red flowers with small black-red flares. Yellow anthers on dark red filaments. Crimson stigmata and a purple sheath. Vigorous with purplish red stems when young. Midseason. 90cm (36in).

Goldfinch (1949)

One of the prettiest of the yellow hybrids, 'Goldfinch' has single pale yellow flowers without any flares. The stamens have large yellow anthers and red filaments. The carpels are greyish green with pale yellow stigmata. Large flowers, well worth growing. Midseason.

Gold Sovereign (1949)

Semi-double, bright gold flowers with small dark flares. Filaments are gold, the stigmata and sheath cream. Vigorous, with medium-sized flowers held well above the leaves. Midseason. 1.1m (3½ft).

Golden Hind (1948–50)

Particularly large flowers, to 20cm (8in) across, are semi-double to double and creamy yellow with as a many as 100 petals. The flares are very dark red and the petals may be edged with pink. Numerous carpels with creamy pink stigmata and a lilac sheath. Robust with broad leaves and very large flower buds. Very desirable. Midseason. 90cm (36in).

Golden Mandarin (1952)

Double, rosette-shaped flowers with pink-edged yellow petals and raspberry-red flares. Some of the stamens are developed into petaloids. The anthers are yellow with red filaments. The carpels are pale green with pink stigmata, enclosed by a dark red sheath. Flowers held well above the foliage. Midseason.

Harvest (1948)

Semi-double, rather full, golden yellow flowers with pink-tinged edges. The central petals are much smaller than the outer ones, all have crimson flares. The anthers are golden yellow with light red filaments. The stigmata are pink and the sheath is lilac. Foliage bronzy green foliage. Midseason. 93cm (37in).

Hesperus (1949)

Unusual flower whose petals are golden yellow in the centre turning red towards the margins and with deep pink veins. The petals are nicely arranged around a small centre of green carpels with pink stigmata. The sheath is dark red. There are golden anthers and short red filaments. Midseason, may flower again in late summer. 1.1m (3½ft).

High Noon (1952) GM

Semi-double, bright lemon-yellow flowers with crimson red flares have nicely arranged petals that are slightly turned into the centre. Anthers golden yellow, filaments light red. Stigmata and sheath cream. Tall. Midseason, flowers again in late summer. To 1.3m (4½ft).

Marchioness (1942)

Single flowers with apricot-coloured petals, fading to golden yellow at the edges. They are well rounded and slightly wavy with raspberry-red flares. Green carpels with pink stigmata and a pale lilac sheath. One of the most attractive of Saunders's lutea hybrids. Midseason. 90cm (36in).

Mystery (1948)

Single, very attractive flower of a most unusual ivory lilac strongly marked with purple veins and with bright crimson flares. Green carpels and cream stigmata are surrounded by a creamy lilac sheath. Golden anthers and light red filaments. Broad, slightly glossy green leaves. Midseason. 90cm (36in).

Renown (1949)

Single, copper-red flowers with darker flares and a hint of gold in the petals. Golden stamens with short red filaments. The sheath is lilac, surrounding green carpels with cream-coloured stigmata. Flowers in late spring and again in midsummer. Midseason. 1.1m (3½ft).

Roman Gold (1941)

Single, bright yellow flowers with 10–12 pointed, slightly crinkled petals with small crimson flares. There are creamy yellow stigmata and a cream sheath. Numerous stamens with red filaments. Free flowering. Midseason. 1.1m (3½ft).

Savage Splendor (1950)

Single flowers with wavy, ivory petals, edged and heavily suffused with purple pigmentation, with purple veins and strongly tinted with gold. Dark flares. Yellow stamens are without anthers but have crimson filaments.

Pink stigmata and a reddish purple sheath. Very unusual colouring. Midseason. 1.2m (4ft).

Spring Carnival (1944)

Single, golden yellow flowers edged with pink. Wavy petals strongly marked with red and pink veins. Large deep red flares. Bright yellow stamens and green carpels with red stigmata. Midseason.

Thunderbolt (1948)

Single with deep crimson-red flowers. The petals are shiny, without flares but sometimes streaked with black or scarlet. Yellow anthers are held on short red filaments. Green carpels with magenta stigmata and a red sheath. Nodding flowers held well above the finely dissected foliage. Free flowering. Midseason. 1.1m (3½ft).

Tiger Tiger (1948)

Single with purple-rose flowers and very dark flares. The filaments are purple-rose, the stigmata creamy pink and the sheath purple-crimson. There are approximately ten carpels. The foliage and stems of this variety are bronze-coloured. Midseason. 1.2m (4ft).

Vesuvian (1948)

Cardinal-red double flowers, with numerous petals, rather hidden by the foliage. They look like extremely large flowers of *P. delavayi* (one of its parents). Stamens are few, with pale yellow anthers and short red filaments. Carpels pale green with purple, crozier-shaped, stigmata. Midseason. 75cm (30in).

THE GRATWICK AND DAPHNIS HYBRIDS

William Gratwick (1904–1988) worked with A. P. Saunders grafting his tree peonies and later started to hybridize peonies for himself in his nursery at Pavilion, in New York State. A number of his tree peonies, such as 'Guardian of the Monastery' and 'Companion of Serenity' are particularly beautiful. Later in his life Gratwick entered into a partnership with Nassos Daphnis an artist from New York. Together they produced a series of dramatic hybrids using Moutan tree peonies and *P. lutea*; these plants have a number prefixed with the letter D.

Ariadne (D-304)

One of the best Daphnis tree peonies with petals of a

peach-colour with magenta edges and dark red flares and suffused with dark red veins. The sheath is peach-coloured, surrounding green carpels with salmon-pink stigmata. Stunning flower, spoilt only by its slightly drooping posture. Midseason.

Companion of Serenity (Gratwick)

Possibly one of the most beautiful tree peonies ever produced, this has semi-double, ruffled petals with pink veins, deeper pink flares and serrated margins. A ring of golden stamens with purple filaments surround an ivory white sheath. Early season.

Demetra (D-19)

Semi-double, yellow flowers with pink edges and maroon flares. The petals become progressively smaller towards the centre of the flower. The stamens have yellow and maroon filaments. The carpels are green with pink stigmata, enclosed by a maroon sheath. Midseason.

Gauguin (D-22)

This lutea hybrid almost defies description! It has single flowers with an overall impression of raspberry-red over amber (or is it the opposite?). The veins are deep raspberry-red and the flares very dark red. The petal edges are flushed with magenta; on the reverse, the outer petals are yellow with raspberry-red blotches. The sheath is dark pink, the stamen anthers large and yellow

The Daphnis hybrid 'Hephestos' has brick-red flowers.

and supported by dark red filaments. Named after Eugéne Gauguin who used brilliant colours in his paintings. Midseason. 1.2m (4ft).

Guardian of the Monastery (Gratwick)

Semi-double tree peony with large lavender petals and purple flares, yellow anthers and white filaments. Pale green carpels and cream stigmata are enclosed by a cream-coloured sheath. Very pretty flower with a large mass of yellow stamens. Vigorous. Midseason.

Hephestos (D-240)

Very large, semi-double, deep brick-red flowers with darker flares. Long narrow anthers with dark red filaments. The sheath is pink enclosing carpels with salmon-pink stigmata. Slightly nodding ruffled flowers. Fragrant. Midseason. 93cm (37in).

Icarus (D-254)

Single, vivid scarlet flowers with satiny, notched petals. The stamens have pale yellow anthers and long dark red filaments. Pale green carpels with red-edged stigmata are surrounded by a scarlet sheath. Striking plant with fragrant flowers. Midseason. 1m (3ft).

Iphigenia (D-303)

Large single flowers with two rows of ruby-red, rounded petals. The inner row are recurved with black flares, the outer ones have a white line on the reverse. The sheath is pink-magenta, surrounding pale green pilose carpels with magenta-pink stigmata. Pretty. Midseason. 93cm (37in).

Kronos (D-23)

Single or semi-double, burgundy-red flowers with darker flares. The sheath is pink, surrounding pale green carpels with salmon-pink stigmata. The stamens have pale yellow anthers and dark red filaments. Midseason. 96cm (36in).

Leda (D-308)

Stunning, semi-double, mauve-pink flowers with purple veins and maroon-red flares on very wavy petals. The sheath is cream and the stamen filaments dark red with anthers yellow. Carpels pale green with cream-coloured stigmata. Wonderful. Midseason. To 93cm (37in).

The Daphnis tree peony 'Tria' frequently has three flowers to a stem, hence its name.

Nike (D-368)
Single, pale yellow flowers flushed peach at the edges and with peach-coloured veins and relatively large maroon flares. Cream-coloured sheath surrounds pale green stigmata. Fragrant, leaves are glossy green. Late spring season. To 1.5m (5ft).

Persephone (D-26)
Semi-double flowers have notched, pale yellow petals marked with raspberry-red flares. The opening flowers look just like rose buds. Golden anthers and yellow filaments, pale green carpels and cream stigmata. A very pretty peony. Midseason.

Red Rascal (Gratwick)
Good, very deep red, single tree peony with cardinal-red petals and darker flares. The flowers have a hint of warmer red in the centre and yellow anthers on red filaments. The sheath is dark pink, surrounding green carpels with pink stigmata. Flowers are held well above the leaves. Midseason.

Tria (D-3)
Flowers deep yellow when they open, fading slightly with age, with raspberry-red flares. The anthers are long, yellow and supported on short red filaments. Pale green carpels with cream stigmata, enclosed by a pink sheath. Aptly named as it often has three flowers on each stem. Flowers are very large. Long flowering period. Midseason. 90cm (36in).

Zephyrus (D-203)
Double, ivory-yellow flowers flushed with mauve, particularly towards the edges. The colour can be so intense that some petals are completely mauve. The flares are large and purple. The carpels are large, green and tomentose with cream stigmata, enclosed by a cream sheath. Flowers are rather hidden by the foliage. Midseason. 90cm (36in).

OTHER HYBRID TREE PEONIES

The hybrid tree peonies of Lemoine, Gratwick and Saunders are very popular and well known. However, in addition to these, there are also a large number of very beautiful plants that have been produced by less prolific breeders. Sir Peter Smithers has undertaken a lot of breeding with 'Rock's Variety' (*P. rockii*) resulting in varieties such as 'Lydia Foote', which has retained the crimson flares of 'Rock's Variety' but has many more petals.

Baron Thyssen Bornemisza (Smithers, 1992)
Semi-double with very large (25cm/10in) mauve flowers and deeper flares. Vigorous and free flowering. The result of a cross between 'Kamada Fuji' and 'Rock's Variety'. Midseason.

Dojean (Smithers, 1990)
Cross between 'Hindo Desekai' and the British form of *P. rockii*. Semi-double, white flowers with red flares (much darker than *P. rockii*) and a crimson-pink sheath. Very vigorous with ruffled petals. Midseason.

Golden Era (Reath, 1984)
David Reath produced some wonderful peonies during his lifetime but this has to be one of the best. It has semi-double, pale yellow flowers with maroon flares and nicely rounded petals. The stamens have yellow anthers and purple filaments. Pilose carpels, with yellow stigmata, are enclosed by a pale yellow sheath. The strong stems hold the flowers well clear of the foliage. Late midseason. 1.1m (3½ft).

Hélène Martin (Jean Cayeux, 1980)
Single, very large white flowers with petals with a yellow stripe down the centre that merges into a carmine-red flare. The stamens have yellow anthers and red filaments. The carpels are greyish green enclosed by a cream-coloured sheath. Very pretty flower. The result of a cross between *P. potanini* var. *trollioides* and the Japanese tree peony 'Gessekai'. Midseason.

Ice Storm (Smithers, 1992)
Single tree peony bearing large, pure white flowers that may be up to 22cm (9in) wide, with strongly recurved petals and a large boss of yellow stamens. Late spring. Midseason.

Joseph Rock
see *P. rockii* (p.49).

Kishu Caprice (Sasaki, 1988)
Very pretty single tree peony with pale mauve flowers and imperial-purple flares on nicely rounded petals. Sheath and filaments are imperial-purple, and there are pointed golden anthers. Very attractive with large medium green leaves, highly recommended. Midseason. 1.5m (5ft).

Lydia Foote (Smithers, 1992)
Semi- to fully double, white flowers with red flares. Vigorous, the foliage has a red line along the leaf stalks. A descendant of 'Rock's Variety'. Late spring. Midseason.

Rock's Variety
see *P. rockii* (p.49).

Sybil Stern (Stern)
Very rare plant with deep red, glossy petals and pale mauve flares. Quite similar to 'Taisho-no-hokori'. Midseason. 1.5m (5ft).

'Kishu Caprice' has pale mauve flowers and deeper flares.

8

ITOH OR INTERSECTIONAL HYBRIDS

In 1948 Mr Toichi Itoh (pronounced Ee-toe) of Tokyo succeeded in crossing the yellow tree peony 'Alice Harding' with the double white herbaceous peony 'Kakoden'. His success in achieving what had hitherto seemed impossible caused quite a stir among peony breeders.

Nine of the 36 seedlings that resulted from his initial cross were of tree peony-like appearance, while the rest were herbaceous in character. Unfortunately Mr Itoh died in 1956, before the seedlings could flower. His assistant Shigao-Oshida continued his work, and in 1963 the plants flowered for the first time. Six of the seedlings turned out to be outstanding and included plants which have since been named 'Yellow Crown', 'Yellow Emperor', 'Yellow Heaven' and 'Yellow Dream'. These were the very first herbaceous peonies with deep yellow, double flowers. In 1949 Toichi Itoh had also experimented with the pollen of a pink tree peony ('Kagura Jishi') on 'Kakoden'. This resulted in two pink herbaceous hybrids by the names of 'Pink Heaven' and 'Pink Purity'. Regrettably these pink hybrids appear to have been lost to cultivation. An American grower, Louis Smirnow approached Mr Itoh's widow and obtained her permission to patent her husband's plants, as a consequence they are sometimes referred to as Itoh-Smirnow Hybrids.

Since the initial break was announced, a number of American breeders have succeeded in making crosses between *P. × suffruticosa* and other herbaceous species. The result has been the production of a new breed of herbaceous peony that exhibits a much wider range of colours than was hitherto thought possible. To reflect the significance of this development the American Peony Society has created a new 'Itoh double hybrid' category for peony flower shows in the USA. Some breeders do not recognise this name and refer to the plants instead as 'Intersectional Hybrids', ie. between the Sections MOUTAN and PAEON.

The majority of Itoh hybrid peonies are very robust plants, inheriting as they do certain features from their arborescent parent. Some are so vigorous that they have to be divided using a saw! The majority are very resistant to wind damage and their foliage remains green for longer than most of the cultivars of *P. lactiflora*. The other big advantage they have over their cousins is an extended flowering time: usually lasting into early summer. One Itoh breeder, Roger Anderson (1988) of Wisconsin, USA, has gone so far as to suggest that the Itoh hybrids are the peonies of the future. He has produced a fantastic range of hybrid peonies with flowers of red and yellow, orange and yellow, purple and white, and even tricolours with red, yellow and orange blooms. While some of these plants are far too outrageous to be generally accepted, his work does illustrate what may be achieved by careful selection of the seedlings of these crosses.

Itoh hybrids are herbaceous in character; their foliage is somewhat reminiscent of a tree peony but dies down in the winter. They do not grow as tall as tree peonies and rarely exceed 1m (3ft) in height. Itoh hybrids are still very expensive and, until recently, could only be obtained from the United States. They currently range in price from £25 ('Yellow Crown') to £60 ('Garden Treasure') each.

Itoh hybrid peonies come as a complete shock to most people. 'Garden Treasure' has rich yellow flowers and was the first to be awarded a Gold Medal.

There have been attempts to graft scions from Itoh hybrids on to *P. lactiflora* rootstocks, as would be done with tree peonies, but so far these have all met with failure. However, there can be little doubt that in the near future someone will succeed in micro-propagating these plants and thus make them more readily available for all. For the time being they remain plants for the connoisseur.

Bartzella (Anderson, 1986)
A semi-double to double Itoh with very large sulphur-yellow flowers, to 20cm (8in) across. The flowers have a lovely fragrance and red flares. Very free flowering and certain to make an impact in the future. 90cm (36in). Late midseason.

Border Charm (Hollingsworth, 1984)
Single to semi-double yellow flowers with slightly feathered and silvered tips to the petals and large red flares. This is a very hardy plant. Late midseason. 60cm (24in).

Cora Louise (Anderson, 1986)
Single or double flowers with pure white petals and lavender flares. Flowers are held well above the leaves. Slightly fragrant. Midseason. 60cm (24in).

First Arrival (Anderson, 1986)
Semi-double with flowers, 10–13cm (4–5in) across, that are lavender-pink when they open, fading to light pink. They have lavender-coloured flares. Absolutely wonderful, very free flowering when established. Late midseason. 60cm (24in).

Garden Treasure (Hollingsworth, 1984) GM
Probably the best of the Itoh hybrid peonies, the result of a cross between the tree peony 'Alice Harding' and a pale anemone-form lactiflora. The flowers are large, semi-double, with bright yellow petals and small scarlet flares. A larger plant than the original Itoh hybrids, it also has larger flowers. The carpels are greyish green with a pink sheath and have similarly coloured stigmata. It flowers over a long period and frequently has as many as 3 flowers to a stem. Very vigorous with slightly glossy dark green leaves. The first Itoh hybrid to be awarded the prestigious APS Gold Medal (1996). Mid- to late season. 75cm (30in).

Hidden Treasure (Seidl, 1989)
Single, sometimes double, medium yellow flowers with light red flares. Although it has strong stems, the flowers are usually partly hidden by the leaves. Hybrid between a creamy white lactiflora and the tree peony 'Alice Harding'. 50cm (20in). Midseason.

Prairie Charm (Hollingsworth, 1992)
Semi-double, light yellow flowers with prominent purple flares. The stigmas, filaments and sheath are creamy white. The carpels are green and the anthers yellow. The flowers have 20–30 petals, some of which may be irregularly toothed. A cross between 'Miss America' (*P. lactiflora*) and 'Alice Harding' (*P. × suffruticosa*). Midseason. 75cm (30in).

Rose Fantasy (Seidl, 1989)
Single, fuchsia-rose flowers with darker flares and silvered edges. Red stigmata and greyish green carpels are enclosed by a creamy white sheath. It suffers from rather weak stems and is suitable for cutting but is not a particularly good garden plant. A cross between a seedling of the lactiflora 'Harriet Olney' and the tree peony 'Chinese Dragon'. Midseason. 90cm (36in).

Viking Full Moon (Pehrson-Seidl, 1989)
Semi-double Itoh hybrid with light yellow flowers, 13–15cm (5–6in) across. These have two layers of petals with dull red flares. The stigmata are a creamy yellow and the carpels are grey-green. Early season. 75cm (30in).

White Emperor (Seidl, 1989)
Semi-double, white flowers with light purple flares. The stamens are cream, the carpels light grey with a cream-coloured sheath. This is a mutation of 'Yellow Emperor'. Early season. 75cm (30in).

Yellow Crown (Itoh-Smirnow, 1974)
Itoh hybrid with yellow, semi-double flowers and red flares. Quite readily available. Midseason. 90cm (36in).

Yellow Dream (Itoh-Smirnow, 1974)
Semi-double, large yellow flowers with very pale flares and slightly crinkled petals. The yellow stamens radiate out from the flower centre and surround green carpels. Strong, rigid stems, fragrant. Midseason. 90cm (36in).

Yellow Emperor (Itoh-Smirnow, 1974)
Semi-double flowers are yellow with light red flares at the base of the petals. The flowers are fragrant. Midseason. 90cm (36in).

Yellow Heaven (Itoh-Smirnow, 1974)
Semi-double, large, deep yellow flowers with dark red flares at the base of the petals and with green carpels

'Yellow Heaven' with its large yellow flowers was bred by Toichi Itoh, the first person to successfully hybridize tree peonies with herbaceous peonies.

and cream stigmata surrounded by a creamy white sheath. The plant forms a nice rounded bush and has extremely thick stems. Free flowering, perfumed. Midseason. 90cm (36in).

9

WHERE TO SEE PEONIES

UNITED KINGDOM

There are regrettably few good collections of peonies in the British Isles. However, many of the organisations and individual owners listed below are involved in extending their collections and the overall picture may be very different in ten years time. The majority of the existing herbaceous peonies that will be found in the gardens of large houses are likely to be those raised by the Kelway family.

David Austin Roses Ltd

While David Austin Roses are most famous for their modern 'English Roses', they also sell a wide range of peonies, many of which can be seen growing in their peony garden. There is a good selection of modern hybrids with striking specimens of 'Moonrise', 'Defender' and 'Ellen Cowley'. The company specializes in selling by mail order and offers a wide range of American hybrids and the older European varieties of *P. lactiflora*.
David Austin Roses Ltd, Albrighton,
near Wolverhampton, WV7 3HB.

Cambridge University Botanic Garden

This small botanic garden, covering approximately 16 hectares (40 acres), has a good collection of species peonies. The taxonomy on the labels is rather dated but the plants are nicely presented. Notable specimens include *P. × suffruticosa* 'Papaveracea', 'Perle Rosé' and 'Mai Fleuri'. The majority of the peonies are planted beside the path near the Bateman Street Gate and in the formal Order Beds.
Cambridge University Botanic Garden, Bateman Street,
Cambridge, CB2 1JF.

Docwra's Manor

A fascinating garden full of interesting plants, many of which were collected by its creators, John and Faith Raven. The soil has a high gravel content, is slightly alkaline and extremely well drained – perfect conditions for peonies. The majority of the peonies here are species, with only a limited number of cultivars. The garden has nice specimens of *P. delavayi*, *P. lutea* var. *ludlowii*, *P. mlokosewitschi* and *P. officinalis*. The garden has a wild feel to it with *Acanthus mollis*, *Eryngium giganteum*, *Cynara cardunculus* (Cardoon) and *C. scolymus* (Globe Artichoke) adding to the dramatic effect.
Docwra's Manor, Shepreth, Royston,
Hertfordshire, SG8 6PS.

Hidcote Manor

see under National Collections, p.151.

Highdown

The garden of the former home of Sir F. C. Stern, now owned by Worthing Borough Council, still contains a large number of his original plants, including a superb specimen of *P. rockii*. Self sown plants of *P. officinalis* ssp. *humilis* and *villosa* tumble over the rocks of the former quarry. (See also Peonies in the Garden, p.33)
Highdown, Goring-by-Sea, near Worthing,
West Sussex, BN12 6NY.

Hodnet Hall

The gardens at Hodnet Hall show what can be achieved with massed peonies. Twelve varieties of *P. lactiflora* are

An impressive way to grow peonies at Penshurst Place. The border is approximately 120 metres long.

arranged in a circle around the roses 'Comte de Chambord', 'Dagmar Hastrup', 'Felicia' and 'Penelope'.
Hodnet Hall, near Market Drayton, Shropshire, TF9 3NN.

Kelways Ltd

Formerly one of the most famous names in British horticulture, Kelways sadly went into receivership in 1993. The new owners have replanted the famous Paeony Valley with approximately 600 varieties of *P. lactiflora*. There is also a nice display garden with specimens of 'L'Espérance', 'Coral Charm' and a large number of *P. mlokosewitschi*. A range of peonies are available for sale.
Kelways Ltd., Langport, Somerset, TA10 9SL.

Penshurst Place.

The garden at Penshurst Place is one of the oldest in England, parts have remained almost unchanged since the sixteenth century. The peony border is in the formal walled garden and, at 120m (130yd), it is so long that peonies at one end start flowering one week after those at the other. (See also Peonies in the Garden p.33).
Penshurst Place, near Tonbridge, Kent, TN11 8DG (The Rt. Hon. Viscount De l'Isle).

Royal Botanic Garden Edinburgh

Edinburgh's botanic garden, established in 1670, is one of the oldest in the British Isles and has one of the most extensive collections of peony species in Britain. They are in island beds with shrubs and other herbaceous plants. Of particular interest is an ancient tree peony, descended from a plant collected by Alexander Duncan in the late eighteenth century and recently transplanted from his former home in Arbroath. This may be the oldest tree peony grown in the western world.
Royal Botanic Garden, Edinburgh, EH3 5LR.

Royal Botanic Garden Kew

This world renowned botanic garden has an extensive collection of peony species, most of which were grown from wild-collected seed. The majority of the species peonies are grown in Order Beds, a traditional system which reflects the relationship of plant families. At the time of writing, a new herbaceous bed was being planted next to Cumberland Gate. This will be entirely devoted to peonies and is expected to incorporate a wider range of cultivated varieties.

Royal Botanic Garden Kew, Richmond, Surrey, TW9 3AB.

Spetchley Park

Owned by Mr & Mrs R. J. Berkeley, Spetchley has an extensive peony collection. The herbaceous borders which surround the walled kitchen garden contain approximately fifty varieties of *P. lactiflora*, including many that were raised by Kelways. The Fountain Gardens are planted with interesting species such as *P. kavachensis*, *P. obovata* var. *willmottiae* and modern American hybrids such as 'Coral Charm'. Tree peonies are scattered throughout the gardens but some obviously lost their labels many years ago.
Spetchley Park, near Worcester, Worcestershire, WR5 1RS.

CHINA

Beijing Botanical Garden (Northern)

Sleeping Buddha Temple Road, Western Suburbs, Beijing.

Beijing Botanical Garden (Southern)

No. 20, Nanxingcun, Xiangshan, Beijing.

Shanghai Botanical Garden

Longwu Road, Shanghai (120 varieties of tree peony).

Xi´an Botanical Garden

Cuihua Road, Xi´an, Shaanxi Province (200 varieties of tree peony).

FRANCE

Giverny

Claude Monet's beautiful garden at Giverny was created between 1883 and 1926. His first garden, close to the house, is a riot of colour throughout the spring and summer with beds of irises, poppies and peonies. Numerous books have been written about this garden and it remains an inspiration to all gardeners.
Jardins Claude Monet, Musée Claude Monet, 27620 Giverny, Eure.

Villa Noailles

This is a terraced garden planted by the Vicomte de

Noailles after the Second World War. One of the terraces is filled with tree peonies and under planted with oxalis, laid out in a trellis pattern. The long terrace is bordered by yew hedges, which protect the peonies from cold winds and reduce the risk of frost damage.
Villa Noailles, 59, Ave Guy de Maupassant, Grasse 06130, Alpes-Maritimes. (By appointment)

NORTH AMERICA (INCLUDING CANADA)

Peonies have never lost popularity in the United States, consequently they are more widely grown than in Europe. There are some substantial collections of tree peonies and the majority of the commercial nurseries have good demonstration gardens.

Hollingsworth Peony Nursery

This small nursery is situated a few miles outside Maryville. Don Hollingsworth has raised many successful varieties, including 'Delaware Chief' and 'Garden Treasure', the only Itoh hybrid to have been awarded a Gold Medal by the APS. The nursery has many varieties from other breeders and a nice collection of tree peonies.

Hollingsworth Peony Nursery, Maryville, Missouri 64468.

Klehm Nursery

Possibly the most influential family in the peony world the Klehm's have introduced many new varieties since the company was established in the mid-nineteenth century. The company supplies peonies to nurseries throughout the world and has a very good demonstration garden with a wide range of peonies on display. Also on show are a good range of *P. lutea* hybrid tree peonies.
Klehm Nursery, North Duncan Road, Champaign, Illinois 61821.

Reath's Nursery

This nursery was originally established by the late Dr David Reath, a well respected peony breeder who raised 'Salmon Dream' (illustrated on the front cover) and is now run by his son Scott. The climate in this area is

The Klehm nursery at Champaign in Illinois has an extensive demonstration garden.

quite severe so the peonies flower very late in the season. The nursery has a large collection of the Saunders' *P. lutea* hybrid tree peonies.
Reath's Nursery, Vulcan, Michigan 49892.

Gilbert H. Wild & Son Inc.

Wild's have a large number of peonies on display, including many which were bred by the original owners. Older American varieties are well represented in the collection; there is less emphasis on the modern hybrids. The peonies flower at least one month earlier than in Illinois and are at their best in early May.
Gilbert H. Wild & Son Inc., Sarcoxie,
Missouri 64862-0338 (Mr. G. Jones).

The following are also of interest:

A&D Peony & Perennial Nursery, 6808 180th SE Snohomish, Washington State.
Alfred L. Boerner Botanical Garden, Whitnall Park, Hales Corner, Milwaukee, Wisconsin.
Andre Viette Farm & Nursery, Route 1, Box 16, Fishersville, Virginia 22939.

The Arnold Arboretum, The Arborway, Jamaica Plains, Massachusetts 02130.
Caprice Farm Nursery, Sherwood, Oregon 97140.
Cornell University, Ithaca, New York.
Cricket Hill Farm, Thomaston, Connecticut – Chinese tree peonies.
Kingswood Centre, 900 Park Avenue West Mansfield, Ohio 44906.
Longwood Gardens, Kenneth Square, Pennsylvania.
Roger Anderson, Route 4, W. 665B Sunset Lane, Fort Atkinson, Wisconsin – Itoh hybrids.
Royal Botanic Gardens, Hamilton, Ontario, Canada.
Swarthmore College, Swarthmore, Pennsylvania – Tree peonies.
The New Peony Farm, Faribault, Minnesota. (By appointment)
The Tischler Peony Garden, 1021 East Division St., Faribault, Minnesota.

In commercial peony nurseries the plants are grown in huge numbers. This is Gilbert H. Wild in Missouri, where they divide the peonies every three years.

US National Arboretum, Washington D.C.
Weston Nurseries, Route 135 Hopkinton,
	Massachusetts.
White Flower Farm, Litchfield, Connecticut –
	Herbaceous peonies.
Winterthur, Wilmington, Delaware.

THE NATIONAL COLLECTIONS SCHEME

Green Cottage, Lydney

The core of Margaret Baber's collection is based around approximately 70 lactiflora cultivars bred between 1824 and 1919. It includes 'Edulis Superba', 'Festiva Maxima', 'Madame Ducel', 'Madame Boulanger', 'Monsieur Charles Leveque' (syn. 'Mademoiselle Leonie Calot'), 'Solange' and 'Whitleyi Major'. The garden is surrounded by trees. While the main collection is grown in rows there are also many other peonies planted out in a cottage garden style setting and in informal herbaceous borders. The collection also has a selection of the Saunders hybrids including 'Campagna', 'Early Windflower' and 'Late Windflower', 'Honor', 'Lovely Rose' and 'Nosegay'. It is open under the National Gardens Scheme in June; the yellow handbook gives directions and times of opening.
Mrs M. Baber, Green Cottage, Redhill Lane, Lydney, Gloucestershire, GL15 6BS.
Tel. (+44) 01594-841918.

Branklyn, Perth

"We started the collection over twenty years ago but more seriously in the late 1970s obtaining specimens from botanic gardens and where possible from seeds of wild origin. *Paeonia* species freely hybridize and this was evident when several of them flowered. Of our 160 taxa we believe we have about forty valid species and varieties of both herbaceous and tree peonies. We continue to add to the collection but only from wild source material. The collection is used for taxonomic research, conservation and its cultural interest. Our garden is small and the collection is planted among our other plants which provide the necessary shelter from the salt-laden winds. They flower surprisingly well."
Mr. & Mrs. R. Mitchell, Branklyn, Dundee Road, Perth, Perthshire, PH2 7BB.
(Visits by appointment only)

Hidcote Manor Gardens

The majority of the peonies at Hidcote are cultivars of *P. mascula* ssp. *arietina*, *P. lactiflora* and *P. peregrina*. There are approximately twenty species of peony grown in the gardens and they have nice specimens of the tree peonies 'L'Espérance', 'Monsieur Maxime Cornu' and 'Madame Louis Henri'. *P. lactiflora* is well represented with approximately forty cultivars. Close to the entrance to the gardens is an attractive unnamed seedling of *P. delavayi*, which has dark green leaves and a very pale midrib. It is said to have an intoxicating fragrance when in flower. There are also many old *P. wittmanniana* hybrids, including 'Avant Garde'.
Hidcote Manor Gardens (National Trust), Hidcote Bartrim, Nr. Chipping Campden, Gloucestershire, GL55 6LR. Tel. (+44) 01386-438333.

PEONY SOCIETIES

The American Peony Society, c/o The Secretary, Greta M. Kessenich, 250 Interlachen Road, Hopkins, Michigan 55343, USA. Tel. (+1) (612) 938-4706. Established in 1904, The APS is responsible for the registration of new peony varieties. It has many members throughout the world. Its quarterly bulletin is packed with useful information about peonies.

The Canadian Peony Society,
	1246, Donlea Crescent, Oakville, Ontario L6J 1V7.
	Tel. (+1) (416) 845-5380.

Hardy Plant Society Peony Group,
	c/o Margaret Baber, Green Cottage, Redhill Lane,
	Lydney, Gloucestershire, England, GL15 6BS.
	Tel. (+44) 01594 841918.

Japanese Peony Society,
	1-2-11 Honcho, Tatebayashi, Gunma 374, Japan.
	Fax. (+81) (276) 72-0022.

The New Zealand Society,
	c/o Mr Terry Banks, Omeo Peonies, 6 Hawley Road,
	R.D.1, Alexandra, NZ.

Species Peony International Network (SPIN)
	c/o Irmtrud Reick, Friedrichstrasse 8,
	74906 Bad Rappenbau-Babstadt, Germany.

APPENDICES

GLOSSARY

(A large number of botanical terms are used in this book, I have tried to keep them to a minimum but in some cases there is no other way of referring to a part of a plant. To muddy the water further several different names are used in books to describe the same feature, for the sake of consistency I have tried to use that which is scientifically correct. As an example the coloured marks at the base of tree peony petals are variously referred to as flares, blotches and petal 'base'. The term used by the American Peony Society for this feature is a flare and I have adhered to this description throughout the book. A more extensive glossary may be found in the RHS Index of Garden Plants (Griffiths, 1994).

Acuminate The tip tapers gradually to a point.

Adpressed Lying flat against the leaf surface or another part of the plant; usually applied to hairs.

Anemone The third stage of doubling in peony flowers. The **stamens** have now widened to produce narrow petals throughout the centre of the flower. No sign of the **anthers** remains. The term is not used by all breeders.

Anther The part of the **stamen** which produces pollen.

Biternate Peonies have compound leaves. They are divided once into three leaflets, each with a **petiole**, and then a second time to give at least nine segments.

Bomb Some of the stamens are **petaloid**, raised and creating a flower in the shape of a pompom. These flowers frequently have a collar of petals of a different colour.

Carpel A single unit of a compound ovary; in peonies each carpel matures to produce a **follicle**.

Carpelodes Carpels that have evolved into petal-like structures. See petaloids.

Caudate Tapers abruptly and then gradually to a point.

Circinate Curled around so that the end is in the centre. The majority of ferns have leaves which unfurl in this way.

Crown A flower whose **stamens** and **carpels** are entirely **petaloid**.

Cuneate Inversely triangular.

Cuneiforme In the shape of a backward-facing arrow.

Dehiscing The process of opening in a seed capsule.

Disc The staminoidal disc is conspicuous in many peonies. It is frequently brightly coloured and protrudes beyond the base of the **carpels**.

Double Generally used to describe very full flowers with many petals. In peonies it is meant to be more precise and is used to describe flowers where the **stamens** and **carpels** are **petaloid** and indistinguishable from the normal petals.

Anthers are absent.

Emarginate With a shallowly notched apex.

Endemic A plant that is confined to a specific geographical location.

Estate Peony Coined by Charles Klehm & Son to describe a range of peonies, with particularly strong stems, that they specifically bred for the cut-flower market.

Filament The part of the **stamen** which supports the **anther**.

Flares Blotches of colour at the base of petals radiating from the centre of the flower. These are sometimes referred to as 'onglets' or 'blotches'.

Follicle A dry fruit derived from a single **carpel** with one or more seeds, dehiscing along a single opening on the upper surface.

Fully double Very densely packed petals in a double flower.

Glabrous Smooth and hairless.

Glaucous Covered with a fine bloom, usually white or grey, which can be rubbed off easily. Can give leaves a blue coloration.

Guard petals The outer petals of many cultivated peonies are enlarged and quite different from the inner petals, they are known as guard petals. Usually well rounded, they are the only true petals present in Japanese-form flowers.

Hirsute Covered with coarse long hairs.

Japanese This is the second stage of doubling in peony flowers. The petals, now known as the **guard petals**, tend to be enlarged and equal in size. The **stamen filaments** are widened and the **anthers** have become very large. These enlarged stamens are known as staminodes.

Maquis Low scrub found in the Mediterranean region. It consists mainly of small drought-resistant trees and shrubs. Macchia in Italian.

Moutan The Chinese name for tree peonies. Often used as a general term for tree peonies. The Japanese equivalent is Botan.

Multipetalled hybrid A bloom that has a flower developed within a flower. This secondary flower may be rudimentary and hidden or gives rise to a duplicate set of floral structures.

Ovule The female reproductive organ in a flower. If fertilized it gives rises to a seed; infertile peony ovules are bright red.

Patent Widespreading (as in petals).

Petaloids Enlarged **stamen filaments** (staminodes) or **carpels** (carpelodes) which, as result of hybridization, have increased in size and assumed the appearance of narrow petals.

Petiole The leaf stalk.

Petiolule The stalk of a leaflet.

Phyragana A species-rich plant community of short shrubs and herbaceous perennials. The ground is usually very rocky and dry and is colonized by 'herbs' such as garlic, rosemary, sage and thyme. Widespread around the Mediterranean. Also known as Garigue (French).

Pilose Covered with an even layer of soft slender hairs.

Pistil The reproductive unit of a flower, composed of one ovary, **style** and **stigma**. Compound flowers have many pistils.

Recurved Curved back on itself.

Rose See fully double.

Semi-double The fourth stage of petal doubling. Flowers of this type of peony generally have enlarged **filaments**, mixed with petals of varying widths. The petals tend to be looser in form and the guard petals may or may not be well differentiated from the others.

Semi-rose The **carpels** are **petaloid**, with the occasional **stamens** showing.

Sessile Stalkless or without a **petiole**.

Sheath A thin structure that covers the carpels in Moutan tree peonies and Itoh hybrids.

Single A flower that usually has a single set of petals and numerous **stamens**.

Sericeous Covered with fine, silky, adpressed hairs.

Senso stricto In the strict sense.

Silvered A general term used by peony specialists to describe flowers whose petals fade to almost white at the edges.

Stamens The male part of the flower, which contains the pollen. Composed of **anthers** and **filaments**.

Staminodes or **Staminodia** Stamens that have evolved into petal-like structures. The singular is staminode (Latin, *staminodium*). See petaloids.

Stigma(s/ata) The tip of the pistil which receives pollen to fertilize the flower of a plant.

Style The elongated part of the **pistil** between the ovary and **stigma**. It is usually very short in peonies.

Subsessile With a very small stalk.

Tomentose Covered with dense short stiff hairs.

Villous Covered with shaggy hairs.

BIBLIOGRAPHY

Albow, N. (1895) Enumeratio Plantarum Transcaucasiae Occidentalis. Trudy Tiflisskago Botanicheskogo Sada, 1, Sup. 1. pp.14–15.

Anderson, G. (1818) 'A monograph of the genus *Paeonia*.' Transactions of the Linnean Society of London, 12, pp.248–290.

Anderson, R. (1988) APS Bulletin, 265, pp.10–11.

Andrews, H (1804) *Paeonia suffruticosa*. Botanists Repository 6, t. 373.

Andrews, H. (1807) *Paeonia papaveracea*. Botanists Repository 7, t. 463.

Baker, J. G. (1884) 'Monograph of the genus *Paeonia*.' Gardener's Chronicle, 21, pp.732, 779–780, 828 and 22, pp.9–10.

Barber, H.N. (1941) Evolution in the Genus *Paeonia*. Nature, 148, pp.227–228.

Bensky, D and Gamble, A. (1993) Chinese Herbal Medicine – Materia Medica translated by D. Bensky and Andrew Gamble. Eastland Press. P.

Bivona Bernardi, A. de (1816) Stirpium rariorum minusque cognitarum in Sicilia. Manipulus 4, p.12.

Busch, N.A. (1901) Flora Caucasus Critica III, 3, 10.

Cooper, F. C. (1970) Peony Flower Pigments. APS Bulletin 197.

Cullen, J & Heywood, V.H. (1964) Notes on the Europaean Species of *Paeonia*. Feddes Repertorium, 69, pp.32–35.

Culpepper, Nicholas (1653) Complet Herbal and English Physician Enlarged.

Davis, P. H. & Cullen (1965) Notes from the Edinburgh Royal Botanic Garden. xxvi, 176 .

De Candolle (1818) Regni Vegetabilis Systema Naturale, 1, 386.

De Candolle (1824) Prodromus Systematis Naturalis Regni Vegetabilis, 1, 65.

Dioscorides De Materia Medica, ed. C.G. Kühn, Leipzig, 1830.

Donn (1804) *Paeonia arborea*. Cat. Hort. Cantabr. Ed. 3, p.102.

Fang, Wen-Pei (1958) (FW) Notes on Chinese Peonies. Acta Phytotaxonomica Sinica 7(4): pp. 297–323.

Farrer, R.J. (1917) 'On the Eaves of the World.' 1, pp.110–113. Arnold.

Griffiths, M. (1994) The new RHS Dictionary. Index of Garden Plants.

Grigson, G. (1958) The Englishman's Flora. Phoenix House Ltd., England.

Haworth-Booth, M. (1963) The Moutan or Tree Peony. Constable, London.

Haw, S.G. & Lauener, L.A. (1990) (HL) A review of the intraspecific taxa of *Paeonia suffruticosa* Andrews. Edinburgh Journal of Botany, 47 (3) pp.273–281.

Heywood, V.H. (1978) Flowering Plants of the World. Oxford University Press.

Hong Tao, Zhang, J. X., Li, J.J., Zhao, W.Z. & Li, M.R. (1992) (HT) Study on the Chinese Wild Woody Peonies I. New Taxa of *Paeonia* L. Sect. Moutan D.C. Bulletin of Botanical Research, Harbin 12 (3): pp.223–234.

Hong Tao & Osti, G. L. (1994) (HT) Study on the Chinese Wild Woody Peonies II. New Taxa of Paeonia L. Sect. Moutan D.C. Op. Cit. 14 (3); pp.237–240.

Huang, Kee Chang (1993) The Pharmacology of Chinese Herbs, pp.306–307. CRC Press, Boca Raton, Florida, USA. IUCN (1978) The IUCN Plant Red Data Book. Morges, Switzerland.

Kemularia-Nathadze, L. M. (1961) Caucasian Representatives of the Genus *Paeonia* L. Translated by Nikolay Kravchuk and Valeriy Kuznetsov. Tr. Tbilisi Botanical Instute, 21, 51p. Tbilisi.

Kemularia-Nathadze, L.M. (1980) K voprocy nomenklatura i takxonomii *Paeonia chamaeleon* Troitsky i ego blizkikh vidov. Zameki Po Sistematike Geografii Rastenii, Tiflis, 36, pp.22–24.

Kessenich, G.M. ed. (1976) A history of the Peonies and their originations. APS.

Kessenich, G.M. ed. (1979) The best of 75 years. APS.

Kessenich, G.M. ed. Peonies 1976–1986. APS.

Klehm, R.G. (1993) The Peony. B. T. Batsford Ltd., London.

Komarov, V. (1921) Not. Syst. Herb. Hort. Petrop. ii, 5.

Komarov, V. L. (1937) Flora URSS, 7, 21-29. Ranales and Rhoeadales. Izdatel 'stvo Akademii' Nauk SSSR. Moskva-Leningrad.

Levéillé, A. A. H. (1915) *Paeonia mairei* Bull. Acad. Internat. Géogr. Bot., Le Mans, 25, p.42.

Linnaeus, C. (1771) Mantissa altera, 247.

Lomakin, A.A. (1897) 'De Paeoniis Novis in Caucaso Crescentibus.' Acta. Hort. Tiflis, 2, pp.280–284.

Lynch, R. I. (1890) 'A new classification of the genus *Paeonia*.' Journal RHS. London 12, pp.428–445.

Miller, P. (1768) The Gardener's Dictionary Ed. 8, no. 1.

Miyabe & Takeda (1910) Gardener's Chronicle xlviii. p.66.

Özhatay, N. & Özhatay, E. (1995) (Ö & Ö) A new white *Paeonia* L. from North-Western Turkey: P. *mascula* Miller subsp. *Bodurii* N. Özhatay. The Karaca Arborteum Magazine, 3, Pt.1 pp.17–26.

Pallas, P.S. (1776) 'Reise durch verschiedene Provinzen des rissischen.' 3, p.286. Leningrad.

Pallas, P.S. (1788) Flora Rossica, 1, ii, pp.92–95. Leningrad.

Pei, Yan-long & Hong, De-yuan (1995) (PH) *Paeonia qiui* – A new woody species of *Paeonia* from Hubei, China. Acta Phytotaxonomica Sinica, 33 (1), pp.91–93.

Phillips, R. & Rix, M. (1991) Perennials, 1, 94–105 Pan Books, London.

Pliny the Elder (1st Century AD) The Natural History of Gaius Plinius Secundus. Book XXV, 29, Book XXVI, 131, Book XXVII, 84.) Translated by W.H.S. Jones Loeb Classical Library, Heinemann, London, 1956.

Reath, D. (1975) Root-grafting of tree peonies. APS Bulletin, 213.

Rehder, A. (1920) New species, varieties and combinations from Herbarium and the collections of the Arnold Arboretum. Journal of the Arnold Arboretum, 1, pp.193–194.

Riedl, H. (1969) Flora Iranica, *Paeoniaceae*. pp.1–6.

Sabine, Joseph (1826) On the *Paeonia* Moutan or Tree Peony, and it's varieties. Trans. of the Horticultural Society of London., 6, pp.465–492.

Sims, (1808) *P. moutan*. Botanical Magazine t. 1154.

Smithers, Sir Peter (1992) 'Rock's peony.' The Garden, RHS, London 117, pp.519–520.

Soó, R. (1960) What is *Paeonia banatica* Rochel? Acta Botanica 6, pp.139–141.

Stapf, O. (1931) *Paeonia tomentosa*. Curtis's Botanical Magazine, 155, t. 9249

Stearn, W.T. & Davis, P.H. (1984) Peonies of Greece. Goulandris Natural History Museum, J.Makris S.A.

Stern, F.C. (1939) The Moutan Tree Peony. Journal RHS. London, 64, pp.550–552.

Stern, F.C. (1946) A study of the Genus *Paeonia*. RHS, London. The University Press, Aberdeen.

Thiébaut, J. (1936) Flore Libano-Syrienne, 1, p. 37, in Mémoires présenté à l'Institut d'Égypte, 31.

Thiselton Dyer, T. F. (1889) The Folk-Lore of Plants.

Tzanoudakis, D.M. (1977). Cytotaxonomic Study of the Genus *Paeonia* in Greece pp.1–32, pls.1–15. Patras.

Vilmorin, A. (1863 & 1909) Les Fleurs de Pleines Terre. Chez Vilmorin-Andrieux et cie., Paris.

Wilson, R. F. (1938 & 1941) Horticultural Colour Chart (in two volumes). The British Colour Council in collaboration with the RHS. Henry Stone & Son Ltd., Banbury.

Wister, J.C. et al. (1995) The Peonies. 2nd Reprint. APS.

Worsdell, W. C. (1908) The affinities of *Paeonia*. Journal of Botany, 46.

Yen, Kun-Ying (1992) The illustrated Chinese Materia Medica. Crude and prepared. Translated by Nigel Wiseman. SMC Publishing Inc., Taipei. 9, 51 & 52.

SYNONYMS

The taxonomic state of the genus *Paeonia* seems to have been in a perpetual state of flux. While one botanist may feel that *Paeonia mascula* should be split into five species, another will consider that these 'species' are only worthy of subspecies status. Some botanists also recognise species that are not generally accepted by others. This debate between the 'lumpers' and 'splitters' has always taken place and has not be aided by recent developments in experimental techniques; if anything the situation has become worse. I have tried to avoid getting involved in such disputes. This book has been written for gardeners, rather than for botanists involved in academic debate. The true situation will only become clear when authentic material becomes available for study.

Paeonia abchasica Mischenko ex Grossheim (1930) = *P. wittmanniana*

Paeonia albiflora Pallas (1788) = *P. lactiflora*

Paeonia arborea Donn (1804) = *P. × suffruticosa* agg.

Paeonia arietina Anderson (1818) = *P. mascula* ssp. *arietina*

Paeonia banatica Rochel (1828) = *P. officinalis* ssp. *banatica*

Paeonia beresowskii Komarov (1921) = *P. veitchii* var. *beresowskii*

Paeonia biebersteiniana Ruprecht (1869) = *P. tenuifolia*?

Paeonia brownii var. *californica* (Nutt. ex Torrey & Gray) Lynch (1890) = *P. californica*

Paeonia byzantina Clusius (1601) = *P. peregrina*

Paeonia carthalinica Ketzcheveli (1959) = *P. tenuifolia*?

Paeonia chinensis Hort. ex Vilm. (1870) = *P. lactiflora*

Paeonia corallina Retzius (1783) = *P. mascula* ssp. *mascula*

Paeonia corallina var. *triternata* (Pallas) Boissier (1867) = *P. mascula* ssp. *triternata*

Paeonia corsica Sieber ex Trausch (1828) = *P. mascula* ssp. *russi* var. *leiocarpa*

Paeonia cretica Tausch (1828) = *P. clusii*

Paeonia daurica Andrews (1807) = *P. mascula* ssp. *triternata*

Paeonia decomposita Handel-Mazzetti (1939) = *P. rockii*

Paeonia decora Anderson (1818) = *P. peregrina*

Paeonia delavayi var. *angustiloba* Rehder & Wilson (1913) = *P. potanini*

Paeonia delavayi var. *lutea* (Franch.) Finet & Gagnepain (1904) = *P. lutea*

Paeonia edulis Salisbury (1805) = *P. lactiflora*

Paeonia foemina Miller (1768) = *P. officinalis*

Paeonia forresti = *P. potanini* var. *trollioides*

Paeonia fragrans (Sabine) Redouté (1827) = *P. lactiflora*

Paeonia fructicosa Dumont de Courset (1811) = *P. × suffruticosa* agg.

Paeonia fulgida Sabine ex Salm-Dyck (1834) = *P. officinalis*

Paeonia humilis Retzius (1783) = *P. officinalis* ssp. *humilis*

Paeonia hybrida Lynch = Probably a hybrid of *P. anomala* and *P. tenuifolia*

Paeonia mascula ssp. *icarica* Tzanoudakis (1977) = *P. mascula* ssp. *hellenica*

Paeonia intermedia C. Meyer ex Ledebour (1830) = *P. anomala* var. *intermedia*

Paeonia japonica (Makino) Miyabe & Takeda (1910) = *P. lactiflora*

Paeonia kurdistanica Zohary (1942) = *P. kavachensis*

Paeonia laciniata Siev. (1795) = *P. anomala*

Paeonia lagodechiana Kemularia-Nathadze (1961) = *P. mlokosewitschi* × *P. mascula* ssp.?

Paeonia lithophila Kotov (1956) = *P. tenuifolia?*

Paeonia lobata Sweet (1824) = *P. peregrina*

Paeonia lusitanica Miller (1768) (species non satis notae) = *P. broteri*

Paeonia majko Ketzchoveli (1959) = *P. tenuifolia* × *P. caucasica.*

Paeonia makaschvilii Kaheladze = *P.* × *chamaeleon*

Paeonia microcarpa Salm-Dyck (1834) = *P. officinalis* ssp. *villosa*

Paeonia microcarpa Boissier & Reuter (1852) = *P. officinalis* ssp. *humilis*

Paeonia modesta Jord. (1903) = *P. officinalis*

Paeonia moutan Sims (1808) = *P.* × *suffruticosa* agg.

Paeonia multifida Salm-Dyck (1834) = *P. peregrina*

Paeonia officinalis ssp. *microcarpa* = *P. officinalis* ssp. *humilis*

Paeonia oreogeton Moore (1879) = *P. wittmanniana*

Paeonia orientalis = *P. mascula* ssp. *arietina*

Paeonia oxypetala Handel-Mazzetti (1920) = *P. mairei*

Paeonia papaveracea Andrews (1807) = *P.* × *suffruticosa* agg.

Paeonia paradoxa Sabine (1817) = *P. officinalis* ssp. *humilis*

Paeonia peregrina Bornm. non Miller = *P. mascula* ssp. *arietina*

Paeonia peregrina var. *romanica* = *P. peregrina*

Paeonia pubens Sims (1821) = *P. mollis*

Paeonia reevesiana (Paxt.) Loud. (1850) = *P. lactiflora*

Paeonia ruprechtiana Kemularia-Nathadze (1961) = ?

Paeonia suffruticosa ssp. *rockii* Haw & Lauener (1990) = *P. rockii*

Paeonia romanica Brandza (1881) = *P. peregrina*

Paeonia russi Bivona (1816) = *P. mascula* ssp. *russi*

Paeonia russoi = *P. mascula* ssp. *russi*

Paeonia sinensis Hort. ex Steud. (1841) = *P. lactiflora*

Paeonia sinjiangensis Pan (1979) = *P. anomala*

Paeonia steveniana (1848) = *P. wittmanniana* var. *glabra*

Paeonia subternata Salm-Dyck (1834) = *P. officinalis*

Paeonia tenuifolia ssp. *biebersteiniana* (Rupr.) Takhtadzjan (1966) = *P. tenuifolia*

Paeonia triternata Pallas (1795) = *P. mascula* ssp. *triternata*

Paeonia troitsky = *P.* × *chamaeleon*

Paeonia trollioides Stapf ex Stern = *P. potanini* var. *trollioides*

Paeonia tomentosa (Lomak.) Busch ex Grossh. (1930) = *P. wittmanniana*

Paeonia vernalis Mandl. (1921) = *P. obovata*

Paeonia whitleyi (1889) = *P. lactiflora* var. 'Whitleyi Major'

Paeonia willmottiae Stapf (1916) = *P. obovata* var. *willmottiae*

Paeonia woodwardii Stapf & Cox (1930) = *P. veitchii* var. *woodwardii*

Paeonia yui Fang 1958 = *P. lactiflora* var. *trichocarpa*

WHERE TO BUY PEONIES

Many companies can supply peonies, although they vary considerably in size. Species peonies are most difficult to obtain: the suppliers are mainly European and many are small nurseries which may be unable to handle export orders. Some American nurseries will export bare roots in the autumn. These require clearance from the US Department of Agriculture before dispatch. Delivery by air takes approximately 10–14 days for most European countries and requires a Phytosanitation Certificate. The large amount of paperwork involved makes it uneconomic for these nurseries to deal with small export orders.

A&D Peony & Perennial Nursery, 6808 180th S.E., Snohomish, Washington 98290, USA. Tel. (+1) (206) 668-9690. (Herbaceous and tree peonies).

Albrecht Hoch, Ahornstraße, 2a, D 1000 Berlin 37 (Zehlendorf), Postfaach 370460, Germany.

Andre Viette Farm & Nursery, State Route 608 Route 1, Box 16, Fishersville, Virginia 22939, USA. (Herbaceous peonies; no export). Tel. (+1) (703) 943-2315.

Brand Peony Farm, Box 862, Saint Cloud, Minnesota 56302, USA.

Busse Gardens, PO Box N, Cokato, Michigan 55321, USA. Tel. (+1) (612) 286-2654.

Caprice Farm Nursery, 15425 SW Pleasant Hill Road, Sherwood, Oregon 97140, USA. Tel. (+1) (503) 625-7241, Fax. (+1) (503) 625-5588. (Herbaceous and tree peonies).

Coombland Gardens, Coneyhurst, Billingshurst, West Sussex, RH14 9DG, England. Tel. (+44) 01403-741549. (Peony species only).

Cricket Hill Garden, 670 Walnut Hill Road, Thomaston, CT 06787, USA. Tel. (+1) (860) 283-1042. (Chinese tree peonies).

David Austin Roses Ltd., Bowling Green Lane, Albrighton, Wolverhampton, WV7 3HB, England. Tel. (+44) 01902-373931, Fax. (+44) 01902-372142. (Herbaceous and tree peonies).

Galen Burrell, P.O. Box 754, Ridgefield, Washington State 98542, USA. (Peony species).

Gartnerei und Staudenkulturen, Wildensbuck, CH-8465, Switzerland.

Gilbert H. Wild & Son, Inc. 1112 Joplin Street, Sarcoxie, Missouri 64862, USA. Tel. (+1) (417) 548-3514, Fax. (+1) (417) 548-6831. (Herbaceous peonies).

Heinz Klose, Rosenstrasse 10, D-34253 Lohfelden, Frankfurt, Germany. Tel. (+49) 561-515555, Fax. (+49) 561-515120. (Herbaceous peonies).

Hollingsworth Peonies, RR3, Box 27, Maryville, Missouri 64468, USA. Tel. (+1) (816) 562-3010, Fax. (+1) (816) 582-8735. (Itoh and herbaceous peonies).

Kelways Ltd., Barrymore Farm, Langport, Somerset, TA10 9EZ, England. Tel. (+44) 01458-250521, Fax. (+44) 01458-253351. (P. lactiflora cultivars and tree peonies).

Klehm Nursery, 4210 North Duncan Road, Champaign, Illinois 61821, USA. Tel. (+1) (800) 553-3715, Fax. (+1) (217) 373-8403. (Herbaceous peonies, P. lutea hybrids and P. x suffruticosa tree peonies).

La Pivoinerie, Latrenne, 47380 Monclar d'Agenais, France.

Marsal Peonies, Old South Road, R.D. Dunsandel, Canterbury, New Zealand. Tel. & Fax. (+64) (3) 325-4003.

Michel Riviére, Pivoines, 'La Plaine', 26400 Crest, France. Tel. (+33) 75.25.44.85, Fax. (+33) 75.76.77.38. (Herbaceous peonies, Itoh Hybrids, P. lutea hybrids and P. x suffruticosa tree peonies).

New Peony Farm, Box 18235 St. Paul, Minnesota 55118, USA. (Herbaceous peonies).

Oriental Leaves, Woodwell Farmhouse Nurseries, Rait, Perthshire, Scotland PH2 7RZ Tel. (+44) 1821-670754, Fax. (+44) 1821-670744. (Chinese tree peonies, including P. rockii and P. ostii).

Phedar Nursery, Bunkers Hill, Romiley, Stockport, SK6 3DS, England. Tel. (+44) 161-430-3772. (Peony species and Chinese tree peonies).

Reath's Nursery, County Road 577 Box 247, Vulcan, Michigan 49892, USA. Tel & Fax. (+1) (906) 563-9777. (Herbaceous and tree peonies).

The Peony Gardens, Lake Hayes Road, No. 1 R.D. Queenstown, New Zealand. Tel. & Fax. (+64) (3) 442-1210.

Sevald Nursery, 4937 3rd Avenue South, Minneapolis, Minnesota 55409, USA.

Staudengartnerei Grafin von Zeppelin, Lauden/Baden, D79295 Salzburg 2, Germany.

Wayside Gardens, Hodges, South Carolina 29695, USA. (No export).

White Flower Farm, Litchfield, Connecticut 06759-0050, USA. (No export). Tel. (+1) (203) 496-1661, Fax. (+1) (203) 496-1418.

INDEX

Page numbers in *italic* refer to picture captions

'Abalone Pearl' 77
'Admiral Harwood' 77
'Adolphe Rousseau' 74, 77-8
'Afterglow' 78, *116*
'A.F.W. Hayward' 78
'Age of Gold' 136
'A la Mode' 78
'Alba' 46, 69, 70
'Alba Grandiflora' 125
'Alba Plena' 66
'Albert Crousse' 34, 35, *73*, 78, 97
Albow, Nicolas 59
'Alhambra' 136-7
'Alice Graemes' 78
'Alice Harding' 78-9, 97, 136, 143
'Alice Palmer' 134-5
'Alstead' 79
'Ama-No-Sode' 79
'Amber Moon' 137
'America' *78*, 79, 87
America, peonies in 34-5
Anderson, Roger 15, 143
Andrews 43, 44
'Anemoniflora Rosea' 31, 66
'Anemoniflora Alba' 71
'Angelo Cobb Freeborn' *72*, 79
'Anna Pavlova' 79
'Ann Berry Cousins' 79
'Anne Rosse' 47
'Annisquam' 79
'Antwerpen' 79
'Arabian Prince' 79
'Archangel' 79
'Argentine' 79, *104*
'Argosy' 33, 137
'Ariadne' 138-9
'Armance Dessert' 79
'Artist' 80
'Asa Gray' 71, 80, *105*
'Asahi-no-sora' 130
'Athena' 80
'Audrey' 80
'Auguste Dessert' 80
'Augustine d'Hour' 80, *116*
'Auten's' 80
'Avalanche' 71, 80
'Avant Garde' 32, 70, 71, 80-1, *80*
'Azuma-kagami' 130

'Bahram' 81
Baker, J.G. 52
'Ballerina' 81
'Balliol' 107
Banks, Sir Joseph 50, 127, 128
'Banksii' 127, 128
'Banzai-mon' 130
'Barbara' 81, *83*
Barber, H.N. 43
'Baroness Schroeder' *74*, 81
'Baron Thyssen Bornemista' 141
'Barrington Belle' 81
'Barrymore' 81
'Bartzella' 144
'Beatrice Kelway' 81
'Belle Center' 81, *104*
'Bethcar' 81, *93*
'Betty Groff' 81
'Big Ben' 81
'Bijou de Chusan' 128
'Black Monarch' 81, *116*
'Black Panther' 137

'Black Pirate' 33, 137
'Blaze' 81
'Bluebird' *82*, 84
'Blush Queen' 84
'Border Charm' 144
'Bowl of Beauty' 21, 33, 77, *83*, 84
'Bowl of Cream' 84
'Break of Day' *83*, 84
'Bridal Gown' *73*, 84
'Bridal Veil' 84
'Bridesmaid' 109
'Bright Knight' 84, *84*
'Brightness' 84
'Buckeye Belle' 21, *21*, 81, 85, *110*
'Bunker Hill' *73*, 85
'Burma Midnight' 85
'Burma Ruby' 77, 85, *85*
'Burning Light' 85, *117*
'Butch' 85, *105*
'Bu-Te' 85
'Butter Bowl' *82*, 85

Calot, Jacques 71
'Calypso' *83*, 85
Cambessedes, Jacques 53
'Canary' 137
'Candeur' 85, *112*
'Candia' 137
'Cardinal's Robe' 85-6
'Cardinal Vaughan' 135
'Carina' 86
'Carmen' 86, *112*
'Carol' *72*, 86
'Cascade' 86, *112*
'Cecilia Kelway' 86
'Chalice' 86
'Champlain' 86
'Charlie's White' *73*, 74, 86
'Charm' 86, 96
'Cheddar Charm' 75, 86
'Cheddar Cheese' 86
'Cheddar Gold' 86
'Cheddar Supreme' 86
'Cheddar Surprise' 86-7
'Cherry Hill' 87
'Cherry Royal' 87
'Cherry Ruffles' 77, 87
'Chief Justice' 87
'Chiffon Parfait' 75, 87
'China Rose' 66
'Chinese Dragon' 137
'Chocolate Soldier' 87, *87*, 90
'Christine' 87
'Christine Kelway' 87
'Chromatella' 136
'Circus Clown' 87
'Claire de Lune' 87-8
'Claire Dubois' 76, 88
'Claudia' 88
'Clemenceau' 88
Clusius (Charles de l'Escluse) 55
'Comanche' 88, *88*
'Commando' 89
'Companion of Serenity' 138, *139*
'Comtesse de Tuder' 128
'Coral Charm' 89
'Coral Fay' 89
'Coral 'n' Gold' 89
'Cora Louise' 144
'Coral Sunset' 89
'Cora Stubbs' 89
'Cornelia Shaylor' 89, *97*

'Couronne d'Or' 89, 97
Cousins, Lyman 75
'Cream Delight' 89
'Crimson Globe' 66
'Crimson Glory' *82*, 89
Crousse, Felix 71
'Crusader' 89
cultivation 26-7, 29, 41-2
'Cytherea' 89

'Dad' 89
'Da Jin Fen' 129
'Dandy Dan' 90, *90*
Daphnis, Nassos 138
'Dauntless' 90
'David Kelway' 90, *112*
'Dawn Glow' 90
'Dawn Pink' 90, *91*
'Da Ye Hu Die' 129
'Daystar' 90
'Defender' 77, 90, *110*
Delavay, Père Jean Marie 44, 47
'Delaware Chief' 77, 90-1
'Demetra' 139
'Denise' 91
Dessert, Auguste 74
'Diana Drinkwater' 91
'Diana Parks' 91
'Dinner Plate' 74, 91
diseases 38, 40
'Docteur H. Barnsby' 91
'Dojean' 141
'Dolorodell' 91
'Doreen' 91, 96
'Do Tell' 91
Douglas Brand' 91
'Dou Lu' 129
'Dragon's Nest' 91
'Dr. Alexander Fleming' 91-2, *97*
'Dresden' 92, *102*
'Duc de Wellington' 92
'Duchesse de Morny' 129
'Duchesse de Nemours' 71, 77, 92, 96
'Duchess of Kent' *29*, 135
'Duchess of Marlborough' *127*, 135
Duncan, Alexander 127

'Earlybird' 92
'Early Glow' 92
'Early Scout' 92
'Early Windflower' 57, 92
'Echo' 92
'Edulis Superba' 71, *72*, 92
'Ellen Cowley' 74, 77, 88, 92
'Elsa Sass' 76, 92
'Emma' 92
'Emma Klehm' 74, 76, 92
'Emperor of India' *93*, 94
'Enchantment' 94, *112*
'English Princess' 94
'Etched Salmon' 94
'Evening Glow' 94
'Evening World' 94
'Eventide' 94

'Fairbanks' 94
'Faire Rosamond' *83*, 94
'Fairy's Petticoat' 94
Falk, Elizabeth 77
'Famie' 94

Farrer, John Reginald 49
Fay, Orville 75
'Feather Top' 94
'Felix Crousse' 71, 77, 94-5, *117*
'Felix Supreme' 95
'Fen Dian Bai' 129
'Festiva Maxima' 35, 76, 77, 95
'Festiva Supreme' 95
'Firebelle' 95
'Fire King' 32, 67, 68
'Firelight' 95
'First Arrival' 144
'Flame' 95, *110*
'Florence Ellis' 95
flowers 18-21
Fortune, Robert 128
'Fragrans' 71, 95
'Fragrans Maxima Plena' 129
'Fuji' *112*
'Fuji-no-mine' 130

'Gardenia' 95
'Garden Peace' 95
'Garden Treasure' 143, *143*, 144
'Gauguin' 139
'Gay Paree' 21, 95, *97*, 98
'Général MacMahon' 80
'Gene Wild' 98
'Germaine Bigot' 74, 98
'Gessekai' 130
'Gilbert Barthelot' 98
Glasscock, James 77
'Gleam of Light' *83*, 98
'Globe of Light' 98
'Gloire de Charles Gombault' 98
'Gloriana' 96, *98*
'Glory Hallelujah' 98
'Glory of Huish' 135
'Glowing Raspberry Rose' 98
'Godaishu' 130
'Golden Era' 141
'Golden Glow' 98
'Golden Hind' 137
'Golden Mandarin' 137
'Goldfinch' 137
'Goldilocks' 98
'Gold Sovereign' 137
'Grandiflora' 98, *112*
'Grandiflora Nivea Plena' 98-9
Gratwick, William 138
'Grover Cleveland' 99, *117*
'Guardian of the Monastery' 139
'Gunpo-den' 130

'Haku-banriu' 131
'Hakuo-jisi' 34, 131, *131*
'Halcyon' 99
'Hana-kisoi' 131
'Harvest' 137
'Héléne Martin' 141
'Helen Hayes' *76*, 99
'Henri Potin' 99
Henry, Louis 136
'Henry Bockstoce' 99
'Hephestos' 139, *139*
'Heritage' 99
'Hesperus' 137-8
'Hiawatha' 99
Hidcote Manor 32
'Hidden Treasure' 144
Highdown 33, *33*

'Highlight' 99
'High Noon' 138
'Hinode-sekai' 131
'Hino-tobira' 131
'Hit Parade' 99, 99
Hodnet Hall 33, 34
'Hoki' 131
Hollingsworth, Don 34-5, 77
'Honey Gold' 82, 99-100
Hong De-yuan 44
Hong Tao 44, 46, 49
'Honor' 100, 101
'Horakumon' 133, 133
'Horizon' 100
'Howki' 133
'Humei' 71, 100

'Icarus' 139
'Ice Storm' 141
'Illini Belle' 100
'Illini Warrior' 9, 100, 102, 119
'Impu-mon' 133
'Ingenieur Doriat' 100
'Inspecteur Lavergne' 77, 100, 104
'Instituteur Doriat' 82, 100
'Iphigenia' 139
'Isani Gidui' ('Isani Jishi') 100
'Isoline' 100
Itoh, Toichi 77, 136, 143
'Ivory White Saucer' 100
'Iwato-kagura' 133

'James Crawford Weguelin' 66
'James Kelway' 100-1
'Janice' 101
'Jan van Leeuwen' 82, 100, 101
'Jean E. Bockstoce' 101
Jia-jue Li 49
'Jitsu-getsu-nishiki' 133
'John Howard Wigell' 101, 102
'Joseph Rock' see Paeonia rockii
'Joy of Life' 93, 101, 103
'June Rose' 73, 103

'Kagura-jishi' 133, 143
'Kakoden' 103, 143
'Kamada-fuji' 130, 133
'Kamada-nishiki' 134
'Kansas' 103
'Kaow' ('Kao') 132, 134
'Karl Rosenfield' 77, 103
Kelway, James 74; William 74
'Kelway's Brilliant' 103
'Kelway's Fairy Queen' 103, 104
'Kelway's Glorious' 33, 35, 74, 103, 117
'Kelway's Majestic' 35, 103
Kelways nursery 35, 74, 134
'Kelway's Scented Rose' 72, 103
'Kelway's Supreme' 103, 105
'Kelway's Unique' 103
Kemularia-Nathadze, L.M. 43, 54
'Kenrei-mon' 134
'King of England' 35, 106
'Kinkaku' 46, 136
'Kinko' 136
'Kinshi' 136
'Kintei' 136
'Kishu Caprice' 141, 141
Klehm, Carl G. 74; Charles C. 74; Roy 7, 31, 74-5

'Koku-ryu-nishiki' 134
Komarov 48, 54, 70
'Kozan' 133
Krekler, William 31, 75, 77
'Krinkled White' 97, 106
'Kronos' 139

'Lady Alexandra Duff' 33, 34, 35, 74, 77, 103, 106
'Lady Beresford' 107
'Lady in Pink' 106
'Lady Orchid' 96, 106
'La Fiancée' 106
'La France' 106
'La Perle' 106
'Largo' 106
'Late Windflower' 57, 106
'Laura Dessert' 74, 106
'Lavender' 56, 56, 77, 106
'Lavender Strain' 56, 106
leaves 15-18
'Le Cygne' 71, 106-7
'Leda' 139
'Legion of Honour' 107, 110
Lemoine, Emile 70, 71, 135-6; Victor 70, 71, 135-6
Lemon, Nicolas 71
'Le Printemps' 70, 71, 107
L'Espérance' 136
'L'Etincelante' 107
'Letitia' 107
Léveillé 59
'Little Dorrit' 107
'Little Red Gem' 107
'Lize van Veen' 66
'Lois Kelsey' 105, 107
'Lord Kitchener' 107
'Lord Selborne' 135
'Lorna Doone' 107
'Lotus Queen' 76, 107
'Lovely Rose' 107, 110
Ludlow 47, 68
'Ludovica' 107
'Luoyang Hong' 129
'Lydia Foote' 141
'Lyric' 107

'Madame Auguste Dessert' 108, 112
'Madame Butterfly' 108
'Madame Calot' 108
'Madame Crousse' 71
'Madame de Verneville' 108
'Madame Ducel' 108
'Madame Edouard Doriat' 108, 117
'Madame Emile Debatene' 108
'Madame Jules Dessert' 108
'Madame Louis Henry' 136
'Madelon' 108, 116
'Mademoiselle Lionie Calot' 108
'Madylone' 108
'Mahogany' 109
'Mai Fleuri' 70, 71, 109
'Many Happy Returns' 108, 109
'Marchioness' 138
'Marechal MacMahon' 80
'Marie Crousse' 109, 112
'Marie Fischer' 109
'Marie Jaquin' 109
'Marie Lemoine' 109, 116
'Marietta Sisson' 109, 117
'Mary Brand' 109

'Massasoit' 109
'May Music' 109
'May Treat' 109
Mechin, Etienne 74
'Messagére' 70, 109
'Mischief' 76, 111
'Mischka' 135
'Miss America' 111
'Miss Eckhart' 111, 116
'Mister Ed' 72, 111
'Mistral' 93, 111
Miyabe 57
Mlokosiewicz, G. 63
Molly the Witch 63-4, 63
'Monsieur Charles Leveque' 108
'Monsieur Jules Elie' 21, 34, 35, 36, 71, 73, 112
'Monsieur Krelage' 111, 116
'Montezuma' 110, 111
'Moon over Barrington' 111
'Moonrise' 75, 77, 111
'Moon River' 111
'Moonstone' 113
'Mother of Pearl' 32, 61, 61
'Mother's Choice' 113
Moutan 127
'Mr. G.F. Hemerik' 113
'Mrs. Edward Harding' 113
'Mrs. Franklin D. Roosevelt' 108, 113, 113
'Mrs. Shirley Fry' 135
'Mrs. William Kelway' 135
'Mutabilis Plena' 32, 66
'My Pal Rudy' 96, 113
'Myrtle Gentry' 113
'Mystery' 138

'Naniwa-nishiki' 134
'Nathalie' 113
'Neon' 113
New Zealand, peonies in 35-6
'Nice Gal' 114
'Nick Shaylor' 112, 114
'Niigata-otomenomai' 134
'Nike' 140
'Norma Vole' 114
'Northern Glory' 61
'Nosegay' 114
'Nova' 114
'Nymphe' 93, 114

'Opal Hamilton' 114
'Orpen' 82, 114
Osti, Gian 47
'Otto Froebel' 32, 68, 89
'Ozieri Alba' 99

Paeonia
P. albiflora see P. lactiflora
P. anomala 9, 12, 13, 31, 43, 51-2, 51, 58, 69; var. intermedia 52
P. arborea 43
P. bakeri 52
P. beresowskii 70
P. broteri 52
P. brownii 25, 52
P. californica 52-3
P. cambessedesii 20, 25, 26, 53, 58
P. caucasica 13, 53-4

P. × chamaeleon 54-5, 54
P. clusii 26, 31, 43, 55, 55
P. coriacea 55-6, 56; var. atlantica 56
P. delavayi 12, 12, 18, 31, 33, 44, 46, 47, 58
P. emodi 18, 20, 26, 56-7, 68; var. glabrata 57
P. hybrida 13
P. japonica 57
P. jishanensis 44, 46
P. kavachensis 57
P. kesrouaensis 57, 59, 69
P. lactiflora 7, 8, 9, 12, 18, 20, 22, 25, 26, 28, 33, 34, 35, 43, 56, 59, 128
P. × lemoinei 46-7, 71, 74, 136-8
P. lobata see P. peregrina
P. lutea 12, 33, 46, 47, 71, 136, 138; var. ludlowii 25, 31, 47, 47
P. macrophylla 42, 59
P. mairei 59-60
P. mascula 7, 12, 14, 25, 43, 60, 71; ssp. arietina 32, 58, 60-1, 60, 61; ssp. bodurii 61-2; ssp. hellenica 62; ssp. mascula 11, 57, 58, 60; ssp. russi 62-3, 62; ssp. triternata 15, 63
P. mlokosewitschi 14, 24, 25, 34, 58, 63-4, 63
P. mollis 34, 64
P. moutan 43
P. obovata 12, 64; var. willmottiae 64-5
P. officinalis 7, 7, 8, 9, 12, 14, 28, 32, 43, 64, 65, 71; ssp. banatica 65; ssp. humilis 15, 31, 33, 65-6; ssp. officinalis 58, 65; ssp. villosa 31, 33, 58, 65, 66
P. orientalis 61
P. ostii 44, 47-8
P. papaveracea 43
P. parnassica 14, 26, 67
P. peregrina 24, 32, 38, 67-8, 68, 71, 110
P. potanini 12, 14, 41, 48, 48, 136
P. qiui 48-9
P. rhodia 25, 26, 31, 43, 68
P. rockii 33, 33, 44, 49-50, 49; ssp. linyanshanii 50
P. × smouthii 58, 68
P. sterniana 68-9, 69
P. steveniana 20
P. × suffruticosa 43, 44, 50, 136
P. szechuanica 44, 50
P. tenuifolia 14, 15, 25, 31, 69
P. tomentosa 20
P. turcica 69
P. veitchii 12, 18, 18, 31, 33, 34, 58, 69-70
P. wittmanniana 20, 22, 24, 32, 33, 42, 42, 58, 59, 70, 71, 80
P. yananensis 44, 50
P. yunnanensis 44, 50-1
'Pageant' 114
'Paladin' 110, 114
Pallas 59, 63
'Paramount' 114
'Pastel Elegance' 114
'Patriot' 114

'Paula Fay' 114-15
'Paul M. Wild' 96, 115
Pei Yan-long 44
Penshurst Place 33-4
'Peppermint' 115
'Perle Rosé' 64
'Persephone' 140
pests 40-1
'Peter Brand' 115, *116*
'Petticoat Flounce' 115
'Phillippe Rivoire' 115
'Philoméle' 71, 115
'Phyllis Kelway' 115, *117*
'Picotee' 115
'Pillow Talk' 115, *117*
'Pink Angel' 115
'Pink Cameo' 115
'Pink Dawn' 33, 115, 118
'Pink Formal' 118
'Pink Hawaiian Coral' 75, 118
'Pink Heaven' 143
'Pink Lemonade' 76, 118
'Pink Parasol Surprise' 118
'Pink Parfait' *97*, 118
'Pink Pom Pom' 118
'Pink Princess' 118
'Pink Purity' 143
'Plena' 69
'Postilion' *27*, *110*, 118
'Pottsii' 118
'Prairie Afire' 118
'Prairie Charm' 144
'Prairie Moon' 118
'President Poincaré' 119
'Primevére' 71, 119
'Princess Margaret' 119
propagation 25-6, 27-9
'Purple Emperor' 61

'Qing Long Wo Mo Chi' 129
'Queen Elizabeth' *93*, 119
'Queen of Sheba' 119

'Raphael' 135, *135*
'Raspberry Charm' 119
'Raspberry Ice' 119
'Raspberry Sundae' 21, 119
'Red Charm' 119
'Red Rascal' 140
'Red Red Rose' 119
'Red Velvet' *100*, 119

Rehder 44, 46
'Reine de Mai' 119
'Reine des Violettes' 129
'Reine Elizabeth' 129
'Reine Hortense' 71, 119
'Reine Supreme' 75, 120
'Renown' 138
'Requiem' 120
'Reward' 120
'Rimpo' 134
'Robert W. Auten' 120
Rock, Josef Franz 33, 49
'Rock's Variety' see *Paeonia rockii*
'Roman Gold' 138
roots 14
'Rosea' 69
'Rosea Plena' 32, 66
'Rosea Superba Plena' 66
'Rose of Delight' 120
'Rose Fantasy' 144
'Rose Garland' *110*, 120
'Roselette' 120
'Rose Shaylor' 120
'Rosy Cheek' 120
'Rosy Gem' 61
'Royal Rose' 120
'Rubra' 66
'Rubra Plena' 65, 66-7, 90
'Russi Major' 70

'Sabini' 66
'Salmon Beauty' 120
'Salmon Chiffon' 120
'Salmon Dream' 79, 121, *121*
'Salmon Glow' 77, 121
'Salmon Suprise' 121
'Sanctus' 121
'Sang-no-Lorrain' 136
'Sarah Bernhardt' (Dessert) see
  'Umbellata Rosea'
'Sarah Bernhardt' (Lemoine) 33,
  34, 71, 77, 87, 121-2
Saunders, Arthur Percy 56, 57,
  68, 74, *74*, 75, *75*, 77, 136, 138
'Savage Splendor' 138
'Scarlet O'Hara' 36, 77, *102*, 122
'Sea Shell' 122
seeds 20; growing from 24-5
'Shaylor's Sunburst' see 'Sunburst'
'Shawnee Chief' 122
'Sheng Dan Lu' 129

Sheriff 47
Shigao-Oshida 143
'Shin-tenchi' 134
'Shirley Temple' 122
'Silver Dawn' 90, 122
'Silver Flare' 107
'Silver Shell' 122
Smirnow, Louis 143
Smithers, Sir Peter 141
'Snow Swan' 122
'Soft Salmon Saucer' 122
soil types 26, 29, 42
'Solange' 71, 122
'Souvenir d'Haraucourt' 122
'Souvenir de A. Millet' 122
'Souvenir de Louis Bigot' 122-3
'Souvenir de Maxime Cornu' 47,
  136
Spetchley Park 32
'Spring Carnival' 138
'Starlight' 123
Stern, F.C. 33, 44, 49, 53, 55, 70
'Steve Nickel' *106*, 123
'Sunbeam' 68
'Sunburst' 123
'Superb' 135
'Sweet 16' 123
'Sweetie' 123
'Sybil Stern' 8-9, 33, 141

'Taisho-no-hokori' *132*, 134, 141
Takeda 57
'Tango' 123
taxonomy 13-14
'The Bride' 125
'The Fawn' 123
'The Mighty Mo' 123
'Thérése' 123
Thiébaut, J. 57, 61
'Thunderbolt' 138
'Tiger Tiger' 138
'Tokio' 123
'Top Brass' *105*, 123
'Toro-no-maki' 123-4
'Torpilleur' 124
'Tourangelle' 74, 124
'Tranquil Dove' 124
'Tria' 140, *140*
'Triomphe de l'Exposition de
  Lille' 124
'Triomphe de Van der Maelan' 129

'Umbellata Rosea' 124
'Una Howard' 103
Upton Grey 31

Veitch nursery 70
Verdier, Charles 66
'Vesuvian' 138
'Viking Full Moon' 144
Vilmorin nursery 66
'Vivid Glow' 124
'Vogue' 124

'Walter Mains' 124
'Water Lily' 109
Wen-Pei Fang 44, 50
'Westerner' 124-5
'White Cap' *124*, 125
'White Emperor' 144
'White Innocence' 125
'White Wings' *102*, 125
Whitley, R. 59
'Whitleyi' 125
'Whitleyi Major' *20*, 34, 59, 125
'Whopper' 125
'Wiesbaden' *104*, 125
'Wilber Wright' 125
Wild, Gilbert 31
'William Gage' 125
'Wilmington' 125
Wilson, E.H. 64, 70
'Wind Chimes' 125
Wissing, Sam 75
Worontzonff, Count M. 70
'Wu Long Peng Sheng' 129

'Yachiyo-tsubaki' 134
'Yae-zakura' 134
'Yama-shakuyaku' 57
'Yao-huang' 130
'Yellow Crown' 143, 144
'Yellow Dream' 143, 144
'Yellow Emperor' 143, 145
'Yellow Heaven' 143, 145, *145*
'Ying Luo Bao Zhu' 129
'Yoyo-no-homare' 134

'Zephyrus' 140
'Zhao Fen' 130
'Zhuang Yuan Hong' 130
'Zhu Sha Lei' 130
'Zuzu' *102*, 125

Acknowledgements

I am very grateful to Professor Sir Ghillean Prance, Director of the Royal Botanic Gardens, Kew, for permission to use the herbarium and other facilities at Kew, Mike Sinnott, Assistant Curator for Herbaceous & Alpine Plants at Kew and Christine Leon of the Medical Toxicology Unit of Guy's and St. Thomas' Hospital Trust. Ron MacBeath, Assistant Curator for Herbaceous & Alpine Plants at the Royal Botanic Gardens, Edinburgh.

I am particularly grateful to the owners and managers of the nurseries who have allowed me access to their collections of peonies and have given me so much other help and advice. This book could never have been published without their assistance. They are Claire Austin of David Austin Roses Ltd., Don and Lavon Hollingsworth of Hollingsworth Peony Nursery, Maryville, Missouri, Greg Jones of Gilbert H. Wild Nurseries Inc., Missouri, David Root of Kelways Ltd. and Roy & Sarah Klehm of Klehm Nursery, South Barrington, Illinois. I would also like to thank Chris and Liz Johnson, the owners of Kelways Ltd., for permission to use their facilities. I would also like to thank the many other nurseries who have been kind enough to send me their brochures.

Chris Beardsley and Worthing Borough Council for access to the plant collection of the late Sir. F.C. Stern at Highdown, Goring-on-Sea. Paul Nicholls and Peter Dennis of Hidcote Manor Gardens, The National Trust. Dr. Deborah Whitehead, Plant Pathologist at the RHS, Miss Gene Wild of Sarcoxie, Margaret Baber of the Hardy Plant Society Peony Group and the staff of the RHS Lindley Library.

Catherine Duncan, Leo Fernig of SPIN, Maggie Hobbis, Martin Jack, Will McLewin, Hanni Roberts, Chris Saunders of Bridgemere Nurseries Ltd. and Lady Christine Skelmersdale. Dorothy Hamilton for supplying information about peonies in New Zealand and Don Hollingsworth for his article about peonies in America.

Finally, I must thank my wife for being so long suffering during the gestation of this book. I hope that the result will justify the sacrifices that were needed!